Wise Words
and Wives' Tales

Other Avon Books by
Stuart Flexner and Doris Flexner

THE PESSIMIST'S GUIDE TO HISTORY

Wise Words and Wives' Tales

THE ORIGINS,
MEANINGS AND
TIME-HONORED WISDOM OF
PROVERBS AND FOLK SAYINGS,
OLDE AND NEW

STUART FLEXNER and DORIS FLEXNER

AVON BOOKS  NEW YORK

For
Jenn and Geoff

The world is your oyster.

WISE WORDS AND WIVES' TALES: THE ORIGINS, MEANINGS AND TIME-
HONORED WISDOM OF PROVERBS AND FOLK SAYINGS, OLDE AND NEW is an
original publication of Avon Books. This work has never before appeared in book form.

AVON BOOKS
A division of
The Hearst Corporation
1350 Avenue of the Americas
New York, New York 10019

First Avon Books Trade Printing: June 1993

AVON TRADEMARK REG. U.S. PAT. OFF. AND IN OTHER COUNTRIES, MARCA REGISTRADA,
HECHO EN U.S.A.

Printed in the U.S.A.

OPM   10 9 8 7 6 5 4 3 2 1

Acknowledgments

Research assistants Mary St. John and Leila Finn delved into dark recesses to collect information on various proverbs, proving that two heads are better than one. Katherine Somervell and Laurel Adams helped correct typescript and compile indexes, again demonstrating the truth of the adage. My heartfelt gratitude to Bruce Wetterau, who managed the compilation and drafted entries. And to my editor, David Highfill, my sincere appreciation for all his efforts on my behalf.

My thanks to you all for refuting the old saw, "Too many cooks spoil the broth." They make it more delicious!

Preface

Throughout history, the wit and wisdom of philosophers, poets and playwrights, sages, saints, and a few sinners, as well as the common folk, has been recorded and come to be known variously as maxims, adages, proverbs, and aphorisms. These pithy expressions tell us how we have looked at life's foibles and virtues over the years in such diverse areas as love, marriage, death, health, wealth, behavior, food, politics, and war.

Many of these folk sayings have a ring of truth and common sense. No doubt most college students would agree, "All work and no play makes Jack (Jill) a dull boy (girl)," a sentiment first expressed in Egypt about 2400 B.C. It pops up again in the middle of the seventeenth century, by which time several prestigious universities had been established. And if you don't quite believe "An apple a day keeps the doctor away," we are reminded at least that a good diet stressing fruits and vegetables should keep us fairly healthy.

On the other hand, daily apple consumption may have been vital at one time if we are to take some of these aphorisms with solemnity. For example, "Doctors bury their mistakes" has been around in some form or other for over five hundred years, perhaps because "Dead men tell no tales," although I suspect a forensic pathologist would not concur. It is not only doctors who have received short aphoristic shrift. I must mention here one of my favorites, "He who is his own lawyer has a fool for a client." The American Bar Association is in full agreement, I am sure, although in all honesty, the original proverb from which this is adapted stated, "He that teaches himself has a fool for his master." Something to keep in mind when perusing all those how-to books and cassettes.

On a more serious note, our attitudes and prejudices are manifest in many expressions. Feminists will disdain, "A woman's place is in the home," first stated way back in 467 B.C. by Aeschylus, the Greek dramatist. It wasn't until 1942 that the mystery writer Agatha Christie referred to it as "a silly old-fashioned prejudice." Feminists may also take umbrage at "Because is a woman's reason," propounded by the English writer Thomas Wilson in 1551 and reiterated jo-

1

cosely by none other than William Shakespeare in *The Two Gentle-men of Verona.*

Good advice abounds in adages with such sayings as "Believe only half of what you see and nothing that you hear." As cynical as this may seem, the ancient Romans thought it was a good idea. In fact, Julius Caesar wrote words to this effect. He noted, too, that "Experience is the best teacher." Unfortunately, one observation he might have appreciated, "He who lives by the sword shall perish by the sword," did not appear until about A.D. 90. He should have been more astute. Other advice we find includes "Business before pleasure," "Don't count your chickens before they hatch," and "Make hay while the sun shines," all of which makes good sense.

Turning philosophical, we have observed, "Every cloud has a silver lining," originating in 1634 with John Milton, or perhaps a silver-fox lining, as adapted later by Saki (H. H. Munro). Although we may not agree with "Everything comes to him who waits," most of us would concede, "Half a loaf is better than no bread," first noted by a Greek playwright as far back as 300 B.C.

Observances on behavior and character appear frequently, as might be expected. A medieval text recorded, "Still waters run deep," which we often ascribe to those quiet people among us who may be seething with great passion or rage. We all know the oft-quoted "A man is known by the company he keeps," so it would be wise to remember, "He who lies down with dogs will rise with fleas," and, therefore, to avoid wicked companions.

Animals have often been mentioned in such adages as "When the cows lie down, it's a sign of rain," which may contain a grain of truth, but we don't suggest you plan the family picnic according to Bossy's inclinations. "When the cat's away, the mice will play" is familiar to all of us and was originally rendered in this form over five hundred years ago, although a variation was recorded by a Roman playwright fifteen hundred years prior. It would seem in matters of integrity we have changed little. Since at least the seventeenth century, we have known, "A dog is man's best friend," an aphorism used to win a legal case in 1876.

Expressions concerning government and politics (which we all know "makes strange bedfellows") have appeared in many guises. "Better death than dishonor" is an idea found in Sophocles' play *Peleus,* written in about 410 B.C. and followed up by the Romans and the English in sundry forms. It is no doubt the predecessor of the contemporary, albeit obsolete, "Better dead than Red," rallying cry of the anti-Communists of recent years. The all-too-familiar "Justice is blind" was conceived over four thousand years ago.

As may be expected, proverbs pertaining to love are prevalent, from the humorous "Love and pease pottage are two dangerous things," first chronicled in 1654, to the debatable "Absence makes the heart grow fonder," noted by the Roman poet Sextus as long ago as 26 B.C. With love may come marriage, which, according to Voltaire, the philosophical eighteenth-century Frenchman, "is the only adventure open to the cowardly"—an adventure he himself did not feel impelled to embark upon.

This book is based on material my late husband gathered and follows the form he wished the book to take. I have compiled these general truths, useful thoughts, astute observations and common experiences as they have appeared in divers forms over the years. I begin the entries with the earliest recorded appearance of these sayings, followed by their variations in form and meaning as they evolved through the centuries to the present day. In many instances, I have kept the original English spellings, which I feel add to their charm and which can be easily, and perhaps amusingly, deciphered. I trust he would have approved of the final compilation.

It was his hope, and it is mine also, that this book will be used not only as a scholarly resource but also as a delight for the insouciant browser. It is also a collection of the humor and wisdom to be found in the human experience—trite and true examples of the way we have viewed ourselves through the ages.

I now close secure in the knowledge that "A word to the wise is sufficient."

—DORIS FLEXNER
Fearrington Village, North Carolina
1992

A

Absence makes the heart grow fonder. The Roman elegiac poet Sextus Propertius rendered the earliest form of this saying in *Elegies* (c. 26 B.C.) as "Always toward absent lovers love's tide stronger flows." But as many a lover can attest, that is true only up to a point. Elsewhere in *Elegies*, Propertius wrote, "A distant journey can change a woman's heart," while his contemporary, the poet Ovid, cautioned that "a short absence is safest." Chaucer, too, echoed this sentiment in *Troilus and Criseyde* (c. 1385): "Absense of hir shal dryve hir out of herte." The seventeenth-century French writer Duc François de La Rochefoucauld successfully melded these contrary themes (a Frenchman would) in his *Maximes* (1665), with the emotionally pragmatic, "Absence diminishes little passions and increases great ones, just as the wind blows out a candle and fans a fire." The modern wording of "Absence makes..." appeared as the opening line of an anonymous English poem in 1602, but it was the British songwriter Thomas Haynes Bayly's book *Isle of Beauty* (1850) that helped make it a popular sentiment in the Victorian drawing rooms of the day.

Abstain from beans. These three words engendered an amusing controversy during the centuries after the Greek philosopher Pythagoras recorded them in *Maxim* (c. 525 B.C.). What did he mean by the saying? The Roman statesman Cicero cleverly pointed out in *De Divinatione* (44 B.C.), "The Pythagoreans make a point of prohibiting the use of beans, as if thereby the soul and not the belly was filled with wind!" The biographer Plutarch, on the other hand, observed in *Moralia* (A.D. c. 95), " 'Abstain from beans' means that a man should keep out of politics, for beans were used in earlier times for voting upon the removal of magistrates from office." Whatever the true meaning, the saying was first recorded in English by Sir Thomas Elyot in *Education* (c. 1535) as "Absteyne from Beanes. Busy not they selfe with ouer mani matters." The English poet John Lyly echoed that sentiment in *Euphues and His England* (1580): "To absteine from beanes, that is, not to meddle in ciuile affaires or businesse of the common weale, for in the old times the election of Magistrates was made

4

by the pullyng of beanes." But the satirist Jonathan Swift here had the last word in a passage from *Strephon and Chloe* (1731): "Keep them to wholesome Food confin'd, / Nor let them taste what causes Wind; / ('Tis this the Sage of Samos [Pythagoras] means, / Forbidding his Disciples Beans)."

Actions speak louder than words.   The importance of actions over words and the frequent disparity between what people say and do, have been the subject of sayings since ancient times. In the ancient Greek epic *Iliad* (ninth century B.C.), Homer wrote of men who were "poor in battle, but better in the forum." Aesop in his fable *The Fox and the Oak-Cutter* (c. 570 B.C.?) observed the outright deceitfulness of "promising in words the best things, but doing in deeds the opposite," and the Chinese sage Confucius held in his *Analects* (c. 500 B.C.), "A superior man is ashamed if his words are better than his deeds." About 425 B.C., the Greek philosopher Democritus wrote, "The word is the shadow of the deed," and not long after in *Oedipus at Colonus*, Sophocles included the passage, "Not by words would I make my life famous, but by deeds." Centuries later, the Roman historian Sallust noted the tendency of some to be "readier of tongue than hand," and wrote, "Think now for yourselves whether words or deeds are worth more." The Buddhist philosopher Dhammapala observed in his fifth-century *Commentaries:* "Like a beautiful flower, full of color but without scent, are the fair but fruitless words of him who does not act accordingly." Erasmus urged, "Help with deeds, not words," in *Adagia* (1523), and in *Macbeth* (c. 1606) William Shakespeare penned the formidable, "I have no words; My voice is in my sword." The British statesman John Pym in 1628 returned to eloquence with "A word spoken in season is like an apple of silver, and actions are more precious than words."

The modern wording of "Actions speak louder . . . " apparently appeared for the first time in the colonial American publication *Colonial Currency* (1736). Benjamin Franklin, whose *Poor Richard's Almanack* of 1755 advised, in appropriately concise terms, "Speak little, do much," repeated the maxim "Actions speak louder . . . " in 1766. The saying was later quoted or adapted by many, among them Abraham Lincoln, who referred to it while writing on sectionalism in 1856. Still current in the twentieth century, the maxim was cleverly adapted in 1940 by an anonymous writer with a bookish bent: "Some talk in quarto volumes and act in pamphlets." *See also* **Talk is cheap**; **There is a difference between saying and doing.**

After black clouds, clear weather.   The English writer Thomas
Usk observed in his allegorical *The Testament of Love* (c. 1387),
"After grete stormes the whether is often mery and smothe,"
and a few years later, a manuscript titled *Tale of Beryn* (c. 1400)
rendered the saying, "After mysty cloudis pere comyth a cler
sonne." John Heywood's *A Dialogue Conteinyng the Nomber in Effect
of All the Prouerbes in the Englishe Tongue* (1546) advised, "Be of
good chere. After clouds blacke, we shall haue wether clere." In
the next century, the English historian William Camden recorded
the exact wording of the current saying in *Remains Concerning
Britaine* (1605): "After black clouds clear weather. After a storm
comes a calm." Though not widely used in modern times, the
saying was nevertheless included in such recent collections of
proverbs as Burton Stevenson's *Home Book of Proverbs* (1948) and
The Oxford Dictionary of English Proverbs (1970).

All is fair in love and war.   In his *Euphues, the Anatomy of Wit*
(1579), the English writer John Lyly painted a cleverly bleak
portrait of love, observing, "Both might and mallice, deceyte and
treacherye, all periurye, any impietie may lawfully be committed
in loue, which is lawless." Another Englishman, the dramatist
John Marston, noted in *The Fawn* (1606), "An old saw hath bin,
Faith's breach for love and kingdoms is no sin." But as desperate
lovers of all eras doubtless discovered for themselves, the lengths
to which they went in pursuit of love sometimes became the
equivalent of war. Thus in 1623, in the English play *The Lovers'
Progress*, love and war were at last linked in the passage, "All
stratagems in love, and that the sharpest war, are lawful." Soon
after, Mrs. Aphra Behn, the first female professional writer in
England, further refined that sentiment in her play *Emperor of
the Moon* (1677): "Advantages are lawful in love and war." In
her novel *Belinda* (1801), the Irish writer Maria Edgeworth
wrote, "In love and war, you know, all stratagems are allowable."
The saying in its modern form apparently appeared first in 1850
in *Frank Fairlegh,* a novel by the Englishman Frank Smedley.
Although this version has remained in use to the present day,
the columnist Walter Winchell in 1941 made a witty and quite
contemporary connection between love and the very real Second
World War: "Name for quick romance: blisskrieg."

All is well that ends well.   *The Proverbs of Hendyng* (c. 1250)
contained what was apparently the earliest recorded version of
this proverb: "Wel is him, that wel ende mai." In 1426, the saying

appeared in a collection of poems as "Al ys good that hath good ende," and the modern version was recorded in John Heywood's *A Dialogue Conteinyng the Nomber in Effect of All the Prouerbes in the Englishe Tongue* (1546). Not long after, William Shakespeare used the proverb for the title of his comedy of 1602, in which a desperate Helena resorted to elaborate deceptions before at last winning the love of the young count of Rousillon. (Shakespeare, incidentally, also borrowed the plot for this play from the *Decameron*.) By the nineteenth century, if not before, the proverb was commonly used throughout Europe. In *Rob Roy* (1818), Sir Walter Scott adapted it to read, "A's weel that ends weel! the warld will last our day." A good ending indeed, and well worth repeating.

All that glitters is not gold.   The warning against being deceived by appearances, "All that glitters..." was first rendered in 1175 by the French monk Alanus de Insulis: "Do not hold everything gold that shines like gold,/Nor every beautiful apple to be good." Later, Chaucer used a similar version in his *Canterbury Tales* (c. 1387), and in the sixteenth century, Edmund Spenser wrote, "Yet gold al is not, that doth golden seeme," in *The Faerie Queene* (1596). A few years later, William Shakespeare made it, "All that glisters is not gold," in *The Merchant of Venice*. The word "glitters" finally appeared in 1773, when "All is not gold that glitters" was quoted in the preface to Oliver Goldsmith's famous comedy *She Stoops to Conquer*. The cause for this particular form was taken up by none other than Dr. Samuel Johnson in 1784, and he succeeded in popularizing it. The proverb appeared in widely different forms in other countries, including the Arabian "Not every crooked neck is a camel." A witty alteration concocted more recently by American poet Ogden Nash in *Look What You Did, Christopher* (1933) still seems true today: "All that glitters is sold as gold."

All the world loves a lover.   The Roman poet Sextus Propertius in *Elegies* (22 B.C.) proclaimed, "There is none would hurt a lover; lovers are sacred." But the current version of the saying apparently did not appear in print until centuries later, when it was included in Ralph Waldo Emerson's *Essays* (1841): "All mankind love a lover." Eugene O'Neill rendered the modern wording in *The Great God Brown* (1926).

All things come in threes.   The earlier version of this saying, "All things thrive at thrice," first appeared in a manuscript dating from about 1598. Over a century later, a different rendering was included in *A Complete Collection of Scotish Proverbs* (1721) by James Kelly: "An Encouragement to those who have miscarried in their Attempts once and again, to try the third time. They will say the third's a Charm, or, there are three things of all things." In *The Adventures of Peregrine Pickle* (1750), Tobias Smollett wrote, "Number three is always fortunate." Though sources list no references to "All things come in threes" from the nineteenth century, the saying was doubtless in use to one degree or another. It has been repeated in print frequently during the twentieth century, notably by P. G. Wodehouse in *If I Were You* (1931) and by mystery writer Agatha Christie in *Dead Man's Folly* (1956). *See also* **Misfortunes never come singly.**

All work and no play makes Jack a dull boy.   The sentiment expressed by this proverb was first recorded thousands of years ago by the Egyptian sage Ptahhotep, who wrote in c. 2400 B.C., "One that reckoneth accounts all the day passeth not a happy moment. One that gladdeneth his heart all the day provideth not for his house. The bowman hitteth the mark, as the steersman reacheth land, by diversity of aim." The more familiar modern saying appeared first in James Howell's *Proverbs in English, Italian, French and Spanish* (1659), and was included in later collections of proverbs. Some writers have added a second part to the proverb, as in *Harry and Lucy Concluded* (1825) by the Irish novelist Maria Edgeworth: "All work and no play makes Jack a dull boy / All play and no work makes Jack a mere toy." Similarly, in a popular nineteenth-century work called *Self-Help* (1859), author Samuel Smiles advises his Victorian audience, "All work and no play makes Jack a dull boy; but all play and no work makes him something greatly worse." The proverb has been quoted in print frequently during the twentieth century, including an instance in John Dos Passos's *The Big Money* (1936).

Answer a fool according to his folly.   This saying is an abridgement of the apparently self-contradictory Old Testament proverb, "Answer not a fool according to his folly, lest thou also be like unto him. Answer a fool according to his folly, lest he be wise in his own conceit." William Caxton, the first English printer, included an early version of the modern proverb in his book *Aesope* (1484): "To foolish demur [question] behoveth a foolish answer." English writer Thomas Nashe rendered the saying in his *Works* (1589): "It is therefore thought the best way ... to answere the fooles, according to their foolishness." In *Fables* (1692), English journalist Roger L'Estrange included a moral consideration with the passage, "It does not yet become a Man of Honour ... to Answer Every Fool in his Folly." But biographer Roger North observed in his *Lives of the Norths* (1740) that "fools are often answered in their folly." The saying has been quoted in print only infrequently during the twentieth century.

Any excuse is better than none.   *See* **Bad excuse is better than none, A.**

Apple a day keeps the doctor away, An.   Allusions to the apple's curative powers date back at least to *Arabian Nights' Entertainments* (c. 1450). One of the tales introduced a magical "apple of Samarkand," which supposedly could cure all diseases. Thomas Cogan's *The Haven of Health* (1612) attributed a somewhat different effect to apples, to wit: "He that will not a wife wed, Must eat a cold apple when he goeth to bed." Here apples supposedly quenched "the flames of Venus." In 1630, according to *The Soddered Citizen* apples quenched a different flame: "Hee gott A terrible heartburnynge, (had hee tane An apple then to beddwards, he had beene cur'd)." The apple's more familiar role of promoting fewer doctor's visits was a recent invention. In the publication *Notes and Queries* (1866), the saying neared its current form: "Eat an apple on going to bed, and you'll keep the doctor from earning his bread." By the early 1920s, that had been reduced to the now popular "An apple a day ... "

Apple never falls far from the tree, An.   Beneath the literal truth of this old saying (one does not need an apple tree to know that), there lies a wry observation about human nature and heredity. Probably applied most often now to someone with obvious failings, the saying asserts the problem was simply passed along from parent to child. The notion is similar to the older "Like father, like son," and "Like mother, like daughter," and seems to have appeared first in German. The American philosopher Ralph Waldo Emerson apparently was the first to use it in English when in an 1839 letter, he wrote that "the apple never falls far from the stem." But here Emerson used it in another sense, to describe that tug that often brings us back to our childhood home.

A century later, however, the saying appeared in its current form and connotation in *Body, Boots, and Britches* by H. W. Thompson.

April showers bring May flowers.   "April, that is messenger to May," as Chaucer described it in *Canterbury Tales* (c. 1387) brought uncertain days of rain and sunshine, and the teasing promise of a sweet spring to come. Probably the earliest reference to April showers was made in 1430 by the English priest and poet John Lydgate, who wrote, "Holsom as the Aprile showr fallying on the herbes newe," in *Reason and Sensuality*. Over a century later, the modern connection between April showers and May flowers was made clear in *Songs, William and Mary* (1560): "When Aprell sylver showers so sweet / Can make May flowers to sprynge." In *Five Hundreth Pointes of Good Husbandrie* (1573), Thomas Tusser shortened the saying to: "Sweete April showers Doo spring Maie flowers." William Shakespeare, in *Anthony and Cleopatra* (1606), penned the eloquent "The April's in her eyes; it is love's spring, / And these the showers to bring it on." The modern wording of the saying was firmly established later in the seventeenth century, appearing as "April showers bring forth May flowers," in John Ray's *A Collection of English Proverbs* (1670). A somewhat different version, "March winds and April showers / Bring forth May flowers," was included in *Proverbs* (1846) by Michael Denham.

Army marches on its stomach, An.   Of the many observations about the nature of armies (as in Napoleon's "An army is a crowd which obeys"), the need for food noted in this proverb is probably the most basic of all. In the Persian classic *Gullistan* (*Rose Garden*, c. 1258), the poet Sa'di wrote, "The well-fed warrior will with ardour fight; / The starved will be as ardent in his flight." William Shakespeare repeated the prescription in *Henry V* (c. 1599): "Give them great meals of beef and iron and steel, / they will eat like wolves and fight like devils." Though probably earlier in origin, the saying, "An army, like a serpent, travels on its belly," was attributed to Frederick the Great, the famous Prussian ruler who transformed his kingdom into a formidable military power in the eighteenth century. About 1800, the British general Arthur Wellesley, Duke of Wellington—perhaps reflecting British national tastes—observed, "No soldier can fight unless he is properly fed on beef and beer." But a French saying held that "the soup makes the soldier." At any rate, the modern "An army marches . . ." was apparently said first by Napoleon, according to an article published in a 1904 issue of *Windsor Magazine,* and the saying has been in use until the present day. It is impossible to resist including one last, understandably anonymous, comment on that often debated question of an army's fighting ability. The best troops, an unnamed nineteenth-century general said, "would be as follows: an Irishman half drunk, a Scotchman half starved, and an Englishman with his belly full."

Arrow shot upright falls on the shooter's head, An.   This lesson no doubt has been forgotten and relearned many times over the centuries (today by wildly firing antiaircraft gunners). An early form of the saying was recorded in ancient times in the apocryphal *Ecclesiasticus* (c. 190 B.C.): "Whoso casteth a stone on high casteth it on his own head." Centuries later, *Songs, Carols . . . from Richard Hill's Commonplace Book* (c. 1530) rendered the saying in English for the first time: "Often times the arow hitteth the shoter," and later that century, the *Garland of a Green Wit* (1595) by R. Turner included the passage, "Thou didst him constraine And causelesse curse, like arrowe shot vpright Returning downe, on thine owne head will light." Over a century later, Richard Kingston wrote in *Apophthegmata Curiosa* (1709), "Like arrows shot against Heaven, fall upon their own heads." There have been other sayings in this vein, of course, such as the Spanish proverb, "He who spits against the heavens gets his spittle back in his face," and the laughably commonplace, "They have simply stepped in their own chewing gum," which appeared in Philip Barry's play *The Philadelphia Story* (1939).

As the twig is bent, so grows the tree.   The twig as a metaphor for a developing child was introduced by Thomas Ingelend, who wrote in *The Disobedient Child* (c. 1560): "As longe as the twygge is gentell and plyent, . . . / With small force and strength it may be bent." Alexander Pope rendered what is essentially the proverb's modern version in *Moral Essays* (1732): "Just as the twig is bent, the tree's inclined." In 1796, George Washington gave it as "It has been said, and truly, 'that as the twig is bent so it will grow,'" and in 1818, the American satirist Thomas Fessenden complained, "'Tis education forms the tender mind. Just as the twig is bent the tree's inclined. This hacknied adage, not more trite than true." The current wording apparently did not appear in print until 1959 in the *Boston Globe,* though it was probably in use well before that time. Among the noted writers who used

the saying were Herman Melville in *Confidence-Man* (1857) and
Sinclair Lewis in *The Man Who Knew Coolidge* (1927).

Ask no questions and be told no lies.   This clever deflection
virtually guarantees that, if pressed on a particular matter, the
speaker will tell the questioner nothing but lies. The saying appeared for the first time in 1773: "Ask me no questions and I'll
tell you no fibs" in Oliver Goldsmith's *She Stoops to Conquer*. In a
letter dated 1775, the American statesman John Adams wrote:
"Of Mr. McPherson's Errand ... ask no Questions and I will tell
you no false News." Later, Sir Walter Scott rendered it as "If
ye'll ask nae questions, I'll tell you no lies" in the novel *Heart of
the Midlothian* (1818), and repeated it in a somewhat different
version that same year in *Rob Roy*. In *Great Expectations* (1860),
Charles Dickens wrote, "Drat that boy ... Ask no questions and
you'll be told no lies." Other noted works in which the saying
appeared include George Bernard Shaw's play *Man and Superman*
(1905) and James Joyce's *Ulysses* (1922).

Bad excuse is better than none, A.   [Any excuse is better ...]
Centuries ago, the Greek poet Pindar observed in his
Pythian Odes (462 B.C.) that an excuse is "that daughter of
Afterthought, who is wise too late." But who has not experienced
that dreaded, red-faced moment when blame was headed one's
way? It is almost impossible to keep silent at such times—to resist
invoking the "daughter of Afterthought"—even when an accu-
sation is completely justified. "A bad excuse ... " was recorded
first in *Rule of Reason* (1551) by the English humanist Thomas
Wilson: "This is as thei saie in English, better a badde excuse,
then none at all." The earliest English comedy, *Ralph Roister
Doister* (1553), by Nicholas Udall, repeated the saying with the
line, "Yea Custance, better (they say) a badde scuse than none."
Later, Henry Porter in *The Two Angrie Women of Abington* (1599)
cautioned, " 'Tis good to have a cloak for the rain; a bad shift

[excuse] is better than none." But perhaps the best advice came from the American writer and moralist Elbert Hubbard, who wrote in his *Epigrams* (1905), "Don't make excuses—make good." Ironically, Hubbard died ten years later in the sinking of the supposedly unsinkable liner *Titanic*, a tragedy for which many excuses were later offered.

Bad luck to walk under a ladder.   This superstition probably comes to us from early Christian times, when ladders became a symbol of misfortune because one had been rested against Christ's crucifix. Much later, in seventeenth-century England and France, the bad luck in walking under a ladder was plain for all to see: Criminals being led to the hangman's noose had to walk under a ladder. The hangman, of course, stepped around it. No doubt this practice gave rise to the superstition that walking under a ladder could lead to being hanged, but other forms of bad luck have been associated with it as well. Some women even believed it would prevent them from becoming married for a year (or forever). For most people, though, walking under a ladder simply meant a generalized misfortune, which could be avoided by spitting through the ladder or three times afterward, or by not speaking until seeing a four-legged animal. Whatever your particular beliefs on this old wives' tale, there is an element of common sense involved. Take the case of a nineteenth-century disbeliever reported in *Notes & Queries* (1866): The man, who "objected . . . to such superstitious nonsense, had a paintbrush dropped right on top of his head while passing under a ladder. He has since been a devout believer."

Bad news travels fast.   Even in ancient times, this proverbial lament about the condition of human society held true. In *Moralia* (A.D. c. 95), the Greek biographer Plutarch wrote, "How much more readily than glad events / Is mischance carried to the ears of men!" Centuries later, English dramatist Thomas Kyd echoed that sentiment with "Euill newes flies faster still than good," in his *Spanish Tragedy* (1592). In his *Barons' Wars* (1603), the Englishman Thomas Drayton gave the idea a poetic turn with "Ill news hath wings, and with the wind doth go; / Comfort's a cripple, and comes ever slow." Later in the seventeenth century, John Dryden rendered it as "Ill news is wing'd with fate, and flies apace," in *Threnodia Augustalis* (1685), and English dramatist Thomas Holcroft in *Road to Ruin* (1792) shortened the saying to essentially its modern form, "Ill news travels fast." This version appeared in works by Charles Dickens (1844, *Martin Chuzzlewit;* 1864, *Our Mutual Friend*) and by Nathaniel Hawthorne (1837, *Twice-Told Tales*), among others. The wording "Bad news travels fast" first appeared in print in the 1920s and has been in regular use in this century.

Barking dogs do not bite. [Barking dogs seldom...; never...] Anyone who has ever hurried past an untethered barking hound has probably hoped for some truth in this proverb. In fact, the saying has been known in one form or other for some time, though that is probably little consolation for those who have actually been bitten. An early Latin proverb warned ominously, "Beware of a silent dog and still water"—the silent dog apparently being more likely to bite than one that barks. A thirteenth-century French proverb noted more optimistically, "Every dog that barks doesn't bite," and about 1350, an English saying assured readers, "Bot as bremely as he [a cur] baies he bit is never the faster." In 1581, Thomas Howell wrote in *His Devises*, "Those dogs byte least, that greatest barkings keepe," and G. Delamothe's *The French Alphabet* (1592) rendered it as "A dogge that barkes farre of, dares not come neare to bite." In 1605, the saying appeared in William Camden's *Remaines Concerning Britaine* as "Great barkers are no biters." Essentially the modern version, "Barking dogs seldom bite," was included in Nathan Bailey's *Dictionarium Britannicum* (1736). In use up to the present day, the saying was cleverly altered by Ogden Nash to "A bargain dog never bites" in his *Funebrial Reflection* (1940).

Be just before you are generous.   Mrs. Eliza Haywood, who penned the first English periodical written by a woman, the *Female Spectator,* reported in a 1744 edition that there was "an old saying, that we 'ought to be just before we are generous.' " Samuel Johnson was said to have observed in about 1776, "It is easier to be beneficent than to be just," and Charles Dickens described the saying in *Martin Chuzzlewit* (1844) as the "most remarkably long-headed, flowing-bearded, and patriarchial proverb." The English dramatist Richard Sheridan quoted it in *School for Scandal* (1777), and Dickens repeated it in *David Copperfield* (1850). James Joyce mentioned the saying in *Ulysses* (1922), but it has not been frequently used in the twentieth century.

Be off with the old love before you are on with the new.   The Roman dramatist Plautus warned in his comedy *Trinummus* (c. 194 B.C.), "He who plunges into love is more lost than if he leapt from a rock." True enough, and many's the lover who realized too late the leap had been into the wrong arms. As early as 1566, the proverbial advice, " 'Tis good to be off wi' the old love / Before you are on wi' the new," appeared as a line in *Damon and Pithias*, a play by the English playwright Richard Edwards. Sir Walter Scott repeated the saying in *The Bride of Lammermoor* (1819), Anthony Trollope mentioned it in *Barchester Towers* (1857) as "the old song" about courting, and George Bernard Shaw found an entirely appropriate place for it in his play *The Philanderer* (1893). The saying has appeared in print with some frequency in the twentieth century, beginning with the English novelist Joseph S. Fletcher's *Safety* (1924). Aldous Huxley shortened it in *Point Counter Point* (1928) to "When it's a case of off with the old love and on with the new." Perhaps reflecting the quickening tempo of life in our century, novelist Esther Forbes in *Rainbow* (1954) referred to a man with "an off-with-the-old, on-with-the-new temperament."

Beauty is in the eye of the beholder.   The first stirrings toward this proverb appear to have come from the English dramatist John Lyly, who wrote in *Euphues in England* (1580), "As neere is Fancie to Beautie, as the pricke to the Rose," and from William Shakespeare, who in *Love's Labour's Lost* (c. 1594) penned the line, "Beauty is bought by judgement of the eye." Almost a century and a half later, Benjamin Franklin in his *Poor Richard's Almanack* of 1741 included the lines, "Beauty, like supreme dominion / Is but supported by opinion," and Scottish philosopher David Hume's *Essays, Moral and Political* (1742) contained the perhaps too analytical "Beauty in things exists merely in the mind which contemplates them." It was not until 1878, however, that the modern wording of the proverb first appeared in *Molly Brown*, by the Irish novelist Mrs. Margaret Hungerford. The saying has been repeated frequently in the twentieth century.

Beauty is only skin deep.   In 1613, Sir Thomas Overbury included the lines, "All the carnall beauty of my wife / Is but skin-deep, but to two senses known," in his poem *A Wife*, and the English writing master John Davies of Hereford recorded essentially the proverb's modern form in *A Select Second Husband* (1616): "Beauty is but skin-deepe." The following century, Samuel Richardson echoed this sentiment in his novel *Pamela* (1740) with "Beauty is but...a mere skin-deep perfection." True enough, but beauty is a perfection of an attractive kind, and not a few writers have disagreed with the notion "Beauty is only skin deep." In *Advice to Young Men* (1830), the Englishman William Cobbett—perhaps keeping in mind the sensibilities of his male audience—wrote, "The less favored part of the sex say, that 'beauty is but skin deep'; . . . but it is very agreeable, though, for all that." A more rancorous response to critics of physical beauty gave rise to the nineteenth-century English saying, "Beauty is only skin deep, but ugly goes to the bone." And that same century, the philosopher Herbert Spencer literally turned the current proverb on itself to make it a clever rebuke in *Personal Beauty* (1863): "The saying that beauty is but skin deep is a skin deep saying."

Because is a woman's reason.   "Beyng asked why they will doe this and that, they aunswere streight. Marie, because, I will doe it, or because it pleaseth me beste so to doe . . . Some women are subject to this aunswere." This passage appeared in Thomas Wilson's *The Rule of Reason* (1551), and not long after, William Shakespeare wrote in *The Two Gentlemen of Verona* (c. 1592), "I have no other but a woman's reason; / I think him so, because I think him so." In *Love's Metamorphosis* (1601), the English dramatist John Lyly explained, "Women's reasons; they would not, because they would not." A year later, the popular playwright Thomas Middleton repeated the idea of "women's reasons" in *Blurt* (1602): "Besides, I have a woman's reason; I will not dance because I will not dance." The saying appeared in its modern form in James Kelly's *Scottish Proverbs* (1721) and subsequent collections of proverbs up to the present day. The English feminist Mary Wollstonecraft noted the proverb in *A Vindication of the Rights of Woman* (1792), saying, "This mode of arguing, if arguing it may be called, reminds me of what is vulgarly termed 'a woman's reason'; for women sometimes declare that they love or believe certain things 'because' they love or believe them."

Beggars can't be choosers.   This proverb was first recorded in John Heywood's *A Dialogue Conteinyng the Nomber in Effect of All the Prouerbes in the Englishe Tongue* (1546) as "Folke saie alwaie, beggers should be no choosers," and from that time forward it has appeared regularly in collections of proverbs and other printed works. The English ecclesiastic Stephen Gosson observed in *School of Abuse* (1579), "Beggars, you know, must bee no choosers." Soon after, in 1594, Francis Bacon repeated the saying, while about the same time, William Shakespeare adapted it for

The Taming of the Shrew (c. 1593). Toward the close of the seventeenth century, John Dryden wrote in a letter, "As for the rarities you promise, if beggars might be choosers, a part of a chine of honest bacon wou'd please my appetite more than all the marrow puddings." Anthony Trollope quoted what was then the familiar form of the saying in *Barchester Towers* (1857), "Beggars mustn't be choosers," and just a few years later, Robert Louis Stevenson recorded what is the modern wording in *The Master of Ballantrae* (1888): "For all this we were to pay at a high rate; but beggars cannot be choosers."

Believe only half of what you see and nothing that you hear.   As Julius Caesar wisely noted in *De Bello Gallico* (c. 52 B.C.), "Men freely believe what they wish [to believe]," a tendency that has led many of us to disappointment and outright misfortune. In an early form of the current proverb, the Roman statesman Cicero advised in *De Divinatione* (44 B.C.), "One does not have to believe everything one hears." Centuries later in 1205, the medieval English poet Layamon wrote in *Brut*, "Yif pu ileuest aehcne mon, Selde pu saelt we don [If thou believest each man, seldom shalt thou do well]." A somewhat similar warning, "Ye shulde not geue credence to alle thing that ye here," was rendered in the *Dialogue of Salomon & Marcolphus* (1492). The modern form of the saying was recorded in *A Woman's Thoughts* (1858), by the English novelist Dinah M. Mulock: " 'Believe only half of what you see, and nothing that you hear,' is a cynical saying, and yet less bitter than at first appears." Somewhat later, the Irish-born writer Oscar Wilde took a different tack in *The Picture of Dorian Gray* (1891), arriving at a clever declaration that perhaps anticipated the twentieth century: "I can believe anything provided it is incredible."

Bellowing cow soon forgets her calf, A.   Centuries ago, farming was still a way of life for many, and they probably had ample opportunity actually to hear a cow bellowing for its calf. But in fact the meaning of this proverb has less to do with the barnyard than with excessive grief, which the adage says does not last long, using the bellowing cow metaphor. Thomas Wilson recorded the earliest mention of this saying in *The Arte of Rhetorique* (1553): "Cowe lacking her Caulf, leaueth lowing within three or four daies at the farthest." The next known references did not appear until the late nineteenth century, when *West Worcestershire Words* by Mrs. Chamberlain gave virtually the modern wording: "A

lowing cow soon forgets her calf," and *Household Tales* (1895) by
S. O. Addy rendered it as "A bletherin' coo soon forgets her
calf." The exact wording of the saying was quoted in Mrs.
Wright's *Rustic Speech and Folk-Lore* (1913), but the saying has not
been quoted in print frequently during the twentieth century.

Best things in life are free, The.   A relatively recent invention,
this proverb reflects more than anything else a kind of modern
romanticism. In fact, the opposite sentiment had a far longer
history, beginning with a proverb usually attributed to Solon:
"Good things are hard." Seneca wrote in *Ad Lucilium* (A.D. c. 64),
"Great things cannot be bought for small sums." Later authors
penned somewhat different versions, as in "The best things are
not most easiest to attain" (1556, *The Castle of Knowledge*, by Robert
Recorde), and the absolutely dire, "The worthiest things ar
wonne with pain in tract of time alwaies" (c. 1570). From the
1600s onward, "The best things are worst to come by" became
fairly standard and appeared in subsequent collections of proverbs. The earliest reference to the modern, unabashedly romantic, "The best things in life are free," dates from the 1927 song
title, "Best Things in Life Are Free," though the saying may well
have been in use before then. It has come into wide use during
this century, though not without an occasional cynically humorous variation, as in "The best things in life may be free, but not
at my age" (1961, *The Big H*, by Bryan Peters).

**Best doctors are Doctor Diet, Doctor Quiet, and Doctor Mer-
ryman, The.**   When this amusing old saw first appeared in the
sixteenth century, doctors and their crude treatments were more
than a little suspect. In fact, the healthy regimen prescribed by
the saying probably had about as much chance of success as the
doctor and his leeches did. The earliest version of the saying
appeared in *Regimen Sanitatis Salernitanum* (c. 1550), which recommended, "If doctors fail you, let these three be your doctors:
a cheerful mind, rest, and moderate diet." A few years later,
William Bullein's *The Government of Health* (1558) gave the prescription its fanciful turn with "The first was called doctor diet,
the seconde doctor quiet, the third doctor mery man." The English writer Robert Burton noted in *The Anatomy of Melancholy*
(1621), "Dr. Merryman, Dr. Diet, and Dr. Quiet, which cure all
diseases," and a century later, the modern version was recorded
by the satirist Jonathan Swift in *Polite Conversation* (1738). Though
the state of medical knowledge had improved considerably by

the nineteenth century, Henry Wadsworth Longfellow preserved
some of the old sentiment against doctors in *The Best Medicines*
(1845) with the lines, "Joy and Temperance and Repose / Slam
the door on the doctor's nose." "The best doctors are..." was
quoted in print only infrequently during the twentieth century,
though James Joyce paraphrased it in *Ulysses* (1922).

Better born lucky than rich.   In these modern, materialistic
times, being born rich may seem the best possible life, but as one
writer noted, some people possess such good fortune that they
could, in fact, "fall down a sewer and find a ring." John Clarke's
collected proverbs, *Paroemiologia,* first recorded the proverbial
preference for good luck in 1639 as "Better to have good fortune
than to be a rich man's child." The modern wording appeared
in *Denham Tracts* (1846) by Michael Denham, and W. Carew Hazlitt's *English Proverbs* (1907) rendered a somewhat different wording, "Better be lucky born than a rich man's son." The proverb
has been quoted up to the present day, though not without some
variations, as in Richard Hofstadter's *Idea* (1969): "If one is lucky
enough it is better to be lucky than clever."

Better death than dishonor.   The Greek dramatist Sophocles
wrote in *Peleus* (c. 410 B.C.), "It is better not to live at all than to
live disgraced." Centuries later, the Roman statesman Cicero
wrote in *De Officiis* (45 B.C.), "When the stress of circumstances
demands it, we must gird on the sword and prefer death to
slavery and disgrace." The Roman poet Juvenal wrote in *Satires*
(c. 120), "Count it the greatest of infamies to prefer life to honor,
and to lose for the sake of living." An English version of the
saying, "Better it is with worshyp to dye than with shame to lyue:
albe hit that Demosthenes sayde: he that fleeth cometh agayne
to batayle," was included in *Tales and Quicke Answers* (c. 1532) by
an unknown author. Later that century, the saying, "Better die
with honour than live with shame," appeared in a translation of
the epic *Orlando Furioso* (1591) by the Italian poet Lodovico
Ariosto. William Shakespeare echoed the sentiment in *Troilus and
Cressida* (c. 1601): "Life every man holds dear; but the brave man
/ Holds honour far more precious-dear than life." Joseph Addison, writing in *Cato* (1712), made it "Better to die ten thousand
deaths, / Than wound my honour." Though it was probably in
use earlier, the modern wording of the proverb apparently did
not appear in print until 1932, in C. Dawes's *Lawless.*

Better late than never.   There is nothing new about being late; almost two thousand years ago, the Greek historian Dionysius of Halicarnassus wrote, "It is better to be late than to never arrive," in *Romaike Archiologia* (c. 25 B.C.). Somewhat later, Livy wrote in *History of Rome* (10 B.C.), "*Potius sero, quam nunquam,*" which translated to "Better late than never" in English. The saying proved popular, and eventually spread to many other languages in Europe and elsewhere. It appeared as early as 1200 in English, and Chaucer rendered it in *Canterbury Tales* (c. 1387) as "Lest ye lese al, for bet than never is late." John Lydgate's *The Assembly of Gods* (c. 1420) gave essentially the modern wording while also holding out hope for those sinners slow in repenting: "He seyde vyce to forsake ys bettyr late than neuer." "Better late than never" no doubt has been repeated many times over the centuries since, but those who are too often behind schedule may want to remember another old saying, "The bones for those who come late."

Better safe than sorry.   The history of this maxim, so familiar in modern times, is somewhat unclear. The earliest rendering is probably "It is good to be sure," a line that appeared in a comedy by Edward Ravenscroft, *The Canterbury Guests* (1695). Over a century later, the Anglican clergyman John Keble, a key figure in the Oxford Movement, elaborated on that sentiment with "Careful always to be on the safe side" (1823). In 1837, the Irish novelist Samuel Lover gave nearly modern wording—"It's better to be sure than sorry"—in *Rory O'More, a National Romance.* The current wording probably appeared for the first time in the 1929 novel *Plain People,* written by the American novelist and essayist Edgar Watson Howe. The saying has been widely used in the twentieth century.

Better the devil you know than the devil you don't.   For those unpleasant choices so often presented by life, the Roman dramatist Plautus advised, "Keep what you have; the known evil is best," in his comedy *Trinummus* (*Three Bob Day,* c. 194 B.C.). Phaedrus, a freed Roman slave and writer of fables, later took the dilemma to extremes in *Frogs Asking for a King* (c. 25 B.C.). The frogs of this tale were unhappy with their ruler, King Log, and suffered the misfortune of getting King Stork instead (a stork eats frogs, among other small animals)—the moral being, "Submit to the present evil, lest a greater one befall you." The Roman historian Livy wrote in *History of Rome* (c. 10 B.C.), "The best known evil is the most tolerable," and Plutarch in *Moralia* (A.D. c. 95) recommended, "Put up with familiar evils, rather than make trial of unfamiliar ones." Centuries later in 1539, John Taverner's *Proverbes or Adagies* offered the consolation, "An euyl thynge knowen is best. It is good kepyng of a shrew that a man knoweth." Later in the sixteenth century, French moralist Michel Montaigne wrote in *Essays* (1595), "The oldest and best known evil is always more tolerable than a new and unexperienced one." The modern wording of the proverb was first recorded in Anthony Trollope's novel *Barchester Towers* (1857). *See also* **Of two evils, choose the lesser.**

Better to be an old man's darling than a young man's slave.   That proverbial wisdom is divided on the subject of May-December marriages should be no surprise; the sayings only reflect the general disagreement in society about such marriages. The English priest John Lydgate opposed them in *Temple of Glass* (c. 1400): "For it ne fit not vnto fresshe May / Forto be coupled to colde Januari." Almost two centuries later, another medieval writer warned, "As Venus and Saturne are at continual warre the one with the other, so the old coupled with the yong, never agree together." But the English poet George Herbert wittily defended such marriages in his posthumously published *Jacula Prudentum* (1640): "An old wise man's shadow is better than a young buzzard's sword," and Thomas Fuller's *Gnomologia* (1732) included the saying, "Better have an old Man to humour, than a young Rake to break your Heart." An early form of the current proverb appeared in John Heywood's *A Dialogue Conteinyng the Nomber in Effect of All the Prouerbes in the Englishe Tongue* (1546): "Many yeres sens my mother saide to me / Her elders would saie: it is better to be / an old mans darling than a yong mans warlyng [a disliked person]." The English writer Nicholas Breton in *Works* (1602) observed, "I see by my neighbours, it is better being an olde mans darling than a young mans worldling." The proverb's modern wording was first recorded by the British playwright James R. Planché in *Extravaganzas* (1842).

Better to be unborn than untaught.   In the words of the English poet Joseph Addison, "What sculpture is to a block of marble, education is to the soul." The current proverb, which stresses the importance of training and educating a child, first appeared in the medieval collection *Proverbs of Alfred* (c. 1275) as "For betere is child vnboren thenne vnbeten." It was repeated in the 1300s with such variations as "Better is a chylde unborn pen vnlerned" (1350). In 1530, *Richard Hill's Commonplace Book* rendered the saying in virtually its modern form: "Better it is to be unborne than untaught." Quoted with some frequency in the 1500s and 1600s, the proverb spawned two variants: the dire "Better unfedde than un-taughte" from *The School of Virtue* (1557), and "It is as good to be unborn as unbred" from Thomas Fuller's *History of the Worthies of England* (published posthumously in 1662). Sir Walter Raleigh, in *Instructions to His Son* (1616), rendered the latter variant as "Better were it to be unborn than illbred," and William Shakespeare's *All's Well That Ends Well* (1602) contained the line, "I will show myself highly fed and lowly taught." The modern wording was recorded in Thomas Fuller's *Gnomologia* (1732) and has been included in books of proverbs up to the present day, though the saying appears to have been quoted infrequently in the twentieth century.

Beware of Greeks bearing gifts.   This saying has its origins in ancient times, when the Greeks apparently were in poor repute. In the *Aeneid* (19 B.C.), the Roman poet Virgil wrote, "Think ye any gifts of the Greeks are free from treachery? . . . I fear the Greeks, even bearing gifts." Virgil was mindful of the legendary Trojan horse, a clever gift that, in Homer's epic tale, the invading Greeks used to conquer the city of Troy. Centuries later, the English wit John Lyly wrote in *Euphues and His England* (1580), "Of olde it was sayd . . . , that all the Grecians knewe honestie, but not one practised it." An unknown but equally biting wit was responsible for an old Albanian saying, "After shaking hands with a Greek, count your fingers."

In a letter of 1777, the English lexicographer Samuel Johnson wrote, "Tell Mrs. Boswell that I shall taste her marmalade cautiously at first . . . Beware, says the Italian proverb, of a reconciled enemy." The novelist Anthony Trollope also adapted the ancient cautions in *Phineas Redux* (1873) with "presents from Greeks had ever been considered dangerous." Though probably in use earlier, the current "Beware of Greeks bearing gifts" did not appear in print until 1941, in *Talking Clock* by Frank Gruber.

Bigger they are the harder they fall, The.   Who has not repeated this popular saying—with muffled satisfaction—at least once in a lifetime? Interestingly, this version is not that old, apparently originating in 1902 with world boxing champion "Ruby Robert" Fitzsimmons. During a newspaper interview before a bout on July 25 in San Francisco, Fitzsimmons was questioned about his chances of beating his much heavier opponent and responded, "The bigger the man, the heavier the fall." Fitzsimmons went on to lose the bout, but that did nothing to discourage use of the saying.

The exact wording of the current version was quoted in print at least as early as 1927, in *The Mosaic Earring* by Nell Martin, and about the same time there appeared some clever variations, such as "The wiser they are, the harder they fall," W. A. Wolff, *Trial* (1928), and "The richer they are the harder they fall," E. D. Torgerson's *Cold Finger* (1933). The idea expressed in the current proverb has been rendered in much older sayings dating from ancient times. The Roman poet Horace wrote, " 'Tis the lofty towers that fall with heaviest crash," in his *Odes* (23 B.C.). In medieval times, Chaucer's *Canterbury Tales* (c. 1387) included the lines, "Evere fro the hyer degree that man falleth, the more is he thral." Another variant, "The highest tree hath the greatest fall" was included in John Clarke's *Paroemiologia* (1639) and subsequent collections up to the present day.

Big oaks from little acorns grow. [Great oaks...; Tall...]

That things great and tall spring from small beginnings has been the subject of numerous proverbs since ancient times. The earliest known saying modeled on a tree's growth was recorded in *The Way of Virtue* (c. 550 B.C.) by the Chinese philosopher Laotze: "The tree that needs two arms to span its girth began from the tiniest shoot..." In 458 B.C., the Greek dramatist Aeschylus wrote essentially the same thought in *The Libation-Bearers:* "From a little seed may spring a mighty stock." A Latin proverb, "Much in little," was echoed by the medieval Italian poet Dante in *Paradiso* (c. 1321): "From little spark may burst a mighty flame," and in Chaucer's medieval English poem *Troilus and Criseyde* (c. 1385), which included the line, "An ook cometh of a litel spyr." The English ecclesiastic Stephen Gosson observed in *Schoole of Abuse* (1579), "But tal Cedars, from little graynes shoote high: great Okes, from slender roots spread wide." Almost a century later, the English poet Richard Corbet returned to the acorn-oak theme with, "An acorn one day proves an oak," in *Poems* (c. 1640), and in 1732 Thomas Fuller's *Gnomologia* gave the saying as "The greatest Oaks have been little Acorns." Essentially the modern wording of the saying appeared a few years later in *Lines Written for a School Declamation* (1797) by David Everett: "Tall oaks from little acorns grow." The exact wording appeared in a 1923 *London*

Times story about a political speech, which included the quote, "Here in England, as nowhere else in the world, 'great oaks from little acorns grow.' "

Bird in the hand is worth two in the bush, A.   The dilemma is probably as old as humanity itself: Should you hold on to what you have, or risk everything to pursue something better, even though it may be beyond your grasp? Surely, many a poor soul who succumbed to the temptation wound up empty-handed in the eons before the Greek poet Hesiod wrote what was probably the earliest recorded version of this proverb (Eighth century B.C.): "He is a fool who leaves what is close at hand to pursue what is out of reach." The same thought appeared two centuries later in Aesop's *Fables.* In one tale, a hawk refused to be outwitted by a sparrow it had just caught—the sparrow vainly argued that it was a mere mouthful for the hawk and should be let go in favor of bigger prey. By about 1400, the current "Bird in the hand . . ." was popular in medieval Europe as a rhymed Latin verse, and the English chronicler John Capgrave recorded the first English version in *Life of St. Katharine* (c. 1450) as "It is more sekyr [secure] a bird in your nest, than to have three in the sky aboue." The exact modern wording appeared in Thomas Shelton's translation of *Don Quixote* (1620), and later in John Bunyan's *Pilgrim's Progress* (1678). The proverb has remained in wide use up to the present day, though not without sometimes amusing variations, as in Benjamin Franklin's "An egg to-day is better than a hen to-morrow" (1734, *Poor Richard's Almanack*).

Bird in the house brings bad luck.   From time to time, a bird may get caught inside a house, by flying in through an open window or even by falling down a chimney. Although certainly upsetting for the bird, these occurrences were once also said to be an omen of death. Swallows falling down a chimney were believed to be a sign of misfortune as early as the seventeenth century, and *Notes & Queries* (1850) reported, "It is said that for a bird to fly in a room, and out again, by an open window, surely indicates the decease of some inmate." During the twentieth century, however, a bird in the house became an omen of more generalized misfortune, still something to be avoided but not nearly as serious as an impending death.

Birds of a feather flock together.   The Greek poet Homer wrote in the *Odyssey* (ninth century B.C.), "As ever, the god is bringing like and like together," a saying also quoted in Plato's dialogue

Lysis (c. 380 B.C.), Aristotle's *Rhetoric* (c. 330 B.C.), and in other ancient Greek writings. The related saying, "Like seeks after like," was attributed to the Greek philosopher Empedocles (c. 450 B.C.), and with slight variations, this form was repeated by the Roman statesman Cicero and the Roman biographer Plutarch. Although the saying "Like will to like" remained in use up to modern times, Aristotle's *Rhetoric* also mentions another variant modeled around the jackdaw (a kind of bird): "Always jackdaw with jackdaw." A Latin proverb later rendered this variant as "Jackdaw always perches by jackdaw," and in c. 190 B.C., the more generalized "Birds dwell with their kind" was quoted in the apocryphal *Book of Wisdom* by Jesus Ben Sirach. Not until the sixteenth century, however, did "Birds of a feather . . ." appear in English as "Byrdes of one kynde and color flok and flye allwayes to gether," a line from *Rescuing of the Romish Fox* (1545) by William Turner. Three decades later, the playwright George Whetstone repeated it in his prose tale *Promos and Cassandra* (1578) as "Byrds of a fether, best flye together."

The seventeenth century saw the addition of a clear moral implication to the proverb. William Secker's *Nonsuch Professor* (1660) included the passage, "We say, 'That birds of a feather will flock together.' To be too intimate with sinners is to intimate that we are sinners." That notion was repeated by the English preacher John Bunyan in *The Life and Death of Mr. Badman* (1680): "They were birds of a feather . . . they were so well met for wickedness." "Birds of a feather . . . " was included in John Ray's *A Collection of English Proverbs* (1670) and later collections up to the present day.

Among the well-known authors who repeated the saying were Henry Fielding in his play *Author's Farce* (1729, "Men of a side Like birds of a feather Will flock together"); American revolutionary writer Thomas Paine in *Another Callender* (1805); English writer Baron Edward Bulwer-Lytton in the novel *Pelham* (1828, "It is literally true in the systematised roguery of London, that 'birds of a feather flock together' "); Charles Dickens in *Martin Chuzzlewit* (1850); the venerable Russian novelist Leo Tolstoy in his masterpiece *War and Peace* (1865, "Birds of a feather may fight together"); James Joyce in *Ulysses* (1922, "Birds of a feather laugh together"); and English writer Wyndham Lewis in *The Apes of God* (1930).

Black cat crossing your path.   Cats in general and black cats in particular became associated with witches and misfortune during the Middle Ages in Europe. Often the unfortunate animals fell victim to witch hysteria, when both the supposed witches and their cats were burned at the stake. In fact, during one anticat hysteria in seventeenth-century France, thousands of cats were burned each month, presumably because they were believed to be witches in disguise. By this time, less deadly superstitions about black cats were already known in England, and as one writer put it, "It is a very unfortunate thing for a man to meet early in a morning...a blacke cat." Such meetings were not regarded as universally unlucky, though. One superstition in nineteenth-century England said it was a good omen for a black cat to run along ahead of a fisherman walking to his boat, but bad luck if the cat crossed in front of him. A later version declared it was good luck for a black cat to come up to you, bad luck if it only approached and then walked away. As if to unravel the mystery of this old wives' tale, a young English boy explained some years ago, "The front of a black cat is lucky, the back unlucky."

Blessed is he who expects nothing, for he shall not be disappointed.   [Blessed are they who...] No doubt many have discovered that, as William Shakespeare once wrote, "Oft expectation fails." Centuries earlier, the Roman playwright Terence offered an equally realistic, if not somewhat cynical, assessment in *Phormio* (161 B.C.): "Whatever happens beyond expectation should be counted clear gain." What better defense against the inevitable disappointments of life could there be than to have no expectations? No doubt modeled on such thoughts, the current proverb originated with the English poet Alexander Pope, who, writing to his friend, the poet John Gay, in 1727, described what he called "a ninth beatitude... 'Blessed is he who expects nothing, for he shall never be disappointed.' " Benjamin Franklin repeated the proverb in 1739, as did the English poet John Wolcot in 1782 in *Ode to Pitt,* and the saying has been repeated up to the present time. One American writer, perhaps reflecting the temper of the times in 1967, rendered the saying as "Blessed are they who expect the worst, for they shall get it!"

Blood is thicker than water.   This proverb on the bonds of family and common ancestry first appeared in the medieval German beast epic *Reinecke Fuchs* (c. 1180, *Reynard the Fox*) by Heinrich der Glichezaere, whose words in English read, "Kin-blood is not spoiled by water." In 1412, the English priest John Lydgate observed in *Troy Book*, "For naturelly blod will ay of kynde / Draw

vn-to blod, wher he may it fynde." By 1670, the modern version
was included in John Ray's collected *Proverbs,* and later appeared
in Sir Walter Scott's novel *Guy Mannering* (1815) and in English
reformer Thomas Hughes's *Tom Brown's School Days* (1857). In
1859, a U.S. Navy commodore also quoted the proverb in a letter
explaining why he had gone to the aid of a British fleet during
a battle with the Chinese that year. More recently, Aldous Huxley's *Ninth Philosopher's Song* (1920) gave the saying quite a different turn with "Blood, as all men know, than water's thicker /
But water's wider, thank the Lord, than blood."

Born with a caul.   An irregularity of birth involving the fetal
membrane, referred to as a caul in earlier times, gave rise to an
old wives' tale. At times, babies are born with the fetal sack draped
over their heads ("wrapped in their mothers' smocks" was the
way the rustics put it). Apparently this was not harmful but was
unusual enough to give rise to the belief that being born with a
caul was (in various ways) a sign of good fortune. Already well-
known in the seventeenth century, the old wives' tale was mentioned variously as a sign of coming wealth, general good luck,
or (for a boy) success with women. In the play *The Sullen Lovers*
(1668), Thomas Shadwell wrote, "Sure I was born with a caul on
my head, and . . . the ladies do so love me." That same century,
Richard Howell's *Proverbs in English, Italian, French, and Spanish*
(1659) included the saying, "He is born with his head coiff'd, viz.
rich." The next century, Richard Steele wrote in his play *The
Lying Lover* (1704), "I can't believe there is anything to that old
whim [born with a caul] . . . but I have strange luck with women."
Swift echoed such sentiments in his *Polite Conversations* (1738),
and Charles Dickens once made joking mention of a caul in *David
Copperfield* (1849), but the saying does not appear to be much in
use in modern times.

Boys will be boys.   [Girls will be girls; Children will do like
children.] The Latin proverb, "Children are children and employ
themselves with childish things," probably gave rise to the current
saying. One of the earliest English versions—"Youth are youth"—
appeared in *The Gentle Craft* (1597) by Thomas Deloney, England's first writer of popular fiction. A few years later, English
Puritan leader Arthur Dent added a distinct note of parental
frustration to this version in *Plain Man's Pathway* (1601): "Youth
will be youthfull, when you haue saide all that you can." William
Walker's *Paroemiologia Anglo-Latina* (1672) gave us "Boys will have

toys; children will do like children," and a century later, the more specific "Young fellows will be young fellows" was in use. The parallel, "Girls will be girls," was probably recorded for the first time in 1826, while the modern wording for "Boys will be boys" appeared some years afterward in Lord Edward Bulwer-Lytton's *The Caxtons* (1849). "Boys will be boys" was thereafter repeated by such noteworthy authors as William Makepeace Thackeray (*The Newcomes*, 1853), Mark Twain (*Huckleberry Finn*, 1884), George Bernard Shaw (*Fanny's First Play*, 1911), James Joyce (*Ulysses*, 1922), and William Faulkner (*Sanctuary*, 1931).

Alas, "Girls will be girls" seems to be used far less frequently in print at least, perhaps because of the general perception that girls are less troublesome than boys. That may well be true, but in fairness we should include two lines Henry Wadsworth Longfellow composed for his little golden-haired daughter Edith one day in 1856: "There was a little girl Who had a little curl / Right in the middle of her forehead, / And when she was good She was very, very good, / But when she was bad she was horrid."

Business before pleasure.   A manuscript entitled *Grobiana's Nuptials* (1640) contained an early mention of business and pleasure: "Well to the businesse. On; businesse is senior to complement." The English Restoration dramatist William Wycherley adapted the underlying idea of the proverb for his play *The Country-Wife* (1675): "Go to your business, pleasure, whilst I go to my pleasure, business." The American colonial Thomas Hutchinson wrote, "Pleasure should always give way to business," in his diary in 1767, and interestingly enough, it was Hutchinson's actions while serving as Massachusetts governor in the 1770s that helped spark the American Revolution. After the Revolution, and about a year before becoming vice president of the United States in 1801, Aaron Burr wrote in a letter, "The rule of my life is to make business a pleasure, and pleasure my business." One of the chief prosecutors at Burr's trial for treason (1807; Burr was acquitted) had a sterner motto, though, which he set forth in a letter of 1816: "Business first, and then pleasure, is my motto." The American jurist Nathan Clifford penned essentially the modern version of the proverb in a letter in 1834: "Business before parties is my motto," and the English novelist and playwright Catherine Grace Frances Gore quoted it exactly in *Stokeshill Place* (1837). Herman Melville repeated the proverb in *Israel Potter, or Fifty Years of Exile* (1855).

C

Caesar's wife must be above suspicion.   Concerning the origin of this proverb, the Roman biographer Plutarch recounted the tale of a political maverick named Publius Clodius, who in 62 B.C. surreptitiously entered Julius Caesar's house disguised as a female harpist. Only women were allowed to attend the ceremony of Bona Dea being held there, and after being discovered, Publius was put on trial for sacrilege. In the meantime, though, Caesar used the occasion to divorce his second wife, Pompeia. When asked at the trial why he had divorced her, Caesar answered, "Because Caesar's wife must be free from suspicion." The English dramatist John Lyly added the unspoken assumption in this saying when he repeated it in *Euphues and his England* (1580): "Al women shal be as Caesar would haue his wife, not onelye free from sinne, but from suspition."

A century and a half later, Samuel Richardson in *Clarissa* (1748) rendered the saying in its modern form, and George Bernard Shaw adapted it for *The Man of Destiny* (1895) with the line, "I beg your pardon. Caesar's wife is above suspicion." But it was J. C. Hare who, in the aptly titled *Guesses at the Truth* (1827), seemed to be writing for an audience in late twentieth-century America: "Caesar's wife ought to be above suspicion...Yet most would be slow to acknowledge...that Caesar himself ought to be so too."

Cat washing over its ears means rain.   This old wives' tale dates back at least to the sixteenth century. *Gospelles of Dystaues* (1507) reported, "Whan ye se a cat syt in a wyndowe...& that ...one of her fete be above her ere ye nede not doubte but y' shall rayne that daye." Likewise, in the next century, a book called *Foure-footed Beastes* remarked that "some observe that if [a cat] put her feete beyond the crowne of her head, that it is a presage of raine." The superstition survived into this century, and as recently as the 1980s, one believer was quoted as saying, "If a cat washes behind its ears [with its paw], it's going to be stormy."

Chain is as strong as its weakest link, A.   A relatively recent invention, this proverb is generally used to point out the possible weakness in any activity involving a group of people. In its earliest form, the saying referred to a thread; *Jacula Prudentum* (1740) by the English poet George Herbert included the proverb, "The thread breaks where it is weakest." At some point afterward the word 'chain' was substituted, and in 1868, the writer Leslie Stephen used virtually the modern wording in an article for the English magazine *Cornhill*: "A chain is no stronger than its weakest link." Arthur Conan Doyle repeated the saying as "No chain is stronger than its weakest link" in *The Affair of the Porlock Letter* (1887), and George Bernard Shaw in *Misalliance* (1910) gave us "The strength of a chain is no greater than its weakest link." Similar minor variations have appeared in print up to recent times.

Charity begins at home.   The English church reformer John Wycliffe recorded the earliest English version of this proverb in c. 1380: "Charite schuld bigyne at hem-self," though an even earlier version was recorded in the Muslim *Sunnah* (c. 800): "A man's first charity should be to his own family, if poor." In 1509, English poet Alexander Barclay wrote in *The shyp of Folys of the Worlde*, "For perfyte loue and also charite, / Which first beginneth of him selve for to be charitable." What was nearly the modern wording of the saying—married to a clever barb on the trials of domestic life—appeared in the English play *Wit Without Money* (1614) by Francis Beaumont and John Fletcher: "Charity and beating begins at home." Not long after, the playwright Richard Brome recorded the saying as it is now known in his play *A Joviall Crew* (1641), and Thomas Fuller in *The Appeal of Injured Innocence* (1659) added what became a frequently noted caution: "Charity begins, but doth not end, at home." The proverb has been included in collections and quoted regularly by writers since the seventeenth century, though not without some tampering for pointed or witty effect: Jonathan Swift in *Blue-Skin's Ballad* (1724, "Some to steal from a Charity think it no Sin / Which at home (says the Proverb) does always begin"); Tobias Smollett in *The Adventures of Roderick Random* (1748); Charles Dickens in *Martin Chuzzlewit* (1850, "But charity begins at home, and justice begins next door"); Ogden Nash in *I'll Stay Out of Your Diet* (1942, "I prefer charity to hospitality because charity begins at home and hospitality ends there"); and Ellery Queen in *The Player on the Other Side* (1963).

Charity covers a multitude of sins.   This saying originated as
"Charity shall cover the multitude of sins," in the first of two
letters attributed to Saint Peter in the New Testament. Probably
written sometime in the first or second century, the letter urged
Christians being persecuted in parts of Asia Minor to follow the
example of Jesus Christ by repaying evil with goodness—as by
answering the multitude of sins against them with charity. Later
quoted in works other than the Bible, the proverb in popular
use lost the sense of forgiveness so important to the original
Biblical passage. Instead, the modern usage took a more literal
turn, more often pointing out the self-serving aspect of some
people's charity—namely those who covered up their wrongdoing with charitable works. It was this sense that François
Rabelais wrote of in his satire *Pantagruel* (1552): "Their ugliness-
concealer, which you call a nose mask, but which the ancients
called charity [because it covers a multitude of sins]." The English
poet George Herbert recorded the proverb's modern wording
in *Priest to the Temple* (1633). Benjamin Franklin adapted the
saying in his *Poor Richard's Almanack* (1744), rendering it as
"Money, like Charity, covers all Crimes," and the American
statesman John Quincy Adams seconded that in 1786, writing
that "20,000 sterling will cover almost as great a number of faults
as charity." Over a century later, Oscar Wilde, in *The Soul of Man
Under Socialism* (1895), gave the saying yet another turn with
"Charity creates a multitude of sins." Similar clever adaptations
("Music covers..."; "Victory covers...") were common in the
twentieth century.

Child is father to the man, The.   The Judaic commentaries
known as the *Babylonian Talmud* (c. 350 B.C.) included the rustic
saying, "When a pumpkin begins to sprout, we can tell whether
it will rot or grow sound." Similarly, the current proverb holds
that the character of a child says much about the adult that child
will become, or, as the poet John Milton put it so eloquently in
Paradise Regained (1671), "The childhood shews the man / As
morning shews the day." Over a century later, William Wordsworth wrote the proverb in its modern form in *My Heart Leaps
Up* (1802), and in 1857, the American writer Herman Melville
repeated it ("...father of the man") in *The Confidence Man* (1857).
In *Character* (1871), Scottish writer Samuel Smiles noted, "The
influences which contribute to form the character of the child
endure through life...The child is father of the man." The
saying has been quoted with some frequency in the twentieth

century, notably in works by the English humorist P. G. Wodehouse (1934, *Brinkley*) and the American novelist J. P. Marquand
(1949, *Point of No Return*).

Children and fools speak the truth.   The earliest version of
this worldly proverb was recorded in, of all places, the state
papers of the reign of Henry VIII (1537) and included yet another category of hapless truthtellers—"a child, a fool and a
drunken man will ever show their conditions and the truth."
Richard Taverner's *Erasmus' Apophthegms* (1539) presented a
shortened version, "Our common prouerbe ... Children, drunk-
ers and fooles, can not lye," while John Heywood's *A Dialogue
Conteinyng the Number in Effect of All the Prouerbes in the Englishe
Tongue* (1546) brought it still closer to the modern form with
"Men say also, children and fooles can not lye."
   Virtually the modern version was recorded by the English lexicographer John Florio in *Firste Fruites* (1578)—"Chyldren and
fooles tel truth," and John Lyly in the play *Endimion* (1591) rendered it as " 'Tis an old said saw. Children and fools speak true."
The saying has been quoted regularly since then, including one
remarkably self-defeating use in a British courtroom in 1921.
The *Evening Standard* newspaper reported that when a solicitor
asked a witness, "Are you telling the truth in this case?" the
witness replied, "Only children and fools tell the truth." Now
there was a situation worthy of a courtroom drama (or comedy).

Children should be seen and not heard.   [Maidens should
be ... ; Women ... ; Girls ... ; Boys ...] The ancient Greek dramatist Aristophanes first recorded this proverb in his satire *The
Clouds* (423 B.C.), though it probably came into use well before
then. A fifteenth-century English work called *Mirk's Festial* (c.
1400) gave the version for a maid: "For hyt ys an old Englysch
sawe: 'A mayde schuld be seen, but not herd." This variant appeared in John Ray's *A Collection of English Proverbs* (1670) and
Jonathan Swift's *Polite Conversation* (1738), while the English
writer Richard Graves objected to the notion of relegating women
to silence in *Spiritual Quixote* (1772): "It is a vulgar maxim that a
pretty woman should rather be seen than heard."
   In his *Memoirs* (1820), the American statesman John Quincy
Adams repeated the version for children, recalling his "dear
mother's constant lesson in childhood, that children in company
should be seen and not heard." Later in the century, Victorian
novelist George Eliot rendered it as "Little gells must ..." in

Scenes of Clerical Life (1858), and Reverend Edward John Hardy in *How to Be Happy Though Married* (1885) came to the defense of children with " 'Little people should be seen and not heard' is a stupid saying." George Bernard Shaw in the introduction to his play *Misalliance* (1914) likewise railed against it: "Impudently proclaim the monstrous principle that little children should be seen and not heard." Nevertheless, the proverb continued to appear in print up to the present day, though not without such additional variants as "Little boys should be seen and not heard," which appeared in English satirist Wyndham Lewis's *Apes of God* (1930).

Children will do like children. *See* **Boys will be boys.**

Cleanliness is next to godliness. The relationship between physical cleanliness and spiritual purity dates back at least to the *Mishna,* the Judaic oral laws compiled about A.D. 400. It contained the passage, "The doctrines of religion are resolved into carefulness; carefulness into vigorousness; vigorousness into guiltlessness; guiltlessness into abstemiousness; abstemiousness into cleanliness; cleanliness into godliness." Much later, the English philosopher Francis Bacon wrote in *Of the Advancement of Learning* (1605), "Cleanness of the body was ever deemed to proceed from a due reverence to God."

But it was the English church reformer and founder of Methodism, John Wesley, who gave us the saying in its modern form in *Sermons: On Dress* (1780): "Slovenliness is no part of religion ... 'cleanliness is indeed next to godliness.' " American poet Henry Wadsworth Longfellow adapted the saying in *The Golden Legend* (1851): "If ... cleanliness is godliness, I fear / A hopeless reprobate, a hardened sinner, / Must be that Carmelite now passing near." George Bernard Shaw quoted the saying in the preface to *Man and Superman* (1903), "Cleanliness which comes next to godliness, if not before it," and it has appeared in print frequently during the twentieth century. A few voices have spoken out against the overzealous application of this proverb, however, among them Charles Dickens, who wrote in *Great Expectations* (1861), "Mrs. Joe ... had an exquisite art of making her cleanliness more uncomfortable and unacceptable than dirt itself. Cleanliness is next to Godliness, and some people do the same by their religion."

Clothes make the man.   The Judaic religious commentary, the
Babylonian Talmud, recorded this proverb in about 500, both in
the current form and in a related variation, "The girdle [belt]
shows who the wearer is." The Dutch scholar Desiderius Erasmus
in *Adagia* (1523) rendered the saying as "The clothes are the
man," and in the next century the venerable Ben Jonson expanded on the idea for his play *The Staple of Newes* (1626):
"Clothes do much upon the wit, as weather / Does on the brain;
thence comes your proverb, / 'The taylor makes the man.' " Striking a more pragmatic note, the American clergyman Henry Ward
Beecher wrote in *Proverbs From Plymouth Pulpit* (1887), "Clothes
and manners do not make the man; but, when he is made, they
greatly improve his appearance." Not everyone agreed with such
sentiments, though, and the Scottish philosopher David Hume
countered in *Essays* (1741) with "Art may produce a suit of
clothes; but nature must produce the man." Likewise, in America,
George Washington wrote in 1783, "Do not conceive that fine
Clothes make fine Men any more than fine feathers make fine
birds." *See also* **Fine feathers make fine birds.**

Confession is good for the soul.   [Open confession is . . .] In
43 B.C., the Roman statesman Cicero wrote in *Ad Octavium,* "May
confession be a medicine to the erring." The same thought
was repeated in a seventeenth-century translation of a manuscript
entitled *Janua Linguarum* (1615): "Confession is physick to a sinner." In 1641, David Fergusson's *Scottish Proverbs* included "Ane
open confessione is good for the soul," and this version was
repeated some years later in James Kelly's *A Complete Collection
of Scotish Proverbs* (1721), as well as in later collections of proverbs.
The shorter version in use today appeared at least as early as
1881 ("Confession may be good for the soul") in James Payn's *A
Grape From a Thorn,* and has been quoted regularly in the twentieth century. It is worth noting that while confession was doubtless good for the soul, it was not always good for the neck. Many
a wrongdoer no doubt discovered this before 1589, when the
bluntly fatalistic proverb, "Confess and be hanged," was first
recorded in English.

Course of true love never did run smoothly, The.   William
Shakespeare gave us this proverbial lover's lament in *A Midsummer Night's Dream* (c. 1594): "Ay me! for aught that I could ever
read, / Could ever hear by tale or history, / The course of true
love never did run smooth." Charles Dickens echoed the senti-

ment, if not the poetry, in *Pickwick Papers* (c. 1836) with "The course of true love is not a railway," and the English novelist Anthony Trollope adapted it for *The Golden Lion* (1872) as "He . . . feels it to be a sort of duty to take care that the course of love shall not run altogether smooth." Mystery writer Agatha Christie noted in *Murder in Mesopotamia* (1936), "It's nice when the course of true love runs smoothly," and H. G. Wells quoted the saying in the appropriately titled *You Can't Be Too Careful* (1942). The English writer Richard Aldington made a slight but revealing change to the proverb in his autobiography *Life for Life's Sake* (1941): "Perhaps the course of true love runs all the truer for not being smooth."

Crime does not pay. Though ancient writers alluded to the notion of the fruitlessness of crime, this maxim appears to have originated in the twentieth century. For example, Cleobulus, one of the Seven Wise Men of ancient Greece, recorded a saying in about 550 B.C.: "A man may thrive on crime, but not for long," and the Roman philosopher Seneca wrote in *Ad Lucilium* (A.D. c. 64), "Crime can never go unpunished, since the punishment of crime lies in the crime itself." Much later, the English poet George Herbert included the saying, "Punishment is lame, but it comes," in his collection of proverbs, *Jacula Prudentum* (1651). Ralph Waldo Emerson wrote in *Essays* (c. 1875), "Wherever a man commits a crime, God finds a witness . . . Every secret crime has its reporter." "*Crime does not pay*" apparently did not become current until the 1920s, however, and in 1928 was adapted in Richard Howells Watkins's *Master of Revels* as "Who said crime didn't pay?" The maxim has appeared in print frequently in the decades since.

Curiosity killed the cat. There is nothing new about the annoying tendency of some people to ask one question too many. Proverbial admonitions to the overly curious date back to ancient times, but "Curiosity killed the cat" is apparently a recent invention. Of the earlier sayings, Saint Augustine recorded in *Confessions* (397) the story of a curious soul who wondered what God did in the eons before creating heaven and earth. "He fashioned hell for the inquisitive," came the stern reply, and proverbial sayings of more recent times have been no less forgiving. The seventeenth-century saying, "He that pryeth into every cloud, may be struck with a thunderbolt," appeared in John Clarke's *Paroemiologia* (1639), and in the nineteenth century, Lord Byron in *Don Juan* (1818) roundly condemned the curious with "I loathe that low vice curiosity." An old saw, "Care [worry] killed the cat," dated from Shakespeare's time, but the connection between a cat and curiosity, however natural it may seem now, was not made until a reference to the current proverb appeared in 1909. The adaptation, "Curiosity can do more things than kill a cat," was recorded in O. Henry's short story *Schools and Schools* (1909), and the exact wording of the proverb appeared later in Eugene O'Neill's *Diff'rent* (1922).

Darkest hour is that before the dawn, The.   *Iphigeneia in Tauris* (c. 414 B.C.) by the Greek playwright Euripides included the passage, "Nay, misery's blackest night may chance, / By Fortune's turn, to show a happy dawn," which was probably the earliest rendering of the thought conveyed by the current proverb. But it was not until 1650 that a similar, though less poetic, saying appeared in English: "It is always darkest just before the day dawneth," in Thomas Fuller's *A Pisgah-Sight of Palestine*. John Wesley, the English church reformer and founder of Methodism, rendered the proverb as "It is usually darkest before daybreak" in his personal journal (1760), and more than a century later the English statesman Benjamin Disraeli wrote in *Endymion* (1880), "The darkest hour precedes the dawn." The exact wording of the saying first appeared in Alexander MacLaren's *Exposition of Deuteronomy* (1906). The saying was quoted and adapted by many writers, including Charlotte Brontë in her novel *Shirley* (1849), Robert Louis Stevenson in his correspondence (1889), P. G. Wodehouse in *Meet Mr. Mulliner* (1928), Dorothy Parker in *The Little Hours* (1930, "... darkest before the deluge"), and Ogden Nash in *Lucy Lake* (1933).

Darkest spot is just under the candle, The.   Though there is a pleasing irony to this saying, it has been little used and may in fact be a fairly recent invention. The earliest reference to it appears to be a passage in the American play *The Darling of the Gods* (1902) by David Belasco: "Do you know the proverb: 'The darkest place is just beneath the candlestick'?" Lee Thayer in her novel *Darkest Spot* (1928) rendered the saying as "The darkest spot is immediately under the candle" and repeated it in slightly different form years later in the novel *Persons Unknown* (1941): "The darkest spot is directly under the candle." The only other reference to the current proverb appeared as "The darkest spot is right under the light" in *Hot Ice* (1933) by Robert Joseph Casey.

Daughter is a daughter all the days of her life, A. *See* **My son is my son till he gets him a wife, but my daughter is my daughter all the days of her life.**

Dead men tell no tales. An old proverb that doubled as the title of a number of stories from the 1920s onward, the saying first appeared about 1552 in Thomas Becon's *The Fruitful Treatise of Fastyng*: "He that hath his body loaden with meat and drink, is no more meet to pray unto God than a dead man is to tell a tale." The playwright John Wilson rendered the saying a century later in his play *Andronicus Comnenius* (1664) with " 'Twere best To knock them i' th' head ... The dead can tell no tales." The exact wording of the current saying was recorded in John Dryden's *The Spanish Friar* (1681). The American writer Henry Brackenridge quoted the saying in *Modern Chivalry* (1804) and philosopher William James repeated it in his correspondence (1904). In the twentieth century, the proverb was regularly quoted in print, as well as being adapted for such book titles as John Goodwin's *When Dead Men Tell Tales* (1928) and Lee Thayer's *They Tell No Tales* (1930).

Death pays all debts. The French author Michel de Montaigne apparently penned the earliest version of this proverb in *Essays* (1580): "Death, they say, acquits us of all our bonds." It was William Shakespeare, however, who gave us essentially the thought behind the current saying, first in *Cymbeline* (1610) with "Are you ready for death? ... the comfort is, you shall be called to no more payments, fear no more tavern bills," and then more closely in *The Tempest* (1611) with "He that dies pays all debts." A later Elizabethan playwright, James Shirley, rendered the saying as "Death quits all scores," in *Cupid and Death* (1653). Sir Walter Scott rendered the saying as "Death pays a' scores" in his novel *Guy Mannering* (1815), but was first to quote the current form, "Death pays all debts," in his later novel *Two Drovers* (1827). The saying, in use up to the present day, has been included in such recent collections of proverbs as Burton Stevenson's *Home Book of Proverbs, Maxims, and Famous Phrases* (1948) and *The Oxford Dictionary of English Proverbs* (1970).

Discretion is the better part of valor.   The importance of discretion was noted as early as 421 B.C. by the Greek playwright Euripides, who wrote in the drama *The Suppliant Women*, "A daring pilot is dangerous to a ship. This too is a manly quality, namely discretion." Centuries later, the first Englishman to operate a printing press, William Caxton, included a similar appreciation of discretion in his translation of *Jason* (1477): "Than as wyse and discrete he withdrewe him saing that more is worth a good retrayte than a folisshe abydinge." William Shakespeare wrote the lines in *Henry IV, Part I* (1597), "The better part of valour is discretion; in the which better part, I have saved my life." A few years later, the English dramatists Francis Beaumont and John Fletcher gave essentially the modern wording in *A King and No King* (1611), rendering it as "discretion the best part of valour." Both the American writer Washington Irving (1804, in a contribution to the *Corrector*) and the American statesman John Quincy Adams (1816, in correspondence: "My discretion got the better part of my valor") adapted the proverb, while the English essayist William Hazlitt reversed elements in *Characteristics: In the Manner of Rochefoucauld's Maxims* (1823, "The better part of discretion is valour"). The exact wording of the current saying was first recorded in *Prince Bismarck* (1855), by Charles Lowe, and it has been used widely in the twentieth century.

Divide and conquer.   [Divide and rule.] Though this maxim is often attributed to the sixteenth-century Italian statesman Machiavelli, he is said to have in fact denounced it. French queen Catherine de Medici's adherence to the principle was noted in a translation of M. Hurault's *Discourse Upon the Present State of France* (1588): "It hath been alwaies her custome to set in France, one against another, that in the meane while shee might rule in these diuisions." In the next century, *Meditations* (1605) by J. Hall gave essentially the modern wording with "Diuide and rule." A few years later, the English philosopher Francis Bacon wrote in a letter (1615) to King James I, " 'Separa et impera,' that same cunning maxim," and soon after the English jurist Sir Edward Coke noted yet another version in *Institutes of the Lawes* (1628),

"Divide et impera, that exploded adage." While "Divide and rule" remained an oft-used version, the current "Divide and conquer" was first recorded (1775) in James Thatcher's journal (published 1823 as *A Military Journal During the American Revolutionary War*) with the observation, "The maxim adopted by our enemies is, 'Divide and conquer.' " This version was repeated (1798) in correspondence by the American revolutionary leader Christopher Gadsden and has been quoted regularly up to the present day. *See also* **United we stand, divided we fall.**

Do or die.   An expression of unshakable determination, this maxim first appeared in an early Scottish text, dated about 1577, as "He knew weill thair was no remedie but ether to do or die." In 1621, the current version was repeated as a line in John Fletcher's play *The Island Princess*, and that same year was included in Bartholomew Robinson's *Adagia in Latine and English*. Among those who have quoted the maxim since are the Scottish poet Robert Burns (1794, *Scots Wha Hae*) and more recently the writer Henry Miller (1939, *Tropic of Capricorn*).

Do unto others as you would they should do unto you.   [Do as you would be done by.] Probably best known as the Biblical Golden Rule, this proverb appeared in various forms in texts from many early cultures. For example, the saying, "According as I did to you, so also to me," appeared in *Teachings* (c. 550 B.C.) attributed to the Babylonian Ahikar, and the Chinese philosopher Confucius wrote in his *Analects* (c. 500 B.C.), "Do not to others what you would not like done to yourself." Aristotle's *Maxim* (c. 340 B.C.) told us, "We should behave to friends as we would wish them to behave to us," and the Hindu epic tale *Mahabharata* (c. 200 B.C.) counseled, "This is the sum of all true righteousness: deal with others as thou wouldst thyself be dealt by. Do nought to others which, if done to thee, would cause thee pain."

In Judaism, there is a clever story about a would-be believer who challenged Rabbi Hillel to teach him Jewish law in its entirety while he stood on one foot. The rabbi is said to have replied, "Whatsoever is hateful unto thee, do it not unto thy neighbor. This is the whole of the Torah, the rest is but commentary." The Biblical Golden Rule appeared in both Luke and Matthew of the New Testament (A.D. c. 65), the former giving the saying as "As ye would that men should do to you, do ye also to them likewise."

It was not until centuries later that the saying first appeared in medieval English, in the *Laws of Alfred* (901): "What you do not wish others to do to you, do not to other men." In about 1470, the English writer Sir Thomas Malory rendered the saying as "Allwayes a good man will do ever to another man as he wolde he done to hymself," and Anthony Woodville's *Dictes and Sayenges of the Philosophirs* (1477) gave it as "Do to others as thou woldest they should do to the [thee]..." The English statesman and author Thomas Wilson in *The Rule of Reason* (1551) quoted the saying as "Do as thou wouldest be done vnto." The first mention of the Golden Rule as applied to this proverb appeared in *Various Injuries and Abuses in Chymical Physick* (1674) by Robert Godfrey, "the Golden Law, 'do as ye would be done by,' " and was repeated by the English Nonconformist minister Isaac Watts in *Logick* (1725) as "Thence arises the Golden Rule of dealing with others as we would have others deal with us." Thomas Hobbes in *Leviathan* (1651) gave the proverb as "Do not that thou thinkest unreasonable to be done by another to they selfe," and John Stuart Mill in *Utilitarianism* (1863) wrote, "To do as one would be done by, and to love one's neighbor as one's self, constitute the ideal perfection of utilitarian morality." Anthony Trollope's *Life of Cicero* (1880) recorded essentially the current version with "do unto others as I would they should do unto me." Among the noted Americans quoting the variant "Do as you would be done by" were Benjamin Franklin in his correspondence (1735), John Quincy Adams in his diary (1787), Thomas Paine in *Age of Reason* (1794), George Washington in correspondence (1799), Andrew Jackson in correspondence (1823), and James Fenimore Cooper in correspondence (1829).

Doctors bury their mistakes. This raffish proverb dates back at least to fifteenth-century times when medical practitioners, such as they were, had far poorer success rates than they do today. The book *Dictes and Sayenges of the Philosophirs* (1477) by Anthony Woodville credited the following to the Greek philosopher Diogenes: "He sawe a peyntour [painter] that was waxe [had become] a physicien, to whom he sayde, thou knowest that man might se at the eye the fawtes that thou didst in thy craft, but nowe they may not be perceyued, for they ar hidde vnther the erthe." The French writer Michel de Montaigne, in *Essays* (1580), told of a bad wrestler turned doctor: " 'Courage,' said Diogenes to him, 'You are right; now you can put into the earth those who formerly laid you on it.' " In *Apophthegms* (1620), Francis Bacon returned to the painter-turned-doctor theme with "You have done well; for before the faults of your work were seen, but now they are unseen." The English playwright Thomas Heywood in his *Pleasant Dialogues* (1637) observed, "What good comes by their physick the sun sees; / But in their art, if they have bad successe, / That the earth covers."

By the next century, this variant, as recorded in James Kelly's *A Complete Collection of Scotish Proverbs* (1721), became "If the Doctor cures, the Sun sees it; but if he kills, the Earth hides it." A somewhat different version first appeared in Giovanni Torriano's *Select Italian Proverbs* (1642) as "Physicians errours are covered over with earth, and rich mens errours with moneyes," and survived to be included centuries later in the 1906 edition of W. Carew Hazlitt's *English Proverbs and Proverbial Phrases*. The modern "Doctors bury..." apparently first appeared in *Monk's Hood* (1931) by Arlo Channing Edington in the passage, "We [doctors] bury our mistakes." An improvement in the quality of medical care no doubt has helped make this proverb little known in modern times, but a witty bit of advice from Benjamin Franklin's *Poor Richard's Almanack* (1732) may still be worth remembering: "He's a fool that makes the doctor his heir."

Dog is man's best friend, A.   As early as the seventeenth century, John Horneck observed in *The Crucifixion of Jesus* (1686), "The dog teaches thee fidelity," and several years later, Alexander Pope made the somewhat one-sided observation in a letter (1709), "Histories are more full of examples of the fidelity of dogs than of friends." In *Table-Talk* (1830), the poet Samuel Taylor Coleridge championed the canine cause with "The dog alone, of all brute animals, has an affection upwards to man," but it was a Missouri senator named George G. Vest who in 1876 probably made the best case for man's best friend. Speaking for the prosecution at the trial of a Missouri farmer who had shot another man's dog for killing farm animals, the senator concluded his remarks by saying, "The one absolutely unselfish friend that man can have in this selfish world, the one that never deserts him, the one that never proves ungrateful or treacherous, is his dog." That emotional speech won the prosecution's case. The current wording of the saying was in use by about the early 1900s and was quoted in Dorothy Gardiner's *Transatlantic Ghost* (1935) as "Truly, the dog was man's best friend." No discussion about a dog's nature would be complete without mention of Samuel Butler's warm-hearted observation: "The great pleasure of a dog is that you may make a fool of yourself with him and not only will he not scold you, but he will make a fool of himself too."

Don't believe everything you hear.   *See* **Believe only half of what you see and nothing that you hear.**

Don't build castles on sand.   [. . . houses on sand.] This saying arose from a passage in Matthew in the New Testament (A.D. c. 70), in which Jesus warned, "And every one that heareth these sayings of mine and doeth them not, shall be likened unto a foolish man, which built his house upon the sand." The poet and dramatist Anthony Munday, in his play *Fedele and Fortunio* (c. 1584) recorded the earliest printed reference to the saying in English: "He fondly reares his fortresse on the sande. That buildes his trust vpon a womans troth." Playwright Thomas Heywood wrote in *Edward IV* (1599) that "thus is her glory builded on sand," and the dramatist Philip Massinger adapted it for *The Great Duke of Florence* (1636) as "Nor can I think His confidence built on sand." Alexander Pope in *Wife of Bath's Prologue* (1714) wrote, "Who builds his house on sands . . . Deserves a fool's cap."

In the twentieth century, the saying was adapted by the American poet Edna St. Vincent Millay, who wrote in *A Few Figs From Thistles: Second Fig* (1921), "Come and see my shining palace built upon the sand." The wording of the current version, probably in use earlier, was recorded by E. Williams in *George* (1961) as "Don't build castles on sand."

Don't count your chickens before they hatch.   *The Milkmaid and Her Pail,* a fable generally attributed to Aesop but possibly of much later origins, probably gave rise to the current proverb. In the tale, a maid carrying a pail of milk begins dreaming about a seemingly endless string of things the milk will bring, including eggs that will hatch into chickens, which will in turn lay more eggs and bring her still more good fortune. Finally, she is knocked back to reality after accidentally spilling the whole pail of milk. The earliest renderings of the proverb in English appeared in a work called *Misogonus* (c. 1577): "My chickings are not hatcht I nil to counte of him as yet," and in *Ephemerides of Phialo* (1579) by the English ecclesiastic Stephen Gosson, "I would not have him to counte his chickens so soone before they be hatcht." Samuel Butler's satire *Hudibras* (1664) included the lines, "To swallow gudgeons ere they're catch'd / And count their chickens ere they're hatch'd." John Ray's *A Collection of English Proverbs*

(1670) rendered the saying as "Count not your chickens before they are hatch't," and Thomas Fuller's collection of proverbs in the next century, *Gnomologia: Adagies and Proverbs* (1732), repeated this version. Sir Walter Scott adapted the saying in his journal (1829) as "We must not reckon our chickens before they are hatched, though they are chipping the shell now," and the American novelist Herman Melville adapted it for *The Piazza Tales* (1856). The cautionary version, "Don't count your chickens ...," appeared in *English Proverbs Explained* (1964) by Ronald Ridout and Clifford Witting.

Don't cross the bridge till you get to it.   Though it may well have been in popular use for some time, this familiar proverb was first recorded in 1850 by the American poet Henry Wadsworth Longfellow, who wrote in his *Journal*, "Remember the proverb, 'Do not cross the bridge till you come to it.'" A year later, Longfellow repeated the saying in *Golden Legend*, adding the observation, "a proverb old and of excellent wit." American humorist Charles Henry quoted it in *Bill Arp, So Called* (1866), replacing "till" with "before," and S. O. Addy in *Household Tales* (1895) included a note of explanation with "One who anticipates difficulty is told not to cross the bridge until he gets to it." The saying has since been quoted regularly by writers, including detective story writer Erle Stanley Gardner (1941, *The Case of the Empty Tin*) and English playwright Tom Stoppard (1967, *Rosencrantz and Guildenstern Are Dead*).

Don't cut off your nose to spite your face.   Vengeful rage has led to many pointless and foolish acts—sometimes any destructive act will do—but none are so stupid as those in which we try to get back at someone else by punishing ourselves. The Romans in ancient times had sayings for it: "It is stupid to seek vengeance on a neighbor by setting one's house on fire," and "Why burn thine own corn in thy passion?" The current proverb was first recorded about 1200 as a Latin saying, "He who cuts off his nose takes poor revenge for a shame inflicted upon him." Centuries later, in a work called *Deceit of Women* (c. 1561), the saying is rendered, "He that byteth his nose of, shameth his face." By the seventeenth century, the saying, "to cut off his nose to spite his face," was quoted as an old French proverb in a French history book, *Historiettes* (c. 1657), and in the eighteenth century was quoted in the writings of American revolutionary leader Christopher Gadsden as "Is not this biting our nose to spite our face?" (1784).

   Robert Smith Surtees, the English writer of sporting stories, used essentially the modern wording, "that would be only like cutting off my nose to spite my face," in *Mr. Sponge's Sporting Tour* (1853), as did Robert Louis Stevenson in *Master of Ballantrae* (1889): "He was in that humour when a man—in the words of the old adage—will cut off his nose to spite his face." The cautionary form "Don't cut off your nose . . ." was recorded in *English Proverbs Explained* (1964) by Ronald Ridout and Clifford Witting, though it probably came into use considerably earlier.

Don't look a gift horse in the mouth. *See* **Never look a gift horse in the mouth.**

Don't marry for money, but marry where money is. Although this saying is of fairly recent vintage, it is but a recent example of many much older proverbs concerning the same subject. The English author V. S. Pritchett in *A Cab at the Door* (1968) wrote, "The saying, often heard in Yorkshire: 'Dinna tha' marry money, go where money is.' " and that same year, William Haggard in *A Cool Day for Killing* recorded the current proverb for the first time: "He'd have heard the ancient saw Never marry for money, but marry where money is." This saying in fact probably is not ancient, but the dilemma certainly is. In the fifth century B.C., the Athenian statesman Themistocles, choosing one of two suitors for his daughter's hand, observed, "I prefer a man without money to money without a man." In medieval England, conventional wisdom took a different turn, and about 1500, sayings such as "Money makythe the man" and "Nowadais money maketh marriage with sum menn rather then love or bewtye." The next centuries brought the contrary advice, "Marry not an old crony, or a fool, for money," which appeared in Robert Burton's *Anatomy of Melancholy* (1621), and "To marry the mixen for the sake of the muck [marry an undesirable person for the money]," which was included in John Ray's *A Collection of English Proverbs* (1732 edition). In the twentieth century, an even sterner warning was offered in *Poor Richard Jr.'s Almanack* (1906): "Marry for money, starve for love."

Don't put all your eggs in one basket. The Latin saying, "Trust not all your goods to one bottom [ship]," was in use long before the current proverb, and William Shakespeare adapted it as "My ventures are not in one bottom trusted" in *The Merchant of Venice* (1596). "Don't put all your eggs..." appeared in the next century, being included in Giovanni Torriano's *A Common Place of Italian Proverbs and Proverbial Phrases* (1666) as "To put all ones Eggs in a Paniard, viz. to hazard all in one bottom." Samuel Palmer's *Moral Essays on Proverbs* (1710) used virtually the modern wording with "Don't venture all your eggs in one basket." Mark Twain gave the saying a clever turn with "The wise man saith, 'Put all your eggs in one basket and *watch that basket.*'" The English writer P. G. Wodehouse apparently recorded for the first time the exact wording of the cautionary form, "Don't put..." in *French Leave* (1956). Widely quoted in the twentieth century, the saying was adapted by, among others, the English novelist Edgar Wallace in *Nine Bears* (c. 1910) and Agatha Christie in *The Man in the Brown Suit* (1924).

Don't swap horses while crossing a stream. [Never swap ...] President Abraham Lincoln, speaking to the National Union League after receiving the group's backing for his renomination as president in 1864, remarked that "they have concluded that it is not best to swap horses while crossing the river." A well-known unofficial version of the speech, however, included wording closer to the current proverb: "I am reminded in this connection of an old Dutch farmer who remarked that it was not best to swap horses while crossing a stream." Later in the century, Charles Francis Butler in *C. G. Gordon* (1889) noted at the siege of Sevastopol during the Crimean War "a vigorous process of 'swopping' at the moment the animals were in the mid-stream of the siege." English writer and poet Robert Graves recorded the saying as "Never swap horses while crossing a stream" in *Good-bye to All That* (1929), and the cautionary version of "Don't swap horses..." was included in *English Proverbs Explained* (1967) by Ronald Ridout and Clifford Witting.

Don't take a hatchet to break eggs. What better way to illustrate the folly of using excessive force than by the humorous juxtaposition of a hatchet and an egg? In fact, the saying is but one of many dating from ancient times that made this same point. The Chinese philosopher Confucius in *Analects* (c. 500 B.C.) asked, "Why use a pole-axe to kill a fowl?" and Plutarch in *Apothegms* (c. 100) rendered it, "Using an ox to hunt a hare." John Ray's *A Collection of English Proverbs* (1670) contained the saying, "He takes a spear to kill a fly." In the next century, we find the earliest mention of the current proverb in Thomas Fuller's *Gnomologia* (1732): "Send not for a Hatchet to break open an Egg with." About the same time, Allan Ramsay in *A Collection of Scots Proverbs* (1737) quoted the saying as "Ne'er tak a fore-hammer to break an egg, when ye can do it wi' a pen knife."

The proverb has been cited infrequently since then, and the only mention in recent years was in a 1956 issue of the British humor magazine *Punch*: "There is an old proverb about taking hatchets to break eggs." A number of other similarly absurd sayings that appeared during the interim are worth noting: "Take not a Musket to kill a Butterfly," (1732, Fuller in *Gnomologia*); "A waste of pomp and ammunition to kill a bug with a battery of artillery," (1876, Mark Twain in *Tom Sawyer*); and perhaps the unlikeliest of all Chinese proverbs, "Do not remove a fly from your friend's forehead with a hatchet," (1938, S. G. Champion in *Racial Proverbs*).

Don't throw good money after bad.   Giovanni Torriano's *A Common Place of Italian Proverbs and Proverbial Phrases* (1666) included the earliest reference to this adage, namely, "The English say, To send good Mony after bad, to lose the Substance, for the Shaddow." Not long afterward, in 1690, Edward Fitzhugh, an American colonial living in the Virginia colony, quoted the saying in his correspondence, "And consequently good money thrown after bad." John Stevens in *A New Spanish and English Dictionary* (1706) quoted the saying as "When a Man throws good Money after bad," and toward the end of the same century, George Washington noted in a letter (1797), "the appearance of throwing good money after bad." The cautionary "Don't throw good money..." was included in the nineteenth century *A Glossary of Words Used in the Dialect of Cheshire* (1877), by Egerton Leigh: "Dunna waste a fresh haft on an oud blade. Don't throw good money after bad."

Don't throw the baby out with the bath water.   [Don't empty out the baby with...] A German proverb of unknown origins, it was current in German at least as early as the seventeenth century, when the astronomer Johannes Kepler included the passage, "This is a caution...lest you throw out the baby with the bath water," in *Tertius Interveniens* (1610). The saying apparently first appeared in English (1853) in the writings of Thomas Carlyle, who reported, "The Germans say, 'You must empty out the bathing-tub, but not the baby along with it.' " George Bernard

Shaw used the proverb in the preface to *Getting Married* (1911), noting, "We shall in a very literal sense empty the baby out with the bath by abolishing an institution [marriage] which needs nothing more than a little ... rationalizing to make it ... useful." Shaw repeated the saying in *Parents and Children* (1914) and again in *Everybody's Political What's What?* (1944). In 1958, the *New York Times* mentioned "that ancient maxim of common sense, not to throw the baby out with the bath," and more recently, the saying appeared in *Art of Learning to Manage* (1979) by J. P. Young: "Do be careful that you don't throw the baby out with the bath water."

Drowning man will clutch at straws, A.   The all-too-vivid imagery of this proverb can be traced back to a passage in Sir Thomas More's *Dialogue of Comfort Against Tribulation* (1534): "Lyke a man that in peril of drowning catcheth whatsoever cometh nexte to hande, ... be it neuer so simple a sticke." William Painter's *The Palace of Pleasure* (1566) repeated the notion with "We see them that feare to be drowned, do take hold of the next thing that commeth to hande," while J. Prince in *Fruitful & Brief Discourse* (1583) rendered wording close to the modern, "We do not as men redie to be drowned catch at euery straw." Thomas Fuller's *Gnomologia* (1732) recorded the saying as "Drowning Men will catch at a Rush," though a few years later Samuel Richardson in *Clarissa* (1748) quoted it as "A drowning man will catch at a straw, the proverb well says." The saying has been quoted regularly up to the present day, and among the notable writers who repeated or adapted it were Benjamin Franklin (1758, 1766, in correspondence), Abigail Adams (1785, in correspondence), John Adams (1813, in correspondence), William Makepeace Thackeray (1848, *Vanity Fair*), Robert Louis Stevenson (1875, in correspondence), and more recently the creator of Tarzan, Edgar Rice Burroughs (1921, *The Mucker*), and detective story writer Erle Stanley Gardner (1951, *Angry*).

E

Early bird catches the worm, The. One might guess that birds became the subject of this ever-popular proverb because they were always up (and chirping) early with the morning sunrise. Whatever the reason, virtually the modern form of the proverb was first recorded in *Remaines Concerning Britaine* (1614) by the English antiquary William Camden: "The early bird catcheth the worme." The saying appeared in John Ray's *A Collection of English Proverbs* (1670) and subsequent books of proverbs, and among the noted writers who later quoted it were the Canadian author Thomas Chandler Haliburton (creator of Sam Slick) in *Wise Saws* (1843), Robert Louis Stevenson in *Treasure Island* (1883, "...that gets the rations"), G. K. Chesterton in *The Fad of the Fisherman* (1922), and P. G. Wodehouse in *Blandings Castle* (1935). And then there was the dauntless writer in the *Times Literary Supplement* of 1957 who wanted to resolve the question of what makes worms get up early in the first place. He revealed, "Worms surface during the night in order to mate: which is why 'the early bird catches the worm.'"

Early to bed and early to rise makes a man healthy, wealthy, and wise. The Judaic commentary *Babylonian Talmud* (c. 450) contained an early version of the current saying, "Rise early and eat, in summer because of the heat, in winter because of the cold ...Six runners may run, but will not overtake the man who has breakfasted early." The first version in English did not appear until about the fifteenth century, however, when it was recorded in *Treatise of Fishing With an Angle* (1496): "As the olde englysshe prouerbe sayth in this wyse, who soo woll ryse erly shall be holy helthy and zely." The saying appeared soon after in John Fitzherbert's *The Boke of Husbandry* (1523) as "At grammar-scole I lerned a verse, that is this, *Sanat, sanctificat et ditat surgere mane.* That is to say, Erly rysyng maketh a man hole in body, holer in soule, and rycher in goodes." The modern form of the saying was rendered the next century in John Clarke's collected proverbs, *Paroemiologia Anglo-Latina* (1639). This version was subsequently included in various books of proverbs, including John

Ray's *A Collection of English Proverbs* (1670, "Early to go to bed
..."), and became a favorite of Benjamin Franklin's, who repeated it in *Poor Richard's Almanack* (1735), *The Way to Wealth, or
Poor Richard Improved* (1758), and in correspondence in 1779. As
popular as this saying proved to be, or perhaps because of it,
there has been no little disagreement with it. On the one hand,
a Chinese proverb (which the Japanese today seem to have taken
to heart) recommended a truly severe lifestyle, with "Be the first
to the field and the last to the couch," which was quoted in *Racial
Proverbs* (1938), by S. G. Champion. But there also have been
voices raised against the rigors of even the comparatively modest
"Early to bed..." James Thurber's *Fables* (1939), for example,
poked fun at the saying with "Early to rise and early to bed makes
a male healthy and wealthy and dead."

Easier said than done.   Known at least from Roman times, the
proverb was first recorded by the comic playwright Plautus in
Asinaria (c. 200 B.C.) as "Such things are easier said than done."
Two centuries later, the Roman historian Livy rendered the modern form of the saying (in Latin) in his *History* (c. 10 B.C.). The
first version printed in English appeared in about 1450 as "Better
saide thanne doon," in *Religious and Love Poems*. John Heywood's
*A Dialogue Conteinyng the Number in Effect of All the Prouerbes in the
Englishe Tongue* (1546) rendered it as "That is ... sooner said than
done," and William Shakespeare wrote, " 'Tis better said than
done," in *Henry VI, Part III* (c. 1592). The English playwright
David Garrick gave the modern version in *Neck or Nothing* (1766)
with the lines, "That's easier said than done." *See also* **There is a
difference between saying and doing.**

Easy come, easy go.   This saying is a well-known lament uttered
by those who have easily obtained—and lost—money or some
prized possession, usually because of carelessness or lack of restraint. A Chinese proverb, "Come easy, go easy," dated from
about 100 B.C., and a version in English, "Lightly come, lightly
go," was first mentioned by Chaucer in his *Canterbury Tales* (1387)
as "And lightly as it comth so wol we spende." While this version
appeared regularly in subsequent collections of proverbs, the
current "Easy come, easy go" apparently did not begin to evolve
until the seventeenth century, when the Massachusetts colonist
and poet Anne Bradstreet wrote, "For that which easily comes,
as freely goes" (1650). But it was the English novelist Samuel
Warren who recorded the exact wording of the modern saying

with " 'Easy come, easy go,' is . . . characteristic of rapidly acquired commercial fortunes," as quoted in *Diary of a Late Physician* (c. 1835). The English philosopher Herbert Spencer repeated the saying in *Education* (1861) with " 'Easy come, easy go,' is a saying as applicable to knowledge as to wealth." In more recent times, T. H. White adapted the saying in *The Sword in the Stone* (1939), and American humorist Thorne Smith quoted it in *Topper* (1926).

Eat, drink, and be merry, for tomorrow we die.   This saying was first rendered in the Old Testament Book of Isaiah (c. 725 B.C.) as "let us eat and drink; for to-morrow we shall die," and was repeated in essentially the same form in the New Testament I Corinthians (A.D. 57). The Roman playwright Seneca quoted the saying as "Let us drink, for we all must die," in *Ad Lucilium* (A.D. c. 65), but it apparently did not appear in print again until much later. By the 1700s, the saying was current in America, and by the beginning of the century, the word "merry" had been added to the Biblical saying. Thomas Jefferson mentioned the saying in his correspondence (1789), and Dante Gabriel Rossetti wrote in *The House of Life* (1870), "Eat thou and drink; to-morrow thou shalt die." Notable writers of the twentieth century who adapted the saying include James Joyce (1922, *Ulysses*), Dorothy Parker (1936, *The Flaw in Paganism*), and detective story writer Erle Stanley Gardner (1943, *The Case of the Drowsy Mosquito*). Gardner adapted the saying to impose a more modern form of death with "Eat, drink, and be merry, for tomorrow and tomorrow and tomorrow roll on their dreary course."

Elephant never forgets, An.   [Women and elephants never forget.] A similar proverb—"The camel never forgets an injury"— was once current among the ancient Greeks, who believed the camel to have an especially good memory and who regarded the elephant as essentially stupid. But times (and our perception of the elephant) have changed, bringing on the more modern form of the saying. Though it may well have been in use somewhat earlier, the saying first appeared in 1910 as "Women and elephants never forget an injury," in *Reginald: Reginald on Besetting Sins* by the English writer Saki (H. H. Munro). Dorothy Parker shortened that to "Women and elephants never forget" in *Ballade of Unfortunate Mammals* (1930). American detective story writer Mickey Spillane used the saying metaphorically in *Long Wait* (1951), with "The guy had a memory like an elephant." Science fiction writer Robert A. Heinlein did likewise with "Pete has an elephant's memory" in *Door Into Summer* (1957). The saying came into common use during this century.

End justifies the means, The. The Greek playwright Sophocles wrote in *Electra* (c. 409 B.C.), "The end excuses any evil," a thought later rendered by the Roman poet Ovid as "The result justifies the deed" in *Heroides* (c. 10 B.C.). These were but the first words on the subject; centuries later in *Essays* (1580), the French moralist Michel de Montaigne observed the tendency "to use bad means to a good end." Gervase Babington in *Exposition of Commandments* (1583) disagreed with such sentiments, writing, "The ende good, doeth not by and by make the meanes good." The American Quaker William Penn in *Some Fruits of Solitude* (1693) also rendered the negative of the saying with "A good End cannot sanctifie evil Means; nor must we ever do Evil, that Good may come of it." The Jesuit Hermann Busenbaum, supporting what was Jesuit doctrine in *Medulla Theologiae* (1650), rendered the saying as "When the end is lawful, the means are also lawful," and the English poet Matthew Prior in *Hans Carvel: Poems* (1718) gave essentially the modern wording of the current saying: "The End must justifie the Means." While the saying (with variations) has since been quoted regularly up to the present day, that underlying idea has remained a subject for contention. The English writer and lexicographer Samuel Johnson wrote in *Irene* (1749), "Be virtuous Ends pursued by virtuous Means, / Nor think th' Intention sanctifies the Deed." In his correspondence of 1805, the American statesman John Quincy Adams noted that "the end too must go some way . . . to justify the means," while soon after, the poet William Wordsworth penned the lines in *Dion* (1814), "Him, only him, the shield of Jove defends, / Whose means are fair and spotless as his ends." Sir Walter Scott in *The Abbot* (1820) rendered the matter-of-fact "the end, sister, sanctifies the means we must use." Giving the contrary in equally succinct terms in *Proverbs From Plymouth Pulpit* (1887), the American clergyman Henry Ward Beecher wrote, "You are not at liberty to execute a good plan with bad instruments."

Enough is as good as a feast. The Greek dramatist Euripides wrote in *The Suppliant Women* (421), "Not in gluttony lies virtue: enough is as a feast." In the Scottish national epic *The Actes and Life of the Most Victorious Conqueror, Robert Bruce* (1376), John Barbour rendered the saying as "He maid thame na gud fest, perfay, And nocht-for-thi yneuch had thai," and soon after, the

English priest John Lydgate wrote, "As good ys ynough as a gret feste" in *Assembly of Gods* (c. 1420). The modern wording of the proverb was first recorded in John Heywood's *A Dialogue Conteinyng the Nomber in Effect of All the Prouerbes in the Englishe Tongue* (c. 1546). The current form was quoted in subsequent books of proverbs, including John Ray's *A Collection of English Proverbs* (1670), and was repeated by such noted writers as Henry Fielding (1732, *Convent Garden Tragedy*), Jonathan Swift (1738, *A Complete Collection of Genteel and Ingenious Conversation*), Charles Lamb (1826, *Essays: Popular Fallacies*), and, more recently, D. H. Lawrence (1928, *Woman Who Rode Away*) and Wyndham Lewis (1930, *The Apes of God*).

Every cloud has a silver lining.   John Milton's masque (dramatic entertainment) *Comus* (1634) gave rise to the current proverb with the lines, "Was I deceiv'd, or did a sable cloud / Turn forth her silver lining on the night?" Charles Dickens, in his novel *Bleak House* (1852), recalled the lines with "I turn my silver lining outward like Milton's cloud," and the American impresario Phineas T. Barnum first recorded the wording of the modern saying in *Struggles and Triumphs* (1869) with " 'Every cloud,' says the proverb, 'has a silver lining.' " In the comic opera *The Mikado, or The Town of Titipu* (1885), William S. Gilbert (of Gilbert and Sullivan) did much to popularize the saying with "Don't let's be downhearted. There's a silver lining to every cloud," and the proverb has been repeated (or adapted) frequently in the twentieth century. The popularity no doubt also inspired the witty alterations, "Every stomach has a silver lining," by P. G. Wodehouse in *Leave it to Psmith* (c. 1910), and "The cloud has a silver-fox lining," by Saki (H. H. Munro) in *Beasts* (1914). A. E. Housman quoted the saying in his correspondence (1918), and e. e. cummings repeated it in *Eimi* (1933). *See also* **Take the good with the bad.**

Every dog has his day.   According to the medieval Dutch scholar Erasmus, this saying came about as a result of the death of the Greek playwright Euripides, who in 405 B.C. was mauled and killed by a pack of dogs loosed upon him by a rival. Thus the saying is usually taken to mean that even the most lowly person will at some time get revenge on his oppressor, no matter how powerful the man may be. The Greek biographer Plutarch recorded the proverb for the first time in *Moralia* (A.D. c. 95), rendering it as "Even a dog gets his revenge," and Richard Taverner included the first version in English—"A dogge hath a day"—centuries later in his *Proverbes or Adages* (1539). Queen Elizabeth I (quoted in *Ecclesiastical Memorials*, 1550), William Shakespeare (1600, *Hamlet*), and the venerable Ben Jonson (1633, *Tales of a Tub*) all quoted this earlier English version. What was virtually the modern form appeared in John Ray's *A Collection of English Proverbs* (1670) as "Every dog hath his day," and with minor variations was quoted regularly thereafter. Among the noted writers who have repeated it were the English satirist Jonathan Swift (1722, *Upon the Horrid Plot Discovered by Harlequin*), Alexander Pope (1726, in his translation of the *Odyssey*), the English writer Thomas Carlyle (1837, *The French Revolution*), and George Bernard Shaw (1897, *Caesar and Cleopatra*). The saying, quoted less frequently in the twentieth century, did appear in Robert A. Heinlein's *6XH* (1961) and in Anthony Burgess's *Nothing Like the Sun* (1964).

Every man has his price.   The Roman satirist Juvenal wrote in his *Satires* (c. 120), "All things at Rome have their price," certainly a forerunner of what has sometimes been called the maxim of worldly cynicism, "Every man has his price." The earliest known reference to the saying in English gave the modern form and appeared in a publication called *The Bee* in 1734: "It is an old maxim that every man has his price." In a letter to Robert Howe (1779), George Washington adapted the saying to read, "Few men have virtue to withstand the highest bidder." The saying in its current form has been quoted widely since the 1700s. Among the notable writers who repeated it were the English churchman and founder of Methodism, John Wesley (1790, *Sermons*); James Joyce (1922, *Ulysses*); detective story writer Erle Stanley Gardner (1941, *Turning Tide*); Norman Mailer (1948, *The Naked and the Dead*); and spy adventure story writer Ian Fleming (1957, *From Russia With Love*).

Every man is master of his fortune.   [. . . is architect of his fortune.] The Roman statesman Appius Claudius Caecus included the Latin saying, "Every man is architect of his own fortune," in *Aphorism* (c. 312 B.C.), a collection of sayings. Plautus repeated it in his play *Trinummus* (c. 194 B.C.) as "A wise man is the architect of his own fortune," and over the centuries the proverb spread to many Western languages. It was first rendered in English by Nicholas Udall in *Floures for Latine Speakyng* (1534) as "Everyman maketh . . . is causer of his own fortunes," and was repeated soon after by Richard Taverner as "A man's owne maners do shape hym hys fortune." Since then a number of well-known writers have quoted the saying with variations, including John Milton in *Eikonoklastes* (1649, "Architects of their own happiness"), John Dryden in *The Hind and the Panther* (1687, "Smiths of their own foolish fate"), Richard Steele in a contribution to *The Tatler* (1709, "Every man is the maker of his own fortune"), and Henry David Thoreau in his journal (1838, "Man is the artificer of his own happiness"). The current wording "Every man is master..." appeared in J. S. Fletcher's *The Massingham Butterfly* in 1926.

Every rose has its thorns.   [No rose without a thorn.] The Persian poet Sadi wrote what is probably the earliest known version of this proverb in *Gullistan* (1258, *Rose Garden*): "Wherever there is a rose there is a thorn." The English cleric John Lydgate, writing almost two centuries later, rendered it as "Ther is no rose...but ther be some thorn" in *Fall of the Princes* (1430). The writer John Lyly in *Euphues and His England* (1580) gave "The sweetest rose hath a prickle," and John Florio's translation, *Montaigne* (1603), included the line, "No good without pains; no roses without prickles." William Shakespeare included the line, "Hath not thy rose a thorn, Plantagenet?" in *Henry VI* (c. 1592), but it was John Ray, in *A Collection of English Proverbs* (1670), who recorded the variant, "No rose without a thorn." Benjamin Franklin made a wry allusion to this saying in *Poor Richard's Almanack* (1734): "You cannot pluck roses without fear of thorns, Nor enjoy a fair wife without danger of horns." Thomas Jefferson wrote in a letter (1786), "We have no rose without its thorn; no pleasure without alloy," and allusions to it were made in correspondence by George Washington (1794), Thomas Paine (c. 1800), and John Quincy Adams (1815). James Joyce also quoted this version in *Ulysses* (1922). The earliest citation for the more recent "Every rose has..." appeared in Stephen Leacock's *Behind the Beyond, and Other Contributions to Human Knowledge* (1916) and has been used infrequently since then.

Everything comes to him who waits.   In *Eclogues* (c. 1530), the English clergyman Alexander Barclay recorded what was probably the earliest version of this adage on patience, "Somewhat shall come who can his time abide." Not long after, a version much closer to the modern form appeared in *Pantagruel* (1548), by the French writer Rabelais: "Everything comes to him who

knows how to wait," while in *Select Italian Proverbs* (1642), Giovanni Torriano included the saying, "He who can wait, hath what
he desireth." The English statesman Benjamin Disraeli gave the
saying as "Everything comes if a man will only wait" in *Tancred,
or the New Crusade* (1847), and the poet Henry Wadsworth Longfellow in *The Student's Tale* (1863) rendered it as "All things come
round to him who will but wait." At the end of the nineteenth
century, John Lubbock, Lord Avebury, quoted the saying in *Use
of Life* (1894) as "Everything comes to those who know how to
wait," and the current wording ". . . to him (or her) who waits"
was in use by the 1920s. The English writer Edgar Wallace quoted
the saying ". . . her who waits" in *Sinister Man* (1925), and Kingsley
Amis adapted it in *Spectrum; A Science Fiction Anthology* (1962).

Exception proves the rule, The. The original meaning of this
proverb turned on a philosophical fine point, namely that an
exception, by its very nature, proved that a rule existed. The
early Latin phrase, "An exception claimed in the case of matters
or persons not excepted strengthens the rule," made the slightly
different point that exceptions only strengthened the case for
having the rule. John Wilson recorded the saying in its modern
form in *The Cheats* (1664), and Samuel Johnson in *Preface to
Shakespeare* (1765) rendered it as "The exception only confirms
the rule." Among the noted authors who quoted or adapted the
saying were the English novelist Tobias Smollett (1771, *The Expedition of Humphrey Clinker*); Lord Byron (1808, in his correspondence); Herman Melville (1850, *White-Jacket, or The World
in a Man-of-War*); Anthony Trollope (1883, *Autobiography*); and
Samuel Hammett (1855, *The Wonderful Adventures of Captain
Priest*). In *A Student's Pastime* (1896), W. W. Skeat took issue with
the general understanding of the original Latin saying, holding,
"The exception *tests* the rule," instead of supporting or demonstrating it. But Arthur Conan Doyle in *The Sign of the Four*
(1890) took what amounts to a rigorous scientific position on the
matter with the matter-of-fact "An exception disproves the rule."

Experience is the best teacher. The great Roman leader Julius
Caesar recorded the earliest known version of this proverb, "Experience is the teacher of all things," in *De Bello Civili* (c. 52 B.C.).
Over a century later, the Roman author Pliny the Elder in *Naturalis Historia* (A.D. 77) wrote, "Experience is the most efficient
teacher of all things," and the Roman historian Tacitus said simply, "Experience teaches," in his *Histories* (c. 109). The earliest

English rendering appeared in 1539 as "Experience is mother of prudence," which was included in Richard Taverner's *Proverbes or Adagies*. Soon after in 1579, Sir Thomas North's translation of Plutarch's *Lives of Noble Grecians and Romans* rendered it as "Experience is the School-mistress of fools." John Ray's *A Collection of English Proverbs* (1670) gave the variant, "Experience is the mistress of fools," and Thomas Fuller's *Gnomologia* (1732) included "Experience teacheth Fools; and he is a great one that will not learn by it." The English poet William Cowper wrote in *The Task* (1784), "Experience, slow preceptress, teaching oft / The way to glory by miscarriage foul." Not long after, the American clergyman and biographer Mason Locke ("Parson") Weems recorded essentially the modern version in his correspondence (1803): "Experience, the best of teachers," while the exact wording, "Experience is the best teacher," appeared in the *Widow Bedott Papers* (1856) by Frances M. Whitcher. Adapted by Herman Melville (1857, *The Confidence Man*) and Louisa May Alcott (1868, *Little Women*) among others, the saying has appeared in print up to the present day.

Eye for an eye, An.   Recorded in the Old Testament Book of Deuteronomy (c. 650 B.C.), this saying appeared in the passage recalling Moses's words, "Thine eye shall not pity, but life shall go for life, eye for eye, tooth for tooth, hand for hand, foot for foot." The words "eye for eye" also appear in the Old Testament Book of Leviticus (c. 570 B.C.). The New Testament Book of Matthew (A.D. c. 65) repeated the saying in, "Ye have heard that it hath been said, An eye for an eye and a tooth for a tooth: But I say unto you, That ye resist not evil: but whosoever shall smite thee on thy right cheek, turn to him the other also." While the saying probably has been understood since Biblical times as a metaphor for revenge and retribution, it is curiously absent from most collections of sayings. In one of the references from outside the Bible, in a letter written in 1814, the American president-to-be Andrew Jackson adapted the saying to reflect realities of the American frontier: "An Eye for an Eye, Toothe for Toothe and Scalp for Scalp."

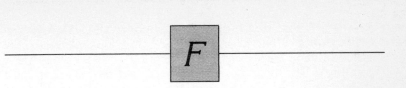

Faint heart never won fair lady. The Greek playwright Euripides wrote in *The Suppliant Women* (421 B.C.), "Faint heart makes feeble hand," which was to say that reticent and downright weak-kneed lovers turned out to be poor mates. Centuries later, the poet John Gower penned the earliest English saying on this theme in *Confessio Amatis* (c. 1390): "Bot as men sein, wher herte is failed, Ther schal no castell [castle] ben assailed." Richard Taverner's *Proverbes or Adagies* (1539) recorded a version closer to the modern saying with "A coward verely neuer obteyned the lue of a faire lady," as did John Lyly's *Euphues and His England* (1580), with "Faint hart neither winneth Castell nor Lady." The proverb in its modern form appeared a short time later in *Remaines Concerning Britaine* (1614, "Faint heart neuer wonne fair Lady"). Among the noted writers who repeated this version in following years were Samuel Richardson in *Sir Charles Grandison* (1753) and Charles Dickens in *Nicholas Nickleby* (1839). The saying has been used infrequently during the twentieth century.

Fair and softly goes far. Virtually the modern form of the proverb was recorded in an English manuscript (c. 1350) as "Fayre and softe me ferre gose," and a few years later Chaucer rendered a variation, "Thei take it wisly faire and softe," in *Troilus and Criseyde* (1385). In the fifteenth-century *Coventry Plays* (c. 1450, by an unknown author), the saying was quoted as "For soft and essele men goo far," and in the sixteenth century, *First Fruites* (1578) by the English lexicographer John Florio quoted it as "Who goeth softly, goeth wel." The current wording appeared in *The Historie of Foure-Footed Beastes* (1607) by Edward Topsell as "Fair and softly goeth far." This form, with minor variations, was included in subsequent collections of proverbs up to the present day. Poet and playwright John Dryden quoted it in *Sir Martin Mar-all* (1668), as did the American statesman John Adams in a letter (1776), and Sir Walter Scott in *The Heart of Midlothian* (1818). The saying has been repeated infrequently in the twentieth century.

Fame is but the breath of the people, and that is often unwholesome.   The Roman ruler and philosopher Marcus Aurelius wrote in *Meditations* (second century), "All is ephemeral—fame as well as the famous," and there has been no less distrust in later centuries for that tempting but ever capricious deity, fame. The Italian poet Dante Alighieri spoke of it in *The Divine Comedy* (1321) with the lines, "The splendors of earthly fame are but a wind, / That in the same direction lasts not long." Another Italian poet, Torquato Tasso, wrote in *La Gerusalemme Liberata* (1581), "Fame, which by the sweetness of her voice, enchants ambitious men and appears so ravishing, is merely...the shadow of a dream, which fleets like the wind and vanishes in a moment." In his *Essays* (1612), the English philosopher Francis Bacon gave an even more cynical description of fame with "Fame is like a River, that beareth up Things Light and Swolne, and Drownes Things waighty and Solide." Thomas Coryat, an Englishman who wrote of his travels in Europe, gave a far more succinct description of fame in *Crudities* (1611): "Fame is but winde." The first mention of fame as "the breath of the people" was made in a passage from *Holy Living* (1650) by the English prelate Jeremy Taylor: "That which would purchase heaven for him he parts with for the breath of the people; which at best is but air, and that not often wholesome." The current wording of the proverb appeared in Thomas Fuller's *Gnomologia: Adagies and Proverbs* (1732) and has been included in some collections of proverbs up to the present day. Though without a doubt a witty and altogether memorable saying, it apparently has been little used and—dare one say it?—not particularly famous.

Familiarity breeds contempt.   In *Sententiae* (c. 43 B.C.), the Roman writer Pubilius Syrus rendered essentially the modern saying in Latin with "Too much familiarity breeds contempt." The proverb's appearance in English was also relatively early: "Familiaritie breedythe contempt" was included in *Satires* (c. 1160) by Alain de L'Isle. About 1200, Pope Innocent III adapted this and another proverb to form a new Latin saying, "Subservience begets friends, truth hatred, familiarity contempt." Almost two centuries later, Chaucer in *Tale of Melibee* (c. 1390) wrote, "Men seyn that 'over-greet hoomlynesse engendreth dispreisynege,'" and in the sixteenth century, "his overmuche familiaritie myght breade him contempte," was recorded in Richard Taverner's *Proverbes or Adagies* (1539). William Shakespeare in *The Merry Wives of Windsor* (1601) wrote the line, "I hope upon familiarity will grow more contempt." Thomas Fuller recorded the exact wording of the saying in *Comment on Ruth* (1654), and the saying was later used by Tobias Smollett in *Adventures of an Atom* (1769), Herman Melville in *Mardi and a Voyage Thither* (1849), Anthony Trollope in *He Knew He Was Right* (1869), and D. H. Lawrence in *Phoenix II* (1928). Mark Twain also reworked the saying in his personal papers, using his wit and understanding of human nature to blend the old adage with a second eternal verity to produce the clever observation, "Familiarity breeds contempt—and children."

February Groundhog Day, half your meat and half your hay. This saying appears to be a more recent version of a centuries-old English adage. The earlier saying revolved around the Christian religious holiday called Candlemas, which like the American Groundhog Day fell on February 2 and was considered something of a turning point during winter. An old English manuscript dating from about 1639 recorded the earliest version of the saying as "At Candlemas a provident husbandman should have halfe his fodder, and all his corne remaininge." The prescribed rations were somewhat different in John Ray's *A Collection of English Proverbs* (1670): "On Candlemas-day, You must have half your straw, and half your hay," a version repeated in the next century in Thomas Fuller's *Gnomologia: Adagies and Proverbs* (1732), and later still in *Weather Lore* (1893), by R. Inwards. The current version apparently was not quoted in print until 1957 (in *Maine Hamlet* by Lura Beam), but probably was in use for some time before that. A related version was mentioned in the *Colorado Quarterly* a year later: "If the ground-hog sees his shadow today (February 2), Save half your corn and half your hay."

Feed a cold and starve a fever. Certainly among the most familiar of proverbs on home remedies, this old saw is by no means a sure cure. In fact, there is even disagreement over what advice is being given. The English lexicographer John Withals observed in *A Short Dictionary Most Profitable for Young Beginners* (1574 edition), "Fasting is a great remedie in feuers," providing what might seem an early basis for the current saying. But the contrary recommendation appeared soon afterward in Stefano Guazzo's *The Civile Conversation* (1586): "It is better to feede a fever, then weaknesse." Centuries later, Edward FitzGerald in *Polonius* (1852) recorded the current proverb for the first time, as well as a note on what was already a common misconception:

"In the case of . . . a Cold—'Stuff a cold and starve a fever,' has been grievously misconstrued, so as to bring on the fever it was meant to prevent." In *The Celebrated Jumping Frog of Calaveras County* (1865), Mark Twain quoted the exact wording of the current saying, but in 1881 the publication *Notes and Queries* explained, " 'Stuff a cold,' &c. The expression is elliptical, for '[if you] stuff a cold, [you will have to] starve a fever,' " which is to say stuffing yourself while you have a cold will supposedly bring on a fever. Despite the confusion and no little uncertainty as to whether it really is a remedy at all, "Feed a cold . . ." has been repeated (and misunderstood) up to the present day. It seems the best advice is still that fairly recent prescription, "Call your doctor."

Fiddle cannot play without the bow, The.   This infrequently used saying is probably an outgrowth of the earlier "He has got the fiddle, but not the stick," which appeared in John Ray's *A Collection of English Proverbs* (1670). Ray gave the further explanation, "i.e. The books but not the learning, to make use of them, or the like." The saying was repeated in Thomas Fuller's *Gnomologia: Adagies and Proverbs* (1732). *Lacon* (1820), a collection of maxims by the English clergyman Charles Caleb Colton, contained the only nineteenth-century reference to the saying, "Those who attempted to imitate them, would find that they had got the fiddle but not the fiddlestick." The current wording of the saying appeared in *The Yearling* (1938), by the American novelist Marjorie Kinnan Rawlings.

Fight fire with fire.   Writing about countering one thing with something of like kind, the French moralist Michel de Montaigne rendered the line, "Fire is put out by fire," in *Essays* (1594). William Shakespeare's *Romeo and Juliet* (c. 1595) echoed that sentiment with the line, "Tut, man, one fire burns out another's burning; One pain is less'ned by another's anguish." Shakespeare returned to the theme in *Cymbeline* (c. 1609) with "One fire drives out one fire; one nail, one nail," and the playwright George Chapman wrote in *Monsieur D'Olive* (1604), "For one heat, all know, doth drive out another, One passion doth expel another still." The English dramatist Sir John Vanbrugh gave the saying in *The Mistake* (1706) as "Fire will fetch out fire," but it was the American novelist James Fenimore Cooper who in *Redskins* (1846) quoted essentially the modern saying with "If 'fire will fight fire,' 'Indian' ought to be a match for 'Injin' any day." The exact wording of the maxim first appeared in *Struggles and Triumphs* (1869), by the American showman Phineas T. Barnum, and it has been in regular use up to the present day.

Figures don't lie, but liars can figure.   The Scottish-born writer Thomas Carlyle flatly declared in *Essay on Chartism* (1839), "You may prove anything by figures." Mark Twain was even more outspoken against numbers in his *Autobiography* (c. 1909): "Figures often beguile me, particularly when I have the arranging of them myself; in which case the remark attributed to Disraeli would often apply ... 'There are three kinds of lies: lies, damned lies, and statistics.'" Such generalized distrust of numbers apparently arose in fairly recent times—no doubt as a result of the increasing importance of numbers in daily life. In the 1700s, for example, the expression, "Figures will not lye," appeared in *Colonial Currency* (1739) and was repeated by the American novelist James Fenimore Cooper, both in his correspondence (1831) and in his novel *The Chain-Bearer* (1845). The clever irony of "... but liars can figure" turned the earlier "Figures will not lie" on itself, and apparently originated about 1890. The current saying, attributed to Ohio Congressman Charles H. Grosvenor, never came into wide use but has been quoted in print during the twentieth century.

Fine feathers make fine birds.   A sixteenth-century saying on the salutary effects of wearing fine clothing, this proverb apparently was recorded first in a Latin translation of Homer's *Odyssey* (1583), the English translation being "Beautiful feathers make a beautiful bird." *The French Alphabet* (1592) by G. Delamothe gave the earliest known English rendering as "The faire feathers, makes a faire foule," and in the next century, Edward Phillips became the first to use the exact wording of the modern saying in his *Mysteries of Love & Eloquence* (1658). John Ray's *A Collection of English Proverbs* (1670) explained the saying with, "Fair feathers make fair fowls. Fair clothes, ornaments and dresses set off persons ... God makes and apparel shapes." The modern version was subsequently quoted by the English cleric and writer John Bunyan in *Pilgrim's Progress* (1678), the novelist Thomas Hardy in *Tess of the D'Urbervilles* (1891), and the American novelist Theodore Dreiser in *A Traveller at Forty* (1913). *See also* **Clothes make the man.**

Fine words butter no parsnips.   John Clarke's collection of sayings, *Paroemiologia Anglo-Latina* (1639), recorded this saying for the first time with the passage, "Fair words butter noe parsnips, *verba non alunt familiam* [Words don't feed the family]." The same message, that flattery and other "fair-sounding" words have little practical value, was repeated by the English journalist and translator Sir Roger L'Estrange in *Erasmus' Colloquies* (1680) as "Your charity upon earth will be rewarded in heaven—those words butter no parsnips," and later in *Fables* (1692) with "Relations, friendships, are but empty names of things, and *Words butter no parsnips.*" The exact wording of the modern version first appeared in *The Citizen* (1761) by the Irish playwright Arthur Murphy. Among the noted writers who quoted or adapted the saying were William Makepeace Thackeray in *Vanity Fair* (1847), Anthony Trollope in *The Last Chronicle of Barset* (1867), and, more recently, Ogden Nash in *My Dear, How Ever Did You Think Up This Delicious Salad?* (1935).

Fingers were made before forks.   Once invoked to excuse eating with the fingers in front of others, this saying can be traced back to a manuscript (1567) that recorded the line, "God made hands before knives, So God send a good lot to the cutler's wives." In the eighteenth century, the English satirist Jonathan Swift rendered the saying as "They say fingers were made before forks, and hands before knives," in *Polite Conversation* (1738). The English novelist Anthony Trollope adapted the saying in *Barchester Towers* (1857) as "fingers were made before forks," and the shortened form was repeated by Charles Lamb's biographer, the English writer E. V. Lucas, in *Landmarks* (1914). James Joyce quoted this version in *Ulysses* (1922), as did Agatha Christie in *Boomerang Club* (1935), and the American novelist John Barth in *End of the Road* (1958, "fingers were invented . . . ").

Fire is a good servant but a bad master.   [Fire and water are good servants but bad masters.] The earliest known version of this saying appeared in the sixteenth-century *Bulwarke of Defence* (1562) by William Bullein: "Water is a very good seruaunt, but it is a cruell master." Somewhat later in *England's Sickness* (1615), Thomas Adams wrote a similar version, this time mentioning fire: "The world, like fire, may be a good seruant, will bee an ill Master." The point in both cases was that fire (or water) were beneficial when kept under control and very dangerous when they were not, as in the case of a forest fire (or a flood). A version of the proverb including both fire and water appeared in James Howell's *Proverbs in English, Italian, French, and Spanish* (1659), John Ray's *A Collection of English Proverbs* (1670), and subsequent collections in the 1700s. The English satirist Jonathan Swift quoted this version (fire and water) in *Polite Conversation* (1738), but it was an American colonial named Jeremy Belknap who first recorded the shortened, modern version in his personal papers in 1787: "Fire is a good servant, but a bad master." The American statesman John Adams adapted the saying in 1808, novelist James Fenimore Cooper quoted it in *The Redskins* (1846), and the show-man Phineas T. Barnum adapted it in *Struggles and Triumphs* (1869). The saying has been repeated only infrequently in the twentieth century.

First impressions are the most lasting.   [. . . untrustworthy.] Proverbial wisdom here appears two-sided, probably because of the natural divisions between those who are trying to impress and those who are deciding whether the impressions are good or bad. First things first, however. A Roman rhetorician named Quintilian gave us a succinct, if somewhat cynical, reason for trying to make a good impression in his *Institutionis Oratoriae* (A.D. c. 80): "It is the worst impressions which are the most lasting." Chaucer provided some further elaboration in *Troilus and Criseyde* (c. 1385) with "impressiounes lighte / Ful lightly been ay redy to the flighte," which said that light impressions fade quickly. The earliest mention of the all-important "first impressions" appeared in the *The Way of the World* (1700) by the English playwright Richard Congreve: "There is a great deal in the first impression."

But an American, Peter Van Schaack, sounded the call for the other side in a letter of 1786, "I know by experience that *first impressions* are not to be implicitly adopted." Not long afterward, the exact wording of the current proverb was recorded (1791) in papers later collected for *William Bingham's Maine Lands, 1790–1820* (published 1954). Charles Dickens seconded the sentiment in *Martin Chuzzlewit* (1844) with "First impressions, you know, often go a long way, and last a long time." Gerard Fairlie in *Stone Blunts Scissors* (1929) rendered the contrary with "First impressions are notoriously untrustworthy," and the English writer J. B. Priestley in *Bright Day* (1946) reaffirmed the positive with "He ought to look neat and tidy . . . It's half the battle . . . making a good first impression." It seems this advice is safe enough for everyone to try at home.

Fish stinks from the head, A.   Once caught, a fish goes bad from the head downward, and this maxim asserts governments and other human endeavors go bad in the same way—from the leaders on down. George Pettie's *Civil Conversation* (1581) made the earliest mention of the saying, "For if the prouerbe be true, That like man like maister, and that a fishe beginneth first to smell at the head." Soon afterward, the lexicographer Randle Cotgrave, in *A Dictionary of the French and English Tongues* (1611), adapted the saying to read, "Fish euer begins to taint at the head; the first thing that's deprau'd in man's his wit." Henry George Bohn's *Dictionary of Quotations* (1860) gave the saying essentially its modern form with "Fish begins to stink at the head," while adding the note, "The corruption of state is first discernible in the higher classes." In a letter of 1915, the British statesman Winston Churchill rendered the saying as "Fish goes rotten by the head." The exact wording of the modern saying appeared in Alec Brown's *Green Lane, or Murder at Moat Farm* (1930). The proverb has been quoted infrequently in this century.

Fool and his money are soon parted, A.   Thomas Tusser's *A Hundreth Good Pointes of Good Husbandrie* (1573) recorded the first known version of this saying in the passage, "A foole and his monie be soone at debate, which after with sorrow repents him too late." John Bridges, in *Defence of Government in Church of England* (1587), rendered nearly the modern version, "A foole and his money is soon parted," while in 1616 Thomas Draxe's *Bibliotheca Scholastica Instructissima* quoted the exact wording. "A fool and his money . . ." subsequently appeared in collections of proverbs and was quoted or adapted by, among others, English novelist Tobias Smollett in *The Adventures of Roderick Random* (1748), novelist Sir Walter Scott in *The Antiquary* (1816, " . . . is parted"), playwright George Bernard Shaw in *Caesar and Cleopatra* (1897), American novelist Jack London in his correspondence (1911), Scottish-born writer Saki (H. H. Munro) in *The Square Egg* (1924), American playwright Maxwell Anderson in *Elizabeth the Queen* (1930), and Agatha Christie in *Mr. Parker* (1934). The saying has been quoted in print frequently in the twentieth century.

Fools rush in where angels fear to tread.   The Spanish Jesuit Baltasar Gracian in *Oraculo Manual* (1647) observed, "Folly rushes in through the door, for fools are always bold." Gracian's line apparently recorded the first of such sentiments, but the current proverb sprang whole from a passage in *An Essay on Criticism* (1709), by the English poet Alexander Pope: "No place so sacred from such fops is barr'd, / Nor is Paul's church more safe than Paul's churchyard: / Nay, fly to altars; there they'll talk you dead; / For fools rush in where angels fear to tread." An American jurist from North Carolina, James Iredell, repeated the saying in a letter of 1789. During the twentieth century, "Fools rush in . . ." has been quoted frequently, and among the noted writers who used it were O. Henry in *The Moment of Victory* (1909, "A kind of mixture of fools and angels—they rush in and fear to tread at the same time"), James Joyce in *Ulysses* (1922, "Prying into his private affairs on the *fools step in where angels* principle"), and Margaret Drabble in *Jerusalem the Golden* (1967). A clever adaptation also appeared in *Poor Richard Jr.'s Almanack* (1906) as "Fools rush in where angels fear to wed."

Forewarned is forearmed.   Originally a Latin maxim that stated simply, "Forewarned, forearmed," this saying first appeared in English in *Songs, Carols, . . . from Richard Hill's Commonplace Book* (c. 1530) as "He that is warned ys half armed." William Shakespeare adapted the saying in *Henry VI* (1591) with the line, "I will arm me, being thus forwarn'd." Benjamin Franklin's *Poor Richard's Almanack* (1736) gave the saying a ribald turn with "Forewarn'd, forearm'd, unless in the case of Cuckolds, who are often forearm'd before warn'd." George Washington adapted the saying to yet another situation in his writings (1778): "To forewarn, and consequently forearm me, against a secret enemy." The exact wording of the modern version was recorded during the next century in *Shadowed to Europe* (1885) by Le Jemlys.

Forgive and forget.   Philo of Alexandria, the "Jewish Plato," recorded the earliest known use of this expression as "I forgive and forget," in *De Iosepho* (A.D. c. 40). An early English text, *Ancren Riwle* (c. 1225), provided the first mention in English, though it is barely recognizable in that contemporary form: "Al thet hurt and al thet sore were uorgiten [forgotten] and uorgiuen uor glednesse [for gladness]." Somewhat later, William Langland wrote in the Middle English poem *Piers Plowman* (1377), "So wil Cryst of his curteisye, / and men crye hym mercy, / bothe fogiue and forgete." John Heywood's *A Dialogue Conteinyng the Nomber in Effect of All the Prouerbes in the Englishe Tongue* (1546) included the line, "Praiyng hir, to forgeue and forget all," and the expression was quoted and adapted widely in subsequent centuries.

William Shakespeare made use of it in a number of plays (*Henry VI, Part III* (1591), *Richard II* (1595), *All's Well That Ends Well* (1602), and *King Lear* (1605), as did another English playwright of the time, Thomas Kyd, in *The Spanish Tragedy* (1584). Among the other noted writers who used the expression were satirist Jonathan Swift (1738, *Polite Conversation*), poet Robert Burton (1621, *Anatomy of Melancholy*), dramatist Richard Sheridan (1775, *The Rivals*), Sir Walter Scott (1823, *Peveril of the Peak*), Herman Melville (1849, *Mardi and a Voyage Thither*), Louisa May Alcott (1868, *Little Women*), and Mark Twain (1872, *Roughing It*).

Fortune favors the bold.   [Fortune favors the brave; ... fools.] The early Greek poet Simonides is credited with devising the maxim, "Fortune assists the brave," in the fifth century B.C., and the current proverb was later rendered almost exactly (in Latin) by the Roman playwright Terence in *Phormio* (161 B.C.). With variations, this saying was also quoted by Cicero in *Tusculanarum Disputationum* (45 B.C.), Virgil in the *Aneid* (19 B.C.), and Ovid in *Metamorphosis* (A.D. 7). The contrary saying, "Fortune favors fools," began as a Latin saying of unknown origins about 150, but was not quoted by important authors in ancient times. The first English rendering of "Fortune favors the brave," closer in sentiment than form, appeared in Chaucer's *Troilus and Criseyde* (c. 1385) as "Fortune, as wel thiselven woost, Helpeth hardy man to his enprise." Chaucer's contemporary, John Gower, came closer to the current saying with "Fortune unto the bolde Is favorable for to helpe," in *Confessio Amantis* (c. 1390). Richard Taverner in *Proverbes or Adagies* (1539) wrote, "Fortune helpeth men of good courage," and the poet Michael Drayton included the line, "Fortune assists the boldest," in *Idea's Mirror* (1594).

About this time, the poet Barnabe Googe recorded essentially the modern wording of the contrary saying with "Fortune favours Fooles as old men saye," in *Eglogs, Epytaphes, and Sonnetes* (1563). The venerable Ben Jonson repeated the proverb in *The Alchemist* (1610) as "Fortune, that favours fools." Allan Ramsay in *The Widow Can Bake* (c. 1724) wrote essentially the modern version of "Fortune favors the bold" with "For fortune aye favours the active and bauld," and British novelist Frederick Chamier rendered the variant, "Fortune, they say, favours the brave," in *Tom Bowling* (1841). With minor variations, this saying has been repeated by poet Edmund Spenser in *The Faerie Queene* (1596), satirist Jonathan Swift in *Strephon and Chloe* (1731), and novelist Anthony Trollope in *Dr. Thorne* (1885).

For want of a nail the shoe is lost, for want of the shoe the horse is lost, for want of the horse the rider is lost.   This proverbial reminder about the sometimes disproportionate importance of minor details was at times carried to still further outlandish extremes with the addition of "for want of a rider the battle is lost, for want of the battle a kingdom is lost." Chaucer's friend, the poet John Gower, recorded the earliest version of the saying in his *Confessio Amantis* (c. 1390): "For sparinge of a litel cost / Ful ofte time a man hath lost / The large cote for the hod [hood]." In the seventeenth century, Thomas Adams's *Sermons* (1861) recorded essentially the modern version as a French "military proverb: 'The loss of a nail, the loss of an army.' The want of a a nail loseth the shoe, the loss of a shoe troubles the horse, the horse endangereth the rider, the rider breaking his rank molests the company so far as to hazard the whole army."

     The current wording first appeared in *Jacula Prudentum*, a collection of proverbs by the English poet George Herbert. Thereafter, it was repeated in *Children's and Household Tales* (1812) by the brothers Grimm, *Poor Richard's Almanack* (1752) and the *Way to Wealth* (1758) by Benjamin Franklin, and *Duty* (1880) by the Scottish biographer Samuel Smiles. The saying has been quoted infrequently during the twentieth century.

Friend in need is a friend indeed, A.   The Roman poet Quintus Ennius observed in *Hecuba* (c. 180 B.C.), "A sure friend is known in unsure circumstances," and some years later the Roman Gaius Petronius in *Satyricon* (A.D. c. 60) echoed the sentiment with "In tight places one's friends are apparent." The earliest related saying in English appeared in about 1035 as "Aet thearfe man sceal freonda cunnian [friend shall be known in time of need]." Another early saying was listed in *Proverbs of Alfred* (c. 1275), by the English philologist Walter Skeat: "A such fere þe is help in mode." The English priest and poet John Lydgate rendered a close variation of the current proverb in *Minor Poems* (c. 1430) with the line, "Ful weele is him that fyndethe a freonde at neede," and the first English printer, William Caxton, gave the saying as "It is sayd, that at the nede the frende is knowen," in a translation of *The Foure Sonnes of Aymon* (c. 1489). The wording was further refined to "A friend thou art in deede, / That helps thy friend in time of nipping neede," in *His Deuises* (1581) by Thomas Howell, and to "He that is thy friend indeed, / He will help thee in thy need," in *The Passionate Pilgrim* (1599) by Richard Barnfield. The exact wording of the current proverb first appeared in the next century, in John Ray's *A Collection of English Proverbs* (1670). Maria Edgeworth, the Irish novelist and friend of Sir Walter Scott, repeated the proverb in *Rosanna* (1802). "A friend in need ..." has been a familiar saying in the twentieth century.

Girls will be girls.   *See* **Boys will be boys.**

Give a man enough rope and he will hang himself.   A clever bit of gallows humor, this saying tells us that if a man with hidden bad intentions (or character) is allowed enough freedom, he will eventually reveal himself (or hang himself). The clergyman Thomas Fuller recorded the earliest reference to this saying in English, "They were suffered to have rope enough, till they had haltered themselves in a *preamunire*," in *History of the Holy Warre* (1639), and virtually the exact wording of the modern saying was quoted a few years later in John Ray's *A Collection of English Proverbs* (1670) as "Give him rope enough, and he'll hang himself." The English novelist Samuel Richardson adapted the saying for *Sir Charles Grandison* (1753) as "Give you women but rope enough, you'll do your own business," and the saying was also quoted or adapted by, among others, George Washington (1799, in his papers), Thomas Paine (1805, *To Mrs. Hulbert*), Charlotte Brontë (1849, *Shirley*), and, more recently, Agatha Christie (1924, *The Man in the Brown Suit*) and American detective story writer Erle Stanley Gardner (1941, *Case of the Empty Tin*).

God helps those who help themselves.   As early as 472 B.C., the Greek playwright Aeschylus wrote in *Persae*, "To the man who himself strives earnestly, God also lends a helping hand." Centuries later in *Erasmus' Adagies* (1545), Richard Taverner rendered the similar saying, "The goddes do helpe the doers." Some few years later, John Baret noted in *An Alveary, or Triple Dictionary* (1580), "Induce God doth helpe those in their affaires, which are industrious," while the English lexicographer John Minsheu, in *Spanish Dialogue* (1599), rendered the saying as "God will him helpe, that seekes for it himselfe."

Nearly the modern wording of the current proverb appeared in James Howell's *Proverbs in English, Italian, French and Spanish* (1659): "God helps him, who helps himself." Yet another close version was included in Benjamin Franklin's *Poor Richard's Almanack* (1736), "God helps them that help themselves." In 1777, the American Revolutionary War hero Samuel Adams penned the exact wording, "God helps those who help themselves," and the saying has been in wide use up to the present day. Herman Melville repeated the saying in *Israel Potter, or Fifty Years of Exile* (1855), George Bernard Shaw used it in *Back to Methusaleh* (1921), Phyllis McGinley adapted it in *Go On, You Scintillate* (1940), and Robert Penn Warren quoted it in *All the King's Men* (1946). Even the *Times Literary Supplement* (1956) has carried the saying, though not without some notice of its diminishing popularity in Britain: " 'God helps those who help themselves' is one of our most popular sayings although not quite so popular today as it was one hundred years ago . . . before the advent of the welfare state."

God keep me from four houses, a usurer's, a tavern, a spital, and a prison.   Here is a prayerful proverb that gives us an amusing look at the perils of sixteenth-century life (and for that matter modern life, give or take a house). Originally a French saying, the proverb was quoted in *Tresor des Sentences* (c. 1550) by Gabriel Meurier as "God keep me from four houses, the tavern, the moneylender's, the hospital, and the prison." The English version appeared in the current form in George Herbert's collected proverbs, *Jacula Prudentum* (1640). Though apparently little used, the saying was included in such recent collections of proverbs as Burton Stevenson's *Home Book of Proverbs* (1948) and *The Oxford Dictionary of English Proverbs* (1970).

Good and quickly seldom meet.   In *Analects* (c. 500 B.C.), the Chinese philosopher Confucius wrote what may be the earliest saying on this theme: "When things are done hastily, they are not done thoroughly." Many centuries later, Chaucer in *Canterbury Tales* (c. 1387) rendered essentially the same sentiment with "Ther nis no werkman, what-so-ever he be, / That may bothe werke wel and hastily." Over two centuries later, George Herbert's collected proverbs, *Jacula Prudentum* (1640), gave the saying in the modern form. It was repeated in John Ray's *A Collection of English Proverbs* (1670) and other later collections of proverbs, including the recent *Oxford Dictionary of Proverbs* (1970), but has been quoted only infrequently in recent times. *See also* **Haste makes waste.**

Good die young, The.   [Whom the gods love dies young; Best go first.] The long history of this saying began with the ancient version, "Whom the gods love dies young," and a touching story of how the proverb originated. As told by the Greek historian Herodotus in *History* (c. 445 B.C.), the story concerns two especially favored youths who, replacing two missing oxen, hitched themselves to a cart and carried their mother to a festival for the goddess Hera. At the temple, the grateful mother asked Hera to reward her sons with the greatest gift anyone might receive, whereupon the boys lay down to sleep and never woke again. The Greek playwright Menander recorded the ancient "Whom the gods love..." in *The Double Deceiver* (c. 300 B.C.); it was repeated by Plautus (190 B.C., *Bacchides*), Plutarch (A.D. c. 95, *Moralia*), and others. The earliest English rendering of the ancient version appeared in *The Troubled Man's Medicine* (1546) by William Hughe: "But among all others, saith the Greek poet, Menander, most happy are they, and best beloved of God, that die when they are young."

Though this saying has appeared in collections of proverbs up to the present day, another version—"The best go first"—appeared in English in the seventeenth century. The English poet John Donne recorded the earliest version of this saying with the line, "And soonest our best men with thee doe goe," in *Sonnet on Death* (c. 1631), and the current wording appeared in print as "The best go first, the bad remain to mend," in H. G. Bohn's *Handbook of Proverbs* (1859). The most recent version, "The good die young," can be traced back to William Wordsworth's *The Excursion* (1814) and the lines, "The good die first, / And they whose hearts are dry as summer dust burn / Burn to the socket." But lines from a seemingly unlikely source, *Thus Spake Theodore Roosevelt* (c. 1924) by the American poet Arthur Guiterman, probably came closest to striking a resonant chord of truth: "The good die young, so men have sadly sung / Who do not know the happier reason why / Is never that they die while they are young, / But that the good are young until they die."

Good fences make good neighbors.   In the eighth century B.C., when there were far fewer people in the world, the Greek poet Hesiod wrote, "A bad neighbor is as great a plague as a good one is a blessing." Of the many things good neighbors do to make themselves a blessing, one is to remember to keep some distance—a low fence, as it were—to allow for the privacy of those living close by. That sentiment was clear in the earliest form of the current proverb, "Love your neighbour, yet pull not down your hedge," which was quoted in George Herbert's *Jacula Prudentum* (1640) and repeated later in Benjamin Franklin's *Poor Richard's Almanack* (1754). Another version written in a letter to an American colonist in 1640 elaborated further on the matter of fences with "A good fence helpeth to keepe peace between neighbours; but let vs take heed that we make not a high stone wall to keepe vs from meeting." Almost two centuries later, the American novelist and jurist Hugh H. Brackenridge wrote in *Modern Chivalry* (1815), "Good fences restrain fencebreaking beasts, and . . . preserve good neighbourhoods," and in 1875 *Proverbial Folk-Lore* by Alan B. Cheales quoted the aphorism, "A hedge between keeps friendship green." But it was the American poet Robert Frost who first wrote the modern version, "Good fences make good neighbors," in the poem "Mending Wall" (1914).

Good name is better than great riches, A.   No less true in these modern times of instant fame (and instant disgrace), this saying was recorded in 474 B.C. by the Greek poet Pindar as "A good name, the best of all treasures," in the *Pythian Odes*. The modern saying probably came from the Old Testament Proverbs (c. 350 B.C.), which included, "A good name is rather to be chosen than great riches." A variant appeared in the later Book of Ecclesiastes (c. 250 B.C.): "A good name is better than precious ointment." Outside the Bible, the first English version was included in Chaucer's *Tale of Melibeus* (c. 1387): "Better it is and more it availleth a man to have a good name, than for to have grete richesses." Almost a century later, virtually the modern wording was quoted in *Dictes and Sayenges of the Philosophirs* (1477) by Earl Rivers: "Good renomme is bettir than richesse . . . " William Shakespeare wrote the memorable lines in *Othello* (1604), "Who steals my purse steals trash . . . But he that filches from me my good name Robs me of that which not enriches him And makes me poor indeed." The saying in its current form (" . . . than great riches") was rendered in Miguel de Cervantes's *Don Quixote* (1615). The saying appears to have been largely forgotten in the twentieth century.

Good things come in small packages.   [Best things come...]
Size of a package does not always determine the value of its
contents, any more than the truth of a saying determines its age;
surprisingly, this maxim appears to be a recent invention. A
French saying, "The best ointments are put in little boxes," appeared in James Howell's *Proverbs in English, Italian, French, and
Spanish* (1659), and may be a remote ancestor of the current
version. So, too, may be the more generic, "Little things are
good," which was included in Giovanni Torriano's *A Common
Place of Italian Proverbs and Proverbial Phrases* (1666). But the
earliest clear reference to the current saying came in a letter of
1877 written by the English novelist Benjamin Farjeon: "As the
best things are (said to be) wrapped in small parcels (proverb),
I select the smallest sheet of paper I can find...to make you
acquainted with the...state of affairs." James Joyce mentioned
the saying in *Ulysses* (1922) with "Fine goods in small parcels,"
while the current "Good things come..." was apparently not
quoted in print until the 1960s.

Good to begin well, better to end well.   A passage in the Old
Testament book Ecclesiastes (c. 250 B.C.) reads, "Better is the
end of a thing than the beginning thereof," and an early English
version of the current proverb expanded on that thought with
"It is nat they that begyn well, but they that persever that shall
come to honour." The latter passage appeared in one of the
earliest French grammars for the English-speaking people, *Les-
clarcissement de la Langue Francoyse*, written in 1530 by the English
grammarian John Palsgrave. The current saying, with its strong
emphasis on carrying through to a good ending, was first recorded the next century in Robert Codrington's *A Collection of
Many Select and Excellent Proverbs Out of Severall Languages* (1664)
and was repeated in John Ray's *A Collection of English Proverbs*
(1670). Though the saying has been included in collections of
proverbs up to modern times, it apparently has not been widely
used.

**Grass always looks greener on the other side of the fence,
The.**   Although the phrasing of this familiar proverb is surprisingly recent, sayings centered on the underlying idea of envy
date back to the sixteenth century. Richard Taverner's *Erasmus'
Adagies* (1545) rendered the saying as "The corne in an other
mans grounde semeth euer more fertyll and plentyfull then doth
oure owne. By this is noted the lyghtnesse, new gangelnesse and

constancye of mankynde which estemeth euen straunge thynges better then his owne." John Withal's *A Short Dictionary Most Profitable for Young Beginners* (1584) rendered this version as "Wee thinke alwayes the corne that growes in another bodies ground to be better then oure owne." James Howell's *Proverbs in English, Italian, French and Spanish* (1659) rendered an even more straightforward version, "My neighbours goat gives more milk then mine." Interestingly, collections of proverbs from the eighteenth and nineteenth centuries did not include any variants of the saying, and it was not until 1956 that the current version was first mentioned, in a play titled *The Grass Is Greener*. In 1957, the English science fiction writer Brian Aldiss wrote in *Space*, "Possibly you recall the old saying about the chlorophyll being greener on someone else's grass," and in 1959 the *New York Times* quoted the exact wording of the current version. The saying has been quoted in print regularly since then.

Great minds think alike.   Often quoted in jest today, this saying originated in the seventeenth century as the comic-sounding "Great wits jump." Daubridgcourt Belchier first recorded the saying in *Hans Beer-Pot* (1618) as "Good wits doe iumpe [agree]." Thomas Shelton's translation of *Don Quixote* (1620) rendered the saying as "Good wits will soon meet," but the version, "Great wits jump [agree]," was quoted in Benjamin Franklin's *Poor Richard's Almanack* (1735), Jonathan Swift's *Polite Conversation* (1738, "Good wits . . .") and Laurence Sterne's *Tristram Shandy* (1761). The expression "Great minds jump" appeared in the late 1800s, and in 1922, the British humor magazine *Punch* recorded the modern version with the line, "Great minds, as the saying is, think alike." The saying has been in wide use during the twentieth century.

Guests and fish stink after three days.   The Roman comic playwright Plautus warned in *Miles Gloriosus* (c. 200 B.C.), "No guest is so welcome that he will not become a nuisance after three days in a friend's house." Indeed, there was remarkable agreement through the ages on the limit of three days, though the raffish comparison with a dead fish did not appear until the sixteenth-century English saying, "Gestes and fish . . . are ever stale within three dayes," which was quoted by the writer John Lyly in *Euphues and His England* (1580). John Ray's *A Collection of English Proverbs* (1670) rendered the saying as "Fresh fish and new come guests, smell by that they are three days old," but it was James Howell's *Proverbs in English, Italian, French and Spanish* (1659) that printed the saying with virtually the modern wording—"Guests and fish stink in three days." A British publication, *Poor Robin Almanack* (1678) repeated that version, while Benjamin Franklin's *Poor Richard's Almanack* rendered the more politely worded "Fish and visitors smell in three days" in 1736. Although these versions have been quoted infrequently up to the present day, the silent screen star Charlie Chaplin noted a more genteel variation in his *Autobiography* (1964): "As mother said, guests were like cakes: if kept too long they became stale and impalatable."

Guilty conscience needs no accuser, A.   Benjamin Franklin observed in *Poor Richard's Almanack* (1747), "A quiet Conscience sleeps in Thunder, / But Rest and Guilt live far asunder." Centuries earlier, the Roman statesman Cato the Elder in *Disticha* (c. 175 B.C.) wrote of another psychological torment suffered by wrongdoers at the hands of their consciences: "The guilty think all men speak of them." In 1591, William Shakespeare articulated the underlying idea of the current proverb with the line, "Suspicion always haunts the guilty mind," in *Henry VI, Part III,* and in 1721 James Kelly's *A Complete Collection of Scotish Proverbs* rendered a close version with the saying, "A guilty Conscience self accuses." The exact wording of the current saying was quoted soon after in *His Life & Adventures* (1744) by Matthew Bishop, and was included in Robert Bland's *Proverbs* (1814) and subsequent collections. Quoted by H. L. Mencken in *Heathen Days* (1943), the saying has not been quoted in print frequently during this century.

Guilty flee when no man pursueth, The.   [Wicked flee . . .] This saying originated with the Old Testament (c. 350 B.C.) proverb, "The wicked flee when no man pursueth: but the righteous are bold as a lion." The Roman philosopher and dramatist Seneca echoed that sentiment with "Wickedness fears the very shadows," in *Ad Lucilium* (A.D. 64), and the earliest English rendering of the current saying appeared in *A Dictionary of the French and English Tongues* (1611) by the lexicographer Randle Cotgrave: "The wicked flies though no man follow him." Giovanni Torriano's *A Common Place of Italian Proverbs and Proverbial Phrases* (1666) rendered the saying as "The wicked man flies without being pursued." Virtually the modern wording was quoted during a criminal trial (1771) in colonial America, "The wicked flee when no man pursueth," this form being used through the nineteenth and into the twentieth century. The word "guilty" began to replace "wicked" during the twentieth century, and the exact wording of the current saying appeared at least as early as 1937, in George Barton's *Triumphs of Crime Detection*. Some years before that, the American attorney Charles Parkhurst was waging a crusade against vice in New York City when he made the wry observation, "The wicked flee when no man pursueth, but they make better time when someone is after them" (c. 1900).

Hair of the dog, A.   For centuries, revelers beset by morning-after hangovers have resorted to taking "a hair of the dog." While the remedy itself may or may not work, the saying arose from an even more doubtful medieval superstition, one that said you could cure a dog bite by putting one of the dog's hairs over the wound. The proverbial remedy for a hangover did not appear until the sixteenth century, however, when it was first recorded in John Heywood's *A Dialogue Conteinyng the Nomber in Effect of All the Prouerbes in the Englishe Tongue* (1546): "I pray the[e] leat me and my felow haue / A heare of the dog that bote vs last night, / And bitten were we both to the braine aright." Appropriately enough, the French writer Rabelais mentioned the saying in his ribald tale *Pantagruel* (1552) with "Will he take a hair of the dog that bit him?" The English lexicographer Randle Cotgrave reported with some amusement in *A Dictionary of the French and English Tongues* (1611), "Our ale-knights often . . . say, Give us a hair of the dog that last bit us." The saying appeared in the major collections of proverbs published thereafter, including James Howell's *Proverbs in English, Italian, French and Spanish* (1659) and John Ray's *A Collection of English Proverbs* (1670). A number of noted writers quoted or used the saying (and perhaps even tried the remedy), including the dramatist Ben Jonson (1614, *Bartholomew Fair*), the satirist Jonathan Swift (1738, *Polite Conversation*), the novelist Sir Walter Scott (1817, *Rob Roy*), and Charles Dickens (1840, *Barnaby Rudge*). "A hair of the dog" was quoted in print frequently during the twentieth century.

Half a loaf is better than no bread.   When life makes getting all we want impossible, this old proverb advises us to be satisfied with the part we can have. The Greek playwright Menander recorded one of the earliest sayings in this vein, "Whenever one offers you no one thing complete, accept the fraction, for obtaining the lesser part will be a good deal better than getting nothing at all" (c. 300 B.C.). The Roman statesman Cicero put it more imaginatively in *Ad Atticum* (44 B.C.): "Better to sail slowly than not to sail at all."

The saying first appeared in English in John Heywood's *A Dialogue Conteinyng the Nomber in Effect of All the Prouerbes in the Englishe Tongue* (1546) as "For better is halfe a lofe than no bread," while the English historian William Camden rendered it in *Remains* (1605, published 1870) as "Better half a loaf than no bread." Later that century, Daniel Rogers warned against giving in to a fit of temper with, "He is a foole who counts not halfe a loafe better then no bread, or despiseth the moonshine because the sunne is down," in *Naaman the Syrian* (1642).

The American clergyman Increase Mather recorded the exact wording of the modern saying for the first time in his writings (1693) with "It is an old proverb, That half a Loaf is better than no bread," which was later repeated by Charles Dickens in *The Old Curiosity Shop* (1840), and more recently by Eugene O'Neill in *Strange Interlude* (1928). In addition, there have been some amusing variants, such as, "Better a mouse in the Pot, than no Flesh at all," "Better half an egg than an empty shell," and "Better are small Fish than an empty Dish," all of which appeared in Thomas Fuller's *Gnomologia: Adagies and Proverbs* (1732).

Hand that rocks the cradle rules the world, The.   A testament to the great influence of mothers and motherhood, this saying was first quoted in 1865 by the American poet William Ross Wallace in *What Rules the World* as "The hand that rocks the cradle / Is the hand that rules the world." The British writer Saki (H. H. Munro) rendered the saying as "It's the nature of the sex. The hand that rocks the cradle rocks the world, in a volcanic sense," in *Toys of Peace* (c. 1916), and a few years later, James Joyce wrote in *Ulysses* (1922), "Her hand that rocks the cradle rules the Ben Howth. That rules the world." The exact wording of the current version was quoted in Robert Carson's *The Bride Saw Red* (1943).

Handsome is as handsome does.   The earliest form of this familiar saying appeared in the poet Anthony Munday's *Sundry Examples* (1580): "As the auncient adage is, goodly is he that

goodly dooth." The playwright Thomas Dekker rendered another version in *The Shoemaker's Holiday* (1600): "By my troth, he
is a proper man; but he is proper that proper doth." Essentially
the modern version was first recorded in John Ray's *A Collection
of English Proverbs* (1670) as "He is handsome that handsome
doth," and was later elaborated upon by Oliver Goldsmith in *The
Vicar of Wakefield* (1766) with "They are as heaven made them,
handsome enough if they be good enough; for handsome is that
handsome does." Thomas Haliburton, creator of Sam Slick, gave
us another variant, "Pretty is as pretty does," in *Wise Saws* (1843),
and the exact modern wording was first recorded in *Spirit of
Times* (1845). Walter Skeat's *A Student's Pastime* (1896) explained
the saying: " 'Handsome is as handsome does,' *handsome* means
neat, with reference to skilfulness of execution." Used earlier by
Herman Melville in *Billy Budd* (published posthumously, 1924)
and Charles Lamb (1826, *Essays: Popular Fallacies*), the saying has
been quoted frequently in the twentieth century. Among those
who repeated it were O. Henry in *Reading Matter* (1909, "Handsome is as handsome palavers"), Jack London in correspondence
(1911), James Joyce in *Ulysses* (1922), Aldous Huxley in *Eyeless
in Gaza* (1936), and detective story writer Ellery Queen in *Door
Between* (1936, "Gentle is . . . ").

Hanging and wiving go by destiny. A roguish sentiment no
doubt repeated in many an alehouse, it was first recorded in *The
Scholehouse of Women* (c. 1541), which was written by an unknown
author who wrote, "Truly some men there bee . . . saye it goeth
by destinie[,] To hang or wed . . . I am well sure Hangynge is
better of the twayne[,] Sooner done, and shorter payne." John
Heywood's *A Dialogue Conteinyng the Nomber in Effect of All the
Prouerbes in the Englishe Tongue* (1546) quoted a shortened version:
"Weddyng is desteny / And hangyng likewise, saith the
prouerbe." It was William Shakespeare, however, who gave us
the exact modern wording in *The Merchant of Venice* (1597), as
well as the devilish corollary, "Many a good hanging prevents a
bad marriage," in *Twelfth Night* (1599). The saying was repeated
by the playwright Thomas Dekker in *The Shoemaker's Holiday*
(1600, "Wedding and hanging . . . "), and was adapted by the poet
Samuel Butler (1664, *Hudibras*), and the satirist Jonathan Swift
(1738, *A Complete Collection of Genteel and Ingenious Conversation*).
The saying has not been widely used in the twentieth century,
at least partly, one would guess, because hanging has gone out
of fashion.

Happy is the bride that the sun shines on, and the corpse the rain rains on.   Two earlier superstitions apparently were fused to form this curious saying, which appeared toward the end of the seventeenth century. Concerning the corpse, the *Puritane, or the Widow of Watling-Streete* (1607) recorded the earliest mention of this superstition with "If, Blessed bee the coarse the raine raynes vpon, he had it, powring downe." The idea here was that a coffin "wet with the dew of heaven" boded well for the deceased, or so a note explained in W. Carew Hazlitt's *English Proverbs and Proverbial Phrases* (1907). About the middle of the seventeenth century, the English poet Robert Herrick recorded the brides' superstition in *Hesperides* (1648) with "Blest is the Bride, on whom the Sun doth shine," and that saying has continued in use up to the present day. However, the two superstitions were also joined together in John Ray's *A Collection of English Proverbs* (1678), which quoted the proverb in its current form. The combined saying was repeated in Francis Grose's *A Provincial Glossary With a Collection of Local Proverbs* (1790), but apparently has been quoted in print only infrequently since then.

Happy is the wooing that is not long a-doing.   Speaking for anxious suitors everywhere, the English poet Richard Edwards penned the lines, "Thrise happie is that woyng [wooing] / That is not long a doyng," which appeared in *The Paradyse of Dainty Deuises* (c. 1566). The playwright George Chapman shortened that in *Sir Gyles Goosecappe* (1606) to "Blest is the wooing that's not long a dooing," a version repeated by the English churchman Robert Burton in *The Anatomy of Melancholy* (1621). The current wording was first recorded in John Ray's *A Collection of English Proverbs* (1670) with "Happy is the wooing that's not long a-doing." The saying was repeated in James Kelly's *A Complete Collection of Scottish Proverbs* (1721), and was later quoted by Henry Fielding in *Tom Thumb* (1730), Benjamin Franklin in *Poor Richard's Almanack* (1730), and Samuel Richardson in *Sir Charles Grandison* (1753). Taking up the cause of unsuccessful wooers, the Irish poet Thomas Moore wrote in *The Time I've Lost in Wooing* (c. 1852), "The time I've lost in wooing, / In watching and pursuing / The light that lies / In woman's eyes, / Has been my heart's undoing." But those who have lost in this game of love can take some small comfort in an eighteenth-century Scottish proverb that said, "A maiden with many wooers often chooses the worst."

Haste makes waste.   The notion of haste being counterpro-
ductive can be traced back at least to the apocryphal *Book of
Wisdom* (c. 190 B.C.) by Jesus Ben Sirach, which contained the
line, "There is one that toileth and laboureth, and maketh haste,
and is so much the more behind." Centuries later, Chaucer
wrote in *Canterbury Tales* (c. 1387), "In wikked haste is no profit,"
and Chaucer's friend John Gower said in *Confessio Amantis* (c.
1390), "Men sen alday that rape rewth [Men say always that
haste rueth]." John Heywood's *A Dialogue Conteinyng the Number
in Effect of All the Prouerbes in the Englishe Tongue* (1546) gave
virtually the modern wording, along with a warning about rush-
ing matrimony: "Show after weddyng, that hast maketh waste."
The exact wording appeared just a few years later in *Memories*
(1575) by the English poet George Gascoigne. A longer version
of the saying was quoted in John Ray's *A Collection of English
Proverbs* (1678): "Haste makes waste, and waste makes want,
and want makes strife between the goodman and his wife."
"Haste makes waste" has been quoted by, among others, Samuel
Butler (1663, *Hudibras*), Benjamin Franklin (1753, *Poor Richard's
Almanack*), and Henry David Thoreau (1852, in his journal).
The saying, widely used in twentieth-century America, has an
amusing counterpart in a Chinese proverb on the futility of
hurrying—"A hasty man drinks his tea with a fork"—which was
recorded in *Racial Proverbs* (1938), by Selwyn G. Champion. *See
also* **Good and quickly seldom meet.**

He laughs best who laughs last.   In its earliest form, this proverb read simply, "He laugheth that winneth," a saying that first
appeared in John Heywood's *A Dialogue Conteinyng the Nomber in
Effect of All the Prouerbes in the Englishe Tongue* (1546). The current
proverb also contains an element of the winner gets the laugh,
but speaks to a more complex set of events. Here, someone who
has been bested in one situation prevails in a subsequent and
final encounter, thereby getting the "last laugh." This version
was first recorded in a seventeenth-century text entitled *The
Christmas Prince* (c. 1607), with the line, "Hee laugheth best that
laugheth to the end." Another version based on essentially the
same idea, "Better the last smile than the first laughter," was
recorded in John Ray's *A Collection of English Proverbs* (1670). The
English dramatist Sir John Vanbrugh quoted the current saying
in *The Country House* (1706) as "He laughs best that laughs last,"
and in the next century, Sir Walter Scott gave the exact wording
of the modern version in *Peveril of the Peak* (1823). The saying

has been in regular use since then, and among the notable authors who quoted or adapted it were the English poet laureate John Masefield (1912, *Widow in Bye Street*), Saki (H. H. Munro, *Unbearable Bassington*, 1912), the English novelist Wyndham Lewis (1925, in correspondence; 1930, *The Apes of God*), Mary Roberts Rinehart (1926, *The Book of Tish*), and Erle Stanley Gardner (1935, *The Case of the Counterfeit Eye*).

He that buys land buys many stones; he that buys flesh buys many bones; he that buys eggs buys many shells; but he that buys good ale buys nothing else.   This rustic saying came to us from a spirited medieval drinking song, *Bring Us in Good Ale* (c. 1410). The words to the original song, recorded by Thomas Wright in *Songs and Carols From a Manuscript of the Fifteenth Century,* read (with bravado), "Bryng us in no befe, for ther is many bonys, / But bryng us in good ale, for that goth downe at onys. / Bryng us in no eggs, for ther is many schelles, / But bryng us in good ale, and gyfe us nothyng ellys." A sixteenth-century work titled *Pedler's Prophesy* (1595) included the line, "You shall be sure to haue good Ale for that haue no bones," but the exact wording of the current version was apparently first recorded in John Ray's *A Collection of English Proverbs* (1670). Thomas Fuller's *Gnomologia: Adagies and Proverbs* (1732) gave a slightly different version, using "...beef buys bones" instead of "...flesh buys many bones" and "...nuts buys shells" instead of "...eggs buys many shells." With minor variations, the saying has been included in collections of proverbs published up to the present day, though it has appeared in print only infrequently outside them.

He that has a great nose thinks everybody is speaking of it.   The first appearance of this eighteenth-century saying came in James Kelly's *A Complete Collection of Scotish Proverbs* (1721), where it was rendered, "He that has a mickle [great] nose, thinks every body is speaking of it. People that are sensible of their guilt, are always full of suspicion." Thomas Fuller's *Gnomologia: Adagies and Proverbs* (1732) gave the exact wording of the saying, and in the next century, Sir Walter Scott made an altogether appropriate mention of it in his diary (1826): "I went to Court for the first time to-day, and, like the man with the large nose, thought everybody was thinking of me and my mishap." The saying subsequently has been included in various collections of proverbs up to the present day, but has been rarely quoted outside them.

He that is down need fear no fall.   It is hard to imagine any
advantage to losing in life, but here is an old bromide that does
precisely that with a clever ironic twist: When you are really down,
at least you don't have to worry about losing anything else. If
that seems a small comfort, remember that when one is really
down, any comfort at all will do. The Latin writer Pubilius Syrus
observed in *Sententiae* (43 B.C.), "The lowly can fall neither far
nor heavily," and the later Greek scholar Diogenianus rendered
it as "He who lies on the ground has no place from which to
fall," in his *Adagia* (c. 125). The earliest English version of the
saying was recorded by the priest Alexander Barclay in *Mirrour
of Good Manners* (c. 1523) as "A man on grounde resting can not
much lower fall." The dramatist Thomas Kyd gave the Latin
version, "He that lies on the ground hath no lower descent to
fall to," in his *Spanish Tragedy* (1587), while Sir Walter Raleigh
wrote in *History of the World* (1614), "I am on the Ground already;
and therefore haue not far to fall." Later that century, Samuel
Butler rendered the saying in *Hudibras* (1663) as "I am not now
in Fortune's power, He that is down can fall no lower." The exact
wording of the current saying was recorded a short time later in
John Bunyan's *Pilgrim's Progress* (1678). Both the current version
and "He that lies upon the ground . . . " have been quoted in print
infrequently outside collections of proverbs.

He who excuses, accuses himself.   Saint Jerome (Eusebius
Hieronymus), whose Latin translation of the Bible became known
as the Vulgate, recorded the earliest version of the current proverb in *Epistles* (c. 370) with the line, "When you seek to excuse,
you accuse." Centuries later, the idea that making an excuse
implied some guilt was made even clearer in the French saying,
"He who excuses himself, accuses himself," which was quoted in
the French work *Tresor des Sentences* (c. 1575) by Gabriel Meurier.
William Shakespeare noted in *King John* (1596) that "oftentimes
excusing of a fault Doth make the fault the worse by the excuse."
Soon after, the lexicographer Randle Cotgrave wrote in *A
Dictionary of the French and English Tongues* (1611), "Excuser Some
when they meane to excuse, accuse themselues." The dramatist
Ben Jonson made a similar observation in *Tale of a Tub* (1633)
with "Squire, these excuses argue more for your guilt." Essen-
tially, the current English version appeared later that century in
Giovanni Torriano's *A Common Place of Italian Proverbs and Prov-
erbial Phrases* (1666) as "Who excuseth himself, himself accuseth."
An interesting and still appropriate variant, "Accusing the Times

is but excusing ourselves," was included in Thomas Fuller's *Gnomologia: Adagies and Proverbs* (1732). The exact wording of the current proverb apparently did not appear in print until the twentieth century, when it was recorded in *Murder Gone to Earth* (1936) by Jonathan Stagge.

He who fights and runs away may live to fight another day.
Denounced for having run away at the Battle of Chaeronea (338 B.C.), the Greek orator Demosthenes was said to have replied with the then common saying, "The man who runs away may fight again." Centuries later, an unknown medieval author echoed that sentiment in *Owl and Nightingale* (c. 1250) with the line, " 'Wel fight that wel flight,' seith the wise." Another manuscript from about 1440 rendered the saying as "It is an olde sawe, he feghtith wele that fleith faste." The French writer Rabelais noted in *Pantagruel* (1548), "Demosthenes saith, That the man that runs away may fight another time," a reference repeated by the English clergyman Robert Burton in *The Anatomy of Melancholy* (1621).

The modern version of the saying was recorded a few years later in a compilation entitled *Musarum Deliciae* (1656), though no attribution was given for the lines, "For he that fights and runs away / May live to fight another day." Among the authors who subsequently quoted or adapted the saying were the English poet Samuel Butler (1678, *Hudibras*), the American writer Washington Irving (1804, in a contribution to the *Corrector*), and the American short story writer O. Henry (1907, *An Afternoon Miracle*).

He who hesitates is lost.
The English poet Joseph Addison gave the earliest rendering of this saying in his play *Cato* (1713): "When love once pleads admission to our hearts...The woman that deliberates is lost." Anthony Trollope repeated the sentiment in *Can You Forgive Her?* (1865) with "It has often been said of a woman that she who doubts is lost," and John H. Beadle's *Western Wilds* (1878) recorded the more generalized, modern wording with the line, "In Utah it is emphatically true, that he who hesitates is lost—to Mormonism." A familiar saying in the twentieth century, "He who hesitates..." was quoted by American novelist Edgar Rice Burroughs in *Gods of Mars* (1912), Eugene O'Neill in *Beyond the Horizon* (1920), and English novelist Wyndham Lewis in *The Apes of God* (1930).

He who is his own lawyer has a fool for a client.   This proverb is probably a recent adaptation of the much older saying, "He that teaches himself has a fool for his master." The medieval clergyman Saint Bernard recorded this earlier proverb in Latin as "He who makes himself his own teacher, makes himself pupil to a fool," while the English translation was quoted by the journalist and translator Roger L'Estrange in *Fables* (1692). This saying was still common in the nineteenth century when the lawyer's version came into existence. The earliest known printed reference, "He who is always his own counseller will often have a fool for his client," appeared in *Port Folio* (1809). Soon afterward, the Irish novelist Maria Edgeworth conjured up an amusing image of the unforeseen consequences of self-counsel in *Ormond* (1817): "King Corny . . . by being his own lawyer . . . has drawn his own will so that any lawyer could drive a coach and six [horses] through it." The English writer Thomas C. Haliburton wrote in *Nature and Human Nature* (1855), "A man who pleads his own cause has a fool for a client," and two decades afterward, Alan B. Cheales recorded the modern wording of the current proverb in *Proverbial Folk-Lore* (1875). The saying has been quoted in print frequently during the twentieth century.

He who lies down with dogs will rise with fleas.   An amusing reminder about the inevitable, unpleasant consequences of keeping bad company, this saying was recorded in *First Fruites* (1578), by the English lexicographer John Florio: "Who sleepeth with dogges, shal rise with fleas." The dramatist John Webster rendered the current wording in the play *The White Devil* (c. 1610). The saying appeared in R. C. Trench's *On the Lessons in Proverbs* (1853) and G. L. Apperson's *English Proverbs and Proverbial Phrases* (1929), but has been quoted in print only infrequently.

He who lives by the sword shall perish by the sword.   The New Testament book Revelation (A.D. c. 90) gave us the earliest version of the saying, "He that killeth with the sword must be killed with the sword." The first English version appeared in Alexander Barclay's *Eclogues* (c. 1530) as "All suche as with the sworde do strike Feare to be serued with the scaberd like." Soon after, John Heywood's *A Dialogue Conteinyng the Nomber in Effect of All the Prouerbes in the Englishe Tongue* (1546) included essentially the same version with "The prouerbe saith he that striketh with the swoorde, Shalbe strikyn with the scaberde." While this variant was repeated throughout the seventeenth century, the

American colonist and founder of Rhode Island, Roger Williams, penned a version closer to the modern saying in a letter of 1652: "All that take the Sword . . . shall perish by it." In 1804, the American statesman Gouverneur Morris gave us virtually the modern wording, writing in his personal papers, "Those who live by the sword shall perish by the sword."

He who rides a tiger cannot dismount. In *Chinese Proverbs* (1875), William Scarborough recorded the earliest version of this saying in English as "He who rides a tiger is afraid to dismount." The implication here is that some things, once started, cannot be easily or safely stopped, and it was to that point that Archibald Colquhoun wrote in *The Mastery of the Pacific* (1902), "The colonies . . . are for her [France] the tiger which she has mounted . . . and which she can neither manage nor get rid of."

He who splits his own wood warms himself twice. Apparently of American origin, this saying referred to a first "warming" (some would call it hard work) experienced during the cutting and hauling of the wood, and the second warming enjoyed when the wood was actually burned. Some have attributed this saying to Abraham Lincoln, and he may well have repeated it, but a reference to the saying, "Wood warms a man twice," appeared in the correspondence of an American named Francis Kinloch in 1819. Lincoln was only about ten years old at that time. The proverb has been quoted in print infrequently during the twentieth century.

He who sups with the devil needs a long spoon. Although this saying conjured up an amusing image of vying with the devil over a stewpot for something to eat, it actually warned against becoming involved in shady dealings of any sort. Chaucer recorded the earliest version of the proverb in *Canterbury Tales* (c. 1387) as "Therfor bihoveth him a ful long spoon / That shal ete with a feend . . ." An early version close to the modern wording appeared in John Heywood's *A Dialogue Conteinyng the Nomber in Effect of All the Prouerbes in the Englishe Tongue* (1546): "He must haue a long spoone, shall eate with the diuell." Later that century, William Shakespeare rendered the saying in *Comedy of Errors* (1592) as "Marry, he must have a long spoon that must eat with the devil." Shakespeare also adapted the saying for *The Tempest* (c. 1611). King James I of England included yet another version in his play *Daemonologie* (1597) with the line, "They that suppe keile with the Deuill, haue neede of long spoons," and the English dramatist John Webster adapted it for *The Devil's Law-Case* (1623), "Here's a Latin spoone, and a long one, to feed with the Devill." With minor variations, early forms of the saying were repeated in collections of proverbs from the mid-seventeenth century onward. In the nineteenth century, the novelist Sir Walter Scott rendered it as "He suld hae a lang-shankit spune that wad sup kail wi' the deil," and a version close to the modern wording was recorded in the *Lay of St. Nicholas* (1838) by the English humorist Richard H. Barham: "Who suppes with the Deville sholde have a long spoone!" The exact modern wording apparently did not appear in print until Robert Walling's *That Dinner* (1928). Among the writers who used the saying were Robert Louis Stevenson (1893, *Catriona*), Graham Greene (1948, *Heart of the Matter*), and Ian Fleming (1959, *Goldfinger*). Former British prime minister Harold Macmillan also made use of the saying to describe Neville Chamberlain's negotiations with Nazi leader Adolf Hitler just prior to World War II. Chamberlain, he wrote, "having no understanding of the man with whom he tried to sup,...never provided himself with the necessary length of spoon."

Hell has no fury like a woman scorned.   Comments upon the fierceness of a woman's wrath have a long history, which may well be a testament to the lasting impression such outbursts have made. The apocrphyal *Book of Wisdom* (c. 190 B.C.) by Jesus Ben Sirach proclaimed, "There is no wrath above the wrath of a woman," and some centuries later, the Roman satirist Juvenal warned in *Satires* (c. 120), "Never is a woman so savage as when her hatred is goaded on by shame." In the medieval English *Somnour's Tale* (c. 1388), Chaucer wrote, "Ther nis, y-wis, no serpent so cruel, / Whan man tret on his tayl, ne half so fel, / As womman is, whan she hath caught an ire." The dramatists Francis Beaumont and John Fletcher wrote in *The Knight of Malta* (1619), "The wages of scorn'd love is baneful hate," and the English dramatist Colley Cibber declared in *Love's Last Shift* (1696), "We shall find no fiend in hell can match the fury of a disappointed woman,—scorned, slighted, dismissed without a parting pang." But it was William Congreve who, a year later, penned essentially the modern saying with the lines, "Heav'n has no rage, like love to hatred turn'd, / Nor Hell a fury like a woman scorn'd," in *The Mourning Bride* (1697). Almost two centuries later, Margaret Holmes referred to the saying in *The Chamber Over the Gate* (1886):

"You know 'Hell hath no fury,' etc...." The complete phrasing of the modern version was first recorded in Carolyn Wells's *Furthest Fury* (1924). The saying has been quoted frequently since then, and has appeared in William McFee's *The Harbourmaster* (1932), Damon Runyon's *Money From Home* (1935), Erle Stanley Gardner's *Case of the Dubious Bridegroom* (1949), and Iris Murdoch's *Case of the Black Prince* (1973).

Here today and gone tomorrow.   The sixteenth-century French Protestant reformer John Calvin recorded this familiar aphorism for the first time in *Life and Conversion of a Christian Man* (1549) with the line, "This prouerbe that man is here today and gone to morrow." A more explicit, if not downright dire, version of "Aliue to day, and dead to morrow" appeared in *Bibliotheca Scholastica Instructissima, or A Treasurie of Ancient Adagies, and Sententious Prouerbes* (1616) by Thomas Draxe. James Kelly's *A Complete Collection of Scotish Proverbs* (1721) included essentially the current version with "Here to Day, and away to Morrow," and the English publication called *Poor Robin Almanack* (1731) expanded on the underlying idea with, "The world is full of Vissitudes [sic], we are here today, and gone to-morrow, as the Shoemaker said when he was going to run away." Among those who quoted the saying were George Washington, in his correspondence (1777), the English writer Thomas Haliburton, creator of Sam Slick, in *Wise Saws* (1843), the American novelist Mary Roberts Rinehart in *Man in Lower Ten* (1909), James Joyce in *Ulysses* (1922), the English writer Malcolm Muggeridge in *Affairs of the Heart* (1949), P. G. Wodehouse in *Angel Cake* (1952), and Ellery Queen in *The Last Woman in His Life* (1970).

Higher the ape goes the more he shows his tail, The.   The French moralist Michel de Montaigne, quoting a criticism of the French in his *Essays* (1580), recorded this laughable bit of proverbial wisdom for the first time as "Frenchmen resemble apes, who, climbing up a tree from branch to branch, never cease going till they come to the highest branch, and there show their bare behinds." The English philosopher Francis Bacon reduced that to a ribald saying in *Promus* (c. 1594), "He doth like the ape that the higher he clymbes the more he shows his ars," while the English poet George Herbert rendered the exact wording of the current, more polite version in *Jacula Prudentum* (1640). Herbert gave an additional explanation, saying, "The higher beggars or base bred persons are advanced, the more they discover the lowness and baseness of their spirits and tempers." Alexander Pope also referred to the saying in *The Dunciad* (1743) with "The higher you climb, the more you shew your A————. Verified in no instance more than in Dulness aspiring. Emblematized also by an Ape climbing and exposing his posteriors'." The saying was used by James Fenimore Cooper in his correspondence (1747), but has not been repeated frequently since.

History repeats itself.   The Greek historian Thucydides laid the foundation for this modern maxim in a passage from his history of the Peloponnesian War (c. 400 B.C.): "I shall be content if those shall pronounce my history useful who desire to have a clear view both of the events which have happened, and of those which will some day . . . happen again in a same or similar way." Centuries later, the unknown author of *Politeuphuia Wits Commonwealth* (1597) rendered a line that was at least similar in sentiment to the current saying, "Time is the repeater of all things," though it was not until the nineteenth century that "History repeats itself" actually appeared in print. The English novelist George Eliot (Mary Ann Evans) recorded it first in *Scenes of Clerical Life* (1857) as "History, we know, is apt to repeat itself." The exact wording was quoted a few years later by Henry Sedley in *Marion Rooke* (1865). Among those who have since used the saying are the American impresario Phineas T. Barnum (1869, *Struggles and Triumphs*), Mark Twain (1875, *Mark Twain's Sketches*), and James Joyce (1922, *Ulysses*). The saying has been used frequently in the twentieth century, though the writer Clement F. Rogers voiced skepticism about the saying in *Verify Your References* (1938): "History repeats itself, says the proverb, but that is precisely what it never really does. It is the historians (of a sort) who repeat themselves."

Home is where the heart is.   Though some attribute this saying to the Latin author Pliny, it appears to be of much more recent origin. A play written in 1870 by J. J. McCloskey (collected in *Davy Crockett and Other Plays,* 1940) included the earliest known rendering of the current saying with the line, "Well, home, they say, is where the heart is." Two years later, Oliver Wendell Holmes wrote in *Homesick in Heaven* (1872), "Home that our feet may leave, but not our hearts," and Elbert Hubbard's *A Thousand and One Epigrams* (1914) repeated the current form of the saying. Twentieth-century writers did not hesitate to pen their own thoughts on what "home" might mean; George Bernard Shaw wrote in *Maxims for Revolutionists* (1903), "Home is the girl's prison and the woman's workshop," which may have seemed a revolutionary statement in the early 1900s. During the World War II years, Craig Rice presented quite a different view in *Having a Wonderful Time* (1943) with "Home is where the bar is." But it was Robert Frost's wry observation in *The Death of a Hired Man* (1914) that probably came closest to home: "Home is the place where, when you have to go there, / They have to take you in."

Honesty is the best policy.   This saying harks back to the sixth-century B.C. *Fables* by Aesop, which included the story of a woodcutter who accidentally dropped his ax in a river. The god Hermes appeared at that moment and, retrieving a golden ax from the water, asked if it were the woodcutter's. When the man replied no, Hermes brought forth a silver ax and again tested him. After the woodcutter again refused to lie, Hermes fetched the right ax and, pleased with the man's honesty, gave him the two others besides. Later, another woodcutter heard about what had happened and threw his ax into the same river. Hermes soon appeared with a golden ax, but was so angry when the second woodcutter claimed it that he disappeared, leaving nothing for the dishonest man—not even the man's own ax, now lost in the river.

In a similar vein, the Roman rhetorician Quintilian wrote in *Institutionis Oratoriae* (A.D. c. 80), "Divine Providence has granted this gift to man, that those things which are honest are also the most advantageous." Centuries later, the first mention of the current saying in English appeared in Edwin Sandys's *Europae Speculum* (1599) as "Our grosse conceipts, who think honestie the best policie." The exact wording of the modern version was recorded soon after in *Thoughts and Apothegms* (1630) by Archbishop Richard Whatley, and the saying was included in Thomas Fuller's *Gnomologia: Adagies and Proverbs* (1732). A host of American statesmen have quoted or adapted the saying in their writings, including Benjamin Franklin (1777, 1779), Alexander Hamilton (1778, 1784), Thomas Paine (1778, 1779), Thomas Jefferson (1785), George Washington (1785, 1786, 1787, 1796), John Quincy Adams (1787), James Monroe (1794), and Andrew Jackson (1827, 1833). In addition, the saying has been used by such writers as Washington Irving (1809, *Knickerbocker History of New York*), Charles Dickens (1850, *David Copperfield*), Louisa May Alcott (1868, *Little Women*), John Galsworthy (1928, *Swan Song*), and George Bernard Shaw (1932, radio address). "Honesty is the best policy" has been quoted in print frequently during the twentieth century.

Hope deferred maketh the heart sick.   The Old Testament Proverbs (c. 350 B.C.) gave us the earliest rendering of this saying as "Hope deferred maketh the heart sick." But the saying did not appear in English until medieval times when the religious reformer John Wycliffe instigated the first English translation of the Old Testament (completed c. 1388, published 1850). At that time, the proverb was rendered as "Hope that is deferrid, tormenteth the soule." Early in the sixteenth century, the playwright John Rastell noted in *Calisto and Melebea* (c. 1529), "For long hope to the hart mych troble wyll do," a sentiment echoed by Roger Edgeworth in *Sermons* (1557): "The hope that is deferred, prolonged, and put of[f], vexeth the minde." Virtually the exact wording of the modern saying was quoted the following century in the King James (English) version of the Bible (1611): "Hope deferred maketh the heart sicke." The proverb was included in collections of proverbs from the eighteenth century onward and was quoted or adapted by, among others, the English novelist Laurence Sterne (1794, *A Sentimental Journey*), the American statesman Andrew Jackson (1814, in his correspondence), the American poet Henry Wadsworth Longfellow (1828, in correspondence), and the English writer Thomas C. Haliburton, creator of Sam Slick (1843, *Wise Saws*). The proverb has been quoted in print infrequently during the twentieth century.

Hope for the best and prepare for the worst.   In *Tragedy of Gorboduc* (1561) by the poets Thomas Sackville and Thomas Norton, we find the earliest mention of this saying with the line, "Good is I graunt of all to hope the best, But not to liue still dreadlesse of the worst." Soon after, John Bridges wrote in *Sermon at St. Paul's Cross* (1571), "I haue good cause to hope the beste, where I know not the worste," and William Averell rendered the saying in *An Excellent Historie of Charles and Julia, Two Welsh Lovers* (1581) as "To hope the best, and feare the worst." In the next decade, Edmund Spenser's *The Faerie Queen* (1590) included the line, "It is best to hope the best, though of the worst affrayd." Roger L'Estrange, in his translation of *Seneca's Morals* (1678), wrote a version close the modern: "I will hope the best, and provide for the worst." Over a century later, the American statesman John Jay quoted the modern version in a letter of 1813: "To hope for the best and prepare for the worst, is a trite but a good maxim." The saying has been quoted in print only infrequently during the twentieth century.

Hope is a good breakfast but a bad supper. It is good to start out the day—or any endeavor—with hope, this proverb tells us, but one should have something of more substance to show for the effort after the day is done. The English philosopher Francis Bacon penned the saying in virtually its modern form in *Apophthegms* (1625) with "Hope is a good breakfast, but an ill supper," and the exact wording appeared a few years later in *Resuscitatio* (1661) by William Rawley. The saying was apparently quoted infrequently in subsequent centuries, though it did appear in John Ray's *A Collection of English Proverbs* (1670), and more recently in Burton Stevenson's *Home Book of Proverbs* (1948) and the *Oxford Dictionary of English Proverbs* (1970). A variant, "Hope is a good sauce but poor food," was included in *Poor Richard Jr.'s Almanack* (1906), by an unknown author.

Hour's cold can suck out seven years' warmth, An. A metaphor for the disproportionate harm that sometimes can happen in a short space of time, this saying was first recorded in James Kelly's *A Complete Collection of Scotish Proverbs* (1721) as "One hour's cold will spoil seven years' warming." A few years later, a related saying appeared in Thomas Fuller's *Gnomologia: Adagies and Proverbs* (1732), "An Hour may destroy what an Age was a building," which in today's nuclear age is closer to the literal truth than it ever was. "An hour's cold..." was quoted in its modern form in *A Collection of Proverbs...Relating to the Weather* (1846) by Michael Denham. Though included in such collections as Burton Stevenson's *The Home Book of Proverbs* (1948) and *The Oxford Dictionary of English Proverbs* (1970), the saying has been quoted in print only infrequently during the twentieth century.

House, a wife, and a fire to put her in, A. A roguish jest, this saying played on an earlier homily about marriage and a wife. In fact, both were recorded when the saying was first quoted in James Kelly's *A Complete Collection of Scotish Proverbs* (1721): "Never look for a wife, till you have a house and a fire to put her in...The jest is in *a fire to put her in;* a house to put her in, and a fire to set her by." The English satirist Jonathan Swift gave the shorter version in *Polite Conversation* (1738), as did Benjamin Franklin's *Poor Richard's Almanack* (1743) with "Ne'er take a wife till thou hast a house (and a fire) to put her in."

House divided cannot stand, A.   This saying came to us from
the New Testament Gospel According to Mark (A.D. c. 70), which
rendered it as "If a house be divided against itself, that house
cannot stand." Centuries later, a related version on divided kingdoms was included in *Fall of Princes* (c. 1439) by the English
clergyman John Lydgate: "Kyngdamys deuyded may no while
endure." In the seventeenth century, Giovanni Torriano's *A Common Place of Italian Proverbs and Proverbial Phrases* (1666) rendered
the saying as "Kingdoms divided soon fall," a variant that has
remained current to the present day. By the beginning of the
eighteenth century, the version "A house divided . . ." was also
current, and the exact wording of the modern version was quoted
(1735) in personal papers belonging to the Wyllys, a prominent
family in colonial Connecticut. The saying was later quoted by
the American statesman Gouverneur Morris in his correspondence (1793), by Abigail Adams in her correspondence (1812, "A
house divided against itself,—and upon that foundation do our
enemies build their hopes of subduing us"), by Andrew Jackson
in his correspondence (1830), and by Abraham Lincoln in a
speech (1857). *See also* **United we stand, divided we fall**.

Hunger is the best sauce.   Attributing the words to Socrates,
the Roman statesman Cicero recorded the earliest version of this
saying in *De Finibus* (c. 45 B.C.) as "The best sauce for food is
hunger, and for drink thirst." Centuries later, the Middle English
poem *Piers Plowman* (c. 1362) referred to the saying in English
for the first time with "Er hunger thee take, And sende thee of
his sauce." Soon after, the Scottish national epic *Bruce* (1375) by
the poet John Barbour included the passage "soucht [sought]
nan othir salso [sauce] thartill Bot appetyt [but appetite], that oft
men takys [overtakes men]." The clergyman Alexander Barclay's
Eclogues (c. 1530) elaborated on the sentiment with "Make hunger
thy sause be thou neuer so nice, For there shalt thou finde none
other kinde of spice." Richard Taverner's *Proverbes or Adagies*
(1539) rendered essentially the modern saying: "He sayd, the
beste sawce is hungre." The exact wording was quoted a few
years later in Richard Eden's *The Decades of the Newe Worlde* (1555).
The saying was included in subsequent collections of proverbs,
and among the noted writers who adapted the saying in subsequent centuries were William Shakespeare in *Two Noble Kinsman*
(1612), Miguel de Cervantes in *Don Quixote* (1615), Henry Fielding in *Joseph Andrews* (1742), and Benjamin Franklin in *Poor Richard's Almanack* (1750, "Hunger is the best Pickle").

Hungry man is an angry man, A.   The Greek poet Theocritus
warned in *Idyls* (c. 270 B.C.), "Never go near a hungry man," and
the Roman playwright Seneca noted still broader political im-
plications of hunger in *De Brevitate Vitae* (A.D. c. 54) with "A
hungry people listens not to reason." The earliest printed reference in English to the current saying, however, did not appear
until William Shakespeare's line in *The Two Gentlemen of Verona*
(1594): "Is it near dinner time?—I would it were, That you might
kill your stomach on your meat And not upon your maid." In
the next century, David Fergusson's *Fergusson's Scottish Proverbs*
(1641) rendered the saying as "Hungry men ar angry," and soon
after James Howell's *Proverbs in English, Italian, French and Spanish*
(1659) quoted the exact wording of the modern saying. The
English satirist Jonathan Swift (1738, *Polite Conversation*) adapted
the saying, as did James Joyce (1922, *Ulysses*). Benjamin Franklin
wrote of the larger consequences of hunger in *Poor Richard's
Almanack* (1755): "Where there is Hunger, Law is not regarded,
and where Law is not regarded, there will be Hunger."

Husband is always last to know, The.   [The wife is always
...] The Roman satirist Juvenal wrote what is perhaps the earliest
version of this saying in his *Satires* (c. 120) with "The head of the
house is the last to know of its dishonor." An English version was
recorded in *Proverbs English, French, Dutch, Italian, and Spanish*
(1659) as "The goodman is the last that knows what's amiss at
home." John Ray's *A Collection of English Proverbs* (1670) repeated
the version, as did Thomas Fuller's *Gnomologia: Adagies and Proverbs* (1732). The English novelist Laurence Sterne referred to the
saying in *Tristram Shandy* (1756), " 'It is with love as with cuck-
oldom'—the suffering party is at least the third, but generally
the last who knows anything about the matter."

The earlier version, "The good man is the last..." remained
in use through the nineteenth century, and was included in the
1907 edition of W. Carew Hazlitt's *English Proverbs and Proverbial
Phrases*. The modern version appeared in print later in the twentieth century, and essentially the current wording was quoted by
Dennis Fairfax in *Masked Ball Murder* (1934): "It's generally the
husband who's the last to know." The American novelist Margaret Mitchell recorded the wife's version in *Gone With the Wind*
(1936) as "You know the old adage; 'The wife is always the last
one to find out.' "

I

Idle brain is the devil's workshop, An.   The notion that keeping occupied also kept a person out of trouble arose at least as early as the sixteenth century, and Jonn Northbrooke apparently recorded this sentiment for the first time with "Idlenesse is Sathan's fetherbed and pillowe," meaning idleness makes the devil's work easy, in *Treatise Against Dicing* (1577). In the next century, the English clergyman William Perkins rendered the saying in *Treatise of Callings* (1602) as "The idle bodie and the idle braine is the shoppe of the deuill." Virtually the modern wording of the current proverb was quoted in John Ray's *A Collection of English Proverbs* (1678) as "An idle brain is the devil's shop," and in the next century, Benjamin Franklin expanded on the theme in *Poor Richard's Almanack* (1758) with "The idle Man is the Devil's Hireling, whose Livery is Rags, whose Diet and Wages are Famine and Diseases." The exact wording of the modern version was apparently first quoted by the Scottish author Samuel Smiles in *Self-Help* (1859): "Steady employment... keeps one out of mischief, for truly an idle brain is the devil's workshop." The proverb has not been quoted in print frequently during the twentieth century.

If a thing is worth doing, it's worth doing well.   The New Testament's I Corinthians (A.D. 57) gave us the saying, "Let all things be done decently and in order," but it was the English statesman Lord Chesterfield who rendered the modern version for the first time in a letter (1746): "Whatever is worth doing at all, is worth doing well." Alan B. Cheales repeated that version in *Proverbial Folk-Lore* (1875), Robert Louis Stevenson quoted it in *Ebb-Tide* (1893), and Charles Dickens apparently made it his favorite motto. Virtually the exact wording of the modern version appeared in H. G. Wells's *Bealby; a Holiday* (1915) as " 'If a thing's worth doing at all,' said the Professor ... 'it's worth doing well.' " A few years earlier, the English writer G. K. Chesterton turned the saying on itself for humorous effect in *What's Wrong With the World* (1910): "If a thing is worth doing, it is worth doing badly."

93

If at first you don't succeed, try, try again. The idea of trying again despite a failure was recorded in an English manuscript (by an unknown author) as early as 1639 with the line, "Nocke anew, nocke anew [try again]." The modern saying did not appear until two centuries later, however, when T. H. Palmer wrote in *Teacher's Manual* (1840), " 'Tis a lesson you should heed, Try, try again. If at first you don't succeed, Try, try again." Somewhat later, W. E. Hickson quoted the saying in *Moral Songs* (1857, "try" was repeated three times instead of two). The saying appeared frequently in print during the twentieth century, and among those who quoted or adapted it were the Canadian economist and writer Stephen Leacock in *Frenzied Fiction* (1919), the American science fiction writer Robert A. Heinlein in *6XH* (1961), and Agatha Christie in *Miss Marple's Final Cases* (c. 1979). *See also* **There is no harm in trying**.

If the cock crows on going to bed, he's sure to rise with a watery head. This curious old saw actually refers to the weather, though it easily could be mistaken for moral advice to a reveler returning from a late-night drinking bout. In fact, the proverb literally means that when the cock crows at night, it will rain, and the cock will wake with a wet head the next morning because of the rain. The notion of a cock's crowing signaling rain first appeared in Reginald Scott's *The Discourie of Witchcraft* (1584) as "When the cocke crow manie times together, a man may ghesse that raine will followe shortlie." The proverb in the modern form appeared in *Proverbs* (1846) by Michael Denham. Richard Inwards repeated the saying with slight variation later in the century in *Weather Lore* (1893): "If the cock crows when he goes to bed, / He gets up in the morning with a wet head." Quoted infrequently in the twentieth century, the saying was included in *Folklore of Maine* (1957) by H. P. Beck.

If the shoe fits, wear it. A familiar saying in twentieth-century America, it was probably adapted from an earlier and somewhat less cryptic English saying, "If the [fool's] cap fits, wear it." In either case, the saying was generally invoked after making an unflattering remark to someone, as if to clinch the insult by getting the intended to try it on and "see if it fits." The English writer John Ozell recorded the earliest version of this saying in *Moliere* (1714): "If the fool's cap fits any body, let 'em put it on," while soon after Thomas Fuller's *Gnomologia: Adagies and Proverbs* (1732) rendered it as "If any Fool finds the Cap fit him, let him wear it." Among the writers who quoted or adapted this version were Samuel Richardson in *Clarissa* (1748), Charles Dickens in *Martin Chuzzlewit* (1844), George Eliot in *Felix Holt* (1866), and Richard D. Blackmore in *Springhaven* (1887). The current "If the shoe fits..." apparently first appeared in eighteenth-century America, the earliest use being in the *New-York Gazette* newspaper (1773): "Let those whom the shoe fits wear it." Another American newspaper, the *New Jersey Gazette*, adapted the saying (1780) to read, "Wishing that every foot may wear the shoe that fits it." Though probably in use earlier, the exact wording of the saying was quoted in print in *Emerald Murder Trap* (1934) by Jackson Gregory.

If you can't lick them, join them.   [If you can't beat them...] Another of the "old" sayings apparently born in this century, this one was first recorded by the American writer Quentin Reynolds in *The Wounded Don't Cry* (1941): "There is an old political adage which says 'If you can't lick 'em, jine 'em.' " A few years later, Holger Cahill used the alternate form, "If you can't beat them...," in *Look South to the Polar Star* (1947), and since then the saying has appeared in print frequently. The English writer Doris Lessing quoted it in *Shikasta* (1979).

Ignorance is bliss.   *See* **Where ignorance is bliss, 'tis folly to be wise.**

Imitation is the sincerest form of flattery.   Certainly a comforting thought for those who are being imitated, this saying was first quoted in *Lacon* (1820) by the English writer Charles Colton. Colton gave the exact wording of the saying, which was repeated by the English writer Robert S. Surtees in *Handley Cross* (1843). Quoted in print infrequently during the twentieth century, it appeared in recent collections of proverbs, including Burton Stevenson's *Home Book of Proverbs* (1948) and *The Oxford Dictionary of English Proverbs* (1970). The saying was used by the English historian Stanley Lane-Poole (1901, *Sir H. Parkes*), T. H. White in *America at Last*), and Robert Cassilis (1979, *Arrow of God*).

Inch in a miss is as good as a mile, An.   *See* **Miss is as good as a mile, A.**

In peace prepare for war.   Though it almost seems a contradiction in terms, this bit of advice has been around since ancient times. The Roman writer Publilius Syrus first recorded the saying as "We should provide in peace what we need in war," in *Sententiae* (c. 43 B.C.). Some centuries later, the Roman writer Vegetius gave the idea a somewhat different turn in his influential treatise on military tactics *Epitoma Rei Militaris* (fourth century): "He who desires peace must prepare for war." The earliest mention of the saying in English, "He forgat the olde adage, Saynge in tyme of peace prouyde for warre," appeared in Edward Hall's *Chronicle, The Union of the Two Noble and Illustre Fameilies of Lancastre & Yorke* (1548). Similarly, Matthew Sutcliffe wrote, "He that desireth peace, he must prepare for warres," in *Practice, and Lawes of Armies* (1593).

The exact wording of the modern version was apparently quoted for the first time by the American revolutionary hero Samuel Adams in his writings (1777): "A good old Maxim, In Peace prepare for war." The saying seemed to be on the minds of other notable Americans as well—Benjamin Franklin referred to it (1766, in his papers), as did Abigail Adams (1774, in correspondence), George Washington (1780, 1781, 1782, in his writings), John Jay (1781, in correspondence), and Andrew Jackson (1837, in correspondence). Some years later, Charles Lowe reiterated the earlier version, "If you want peace, you must prepare for war," in *Prince Bismarck* (1885). The saying has been quoted in print only infrequently during the twentieth century.

In the morning drink one dram, eat one piece of garlic, and smoke one pipe of tobacco.   Proverbs generally have at least some good advice to offer, but this prescription for starting the day is just plain awful. Originally a French saying, it was first recorded in English by one Lieutenant Jabez Fitch, who claimed in his diary (1777) that he "arose very early in the Morning & paid a strict Attention to a perticular French Proverb." The idea of munching on a clove of garlic is too much for modern sensibilities, conjuring up fears of eight A.M. heartburn attacks and of the terrible comments people at the office would make after one whiff of the garlic breath. And the garlic may be the only redeeming part of the regime as far as we are concerned today—at least recent scientific studies tend to find health benefits in eating garlic, though not necessarily in the morning or in such quantity. As for the two other items on the morning menu, they probably could not be much worse from a health point of view.

Although some doctors say a shot of liquor a day may actually be good for you, first thing in the morning seems about the worst time. As for the tobacco, nary a doctor anywhere would recommend smoking these days.

In wine there is truth. The Greek poet Alcaeus recorded what were probably the earliest words on this subject with "Wine, my dear boy, and truth" (c. 600 B.C.). Echoing the sentiment that those who drink wine tend to be truthful (or perhaps just less disingenuous), Plato wrote in *Symposium* (c. 380 B.C.), "Wine, as the saying goes, is truthful." The Roman writer Pliny the Elder rendered the modern form of the saying (in Latin) in *Historia naturalis* (A.D. 77) with the line, "It has become a common proverb that in wine there is truth." Centuries later, the first version in English, "*In vino veritas. In wyne is trouthe*," was recorded in Richard Taverner's *Erasmus' Adagies* (1545). The French writer Rabelais observed in *Pantagreul* (1552), "In wine is the truth hidden," and the English writer John Lyly expanded on the theme in *Mother Bombie* (c. 1590) with "I perceiue sober men tell most lies, for *in vino veritas*. If they had drunke wine, they would haue tolde the truth." Benjamin Franklin rendered the saying in *Poor Richard's Almanack* (1755) as "When the Wine enters, out goes the Truth." The saying proved a popular one in the nineteenth century, being used in one form or another by, among others, Washington Irving (1804, in a contribution to the *Corrector*), Charles Dickens (1839, *Nicholas Nickleby*), Oliver Wendell Holmes (1850, *The Banker's Secret*), Herman Melville (1857, *The Confidence Man*) and Anthony Trollope (1869, *He Knew He Was Right*). The exact modern wording appeared for the first time in James Paulding's play *The Bucktails* (1815). The proverb has been quoted in print frequently during the twentieth century.

Into every life some rain must fall. Here in more pleasant terms is the modern equivalent of "No man shall pass his whole life free from misfortune." Written by the Greek dramatist Aeschylus in *The Libation-Bearers* (c. 458 B.C.), this version was probably the earliest of such sayings. In *Prometheus Bound* (c. 470 B.C.), Aeschylus echoed the theme with "Misfortune wanders impartially abroad and alights on all in turn," and Euripides wrote in *Hercules Furens* (c. 420 B.C.), "No mortal hath escaped misfortune's taint." Compared with these older efforts, the current proverb seems far less grim, and without question it is much more recent. Though it may well have been in use beforehand, the saying was first recorded in 1935 by Harriette Ashbrook in *Most Immoral Murder*, and was repeated soon after in Ruth Darby's *Death Conducts a Tour* (1940, "Into each life some rain is bound to fall"). Among the other writers who used the saying was P. G. Wodehouse in *Jeeves in the Offing* (1960).

It is an ill wind that blows nobody good.   An apology, of sorts, invoked by those who profit while others suffer misfortune, this saying was first recorded as "An yll wynde that blowth no man to good, men saie," in John Heywood's *A Dialogue Conteinyng the Number in Effect of All the Prouerbes in the Englishe Tongue* (1546). William Shakespeare used the saying twice: first in *Henry VI, Part III* (1591, "Ill blows the wind that profits nobody"), and later in *Henry IV, Part II* (1598, "the ill wind that blows no man to good"). The exact wording of the modern saying was recorded in the next century, in the play *Captain Underwit* (c. 1640) by an unknown author. Among the authors who subsequently repeated this version were English dramatist William Congreve (1693, *The Old Bachelor*), satirist Jonathan Swift (1738, *Polite Conversation*), Tobias Smollett (1769, *Adventures of an Atom*), James Fenimore Cooper (1823, *The Pioneers*; 1823 *The Pilot*), Charles Dickens (1837, *Pickwick Papers*); 1839, *Nicolas Nickleby*), Mark Twain (1869, *The Innocents Abroad*), and P. G. Wodehouse (1929, *Fish Preferred*).

It is better to give than to receive.   The New Testament Acts of the Apostles (A.D. c. 70) gave us the earliest version of this saying: "It is more blessed to give than to receive." The first version in English was recorded by the English poet John Gower in *Confessio Amantis* (c. 1390) as "Betre is to yive than to take," and in the next century, Henry Parker wrote, "It is . . . more blysseful to giue than to take," in *Diues et Pauper* (1493). That version was included in John Heywood's *A Dialogue Conteinyng the Number in Effect of All the Prouerbes in the Englishe Tongue* (1546) and was repeated in the next century as well, notably by John Davies, who rendered the contrary thought: "It's better giue then take: Not so; For better giue then take a blow," in *Vpon the English Prouerbes* (1611). Some years earlier in about 1590, essentially the modern wording was recorded in *Timon V* (by an unknown author) as "Plato in his Acrostikes saith it is better to giue than to receaue." This version was repeated by the American clergyman Cotton Mather in *Magnalia Christi Americana* (1702). Later that century, Benjamin Franklin devised the witty adaptation, "What's given shines, what's receiv'd is rusty," for his *Poor Richard's Almanack* (1735).

It is the thought that counts. How many loud ties, useless kitchen items, and other such underappreciated gifts have been rescued by this oft-repeated saying? In fact, only those that have been given since the 1930s, though it is hard to imagine that there was not some other homily for poorly chosen gifts presented before then. What was probably the first recorded rendering of "It is the thought that counts" appeared in *Weather in the Streets* (1936) by Rosamond Lehmann. Though the saying is in common use today, it apparently has not been quoted in print frequently since its appearance in the 1930s.

It never rains but it pours. This old adage tells us that just as raindrops fall one after another, troubles (or other things) likewise often follow one another. Queen Anne's physician, John Arbuthnot, recorded the earliest version of the saying, "It Cannot Rain but it pours," using it for the title of a book he wrote in 1726. His friend, the satirist Jonathan Swift, repeated this version (1726) in the title of a paper written with Alexander Pope.

The exact wording of the modern saying first appeared in a letter written (1771) by the English poet Thomas Gray. In the next century, the English reformer and writer Reverend Charles Kingsley observed in *Yeast* (1851), " 'It never rains but it pours,' and one cannot fall in with a new fact or a new acquaintance but next day twenty fresh things shall spring up as if by magic." Later, Ogden Nash wrote a clever barb in *I'll Take a Bromide, Please* (1940) with "Wilde and his epigrams are shown up as brilliant bores / Before the unpretentious penetration of the comment that It never rains but it pours." Over the centuries, the saying was repeated in one form or another by, among others, Benjamin Franklin (1755, in his writings), James Fenimore Cooper (1845, *Satanstoe*), novelist Robert Surtees (1853, *Mr. Sponge's Sporting Tour*), writer J. B. Priestley (1930, *Angel Pavement*), T. H. White (1939, *The Sword in the Stone*), Michael Innes (1946, *Unsuspected Chasm*), and American writer John Cheever (1957, *The Wapshot Chronicle*).

It takes a thief to catch a thief. [Set a thief to catch a thief.] A bit of seemingly self-contradictory worldly wisdom, this maxim echoes a theory put forward by the Roman statesman Cato the Younger in the first century B.C.: "The authors of great evils know best how to remove them." The earliest version of the current saying was not nearly so grave, however, being simply "As they say, set a fool to catch a fool," a line rendered by Edmund Gayton in *Festivious Notes Upon Don Quixote* (1654). The early form of the saying, "Set a thief to catch a thief," appeared soon afterward in Robert Howard's *Four New Plays* (1665). This version was included in subsequent collections of proverbs, such as John Ray's *A Collection of English Proverbs* (1670), and was adapted by, among others, James Boswell in *The Life of Samuel Johnson, LL.D.* (1791), Washington Irving in *Tales of a Traveller* (1824, "Set a rogue..."), Herman Melville in *White Jacket* (1850, "Set a rogue ..."), and P. G. Wodehouse in *Little Nugget* (1914). The current wording of "It takes a thief..." apparently did not appear in print until the 1930s, when James H. Wallis quoted it in *Capital City Mystery* (1932).

It takes all kinds to make a world.   [... to make the world go 'round.] Often invoked when speaking of those considered odd, this adage first appeared in Thomas Shelton's English translation of *Don Quixote* (1620) as "In the world, there must bee all sorts." Quoting the English philosopher John Locke, Samuel Johnson wrote in a letter (1767), "Some lady surely might be found ... in whose fidelity you might repose. The World, says Locke, has people of all sorts." Virtually the modern version, "It takes all sorts to make a world," appeared in *The Story of a Feather* (1844) by the English writer Douglas Jerrold. However, the exact wording did not appear in print for almost another century, in Leslie Ford's *Old Lover's Ghost* (1940). Among the writers who used the modern saying in one form or another were George Bernard Shaw (1891, *Misalliance*; 1897, *The Devil's Disciple*; 1903, *Man and Superman*); Saki (H. H. Munro; 1924, *The Square Egg*); Eugene O'Neill (1926, *The Great God Brown*); Edgar Wallace (1930, *The Silver Key*), Agatha Christie (1941, *The Moving Finger*), Michael Innes (1943, *The Weight of Evidence*), and Kurt Vonnegut (1963, *Cat's Cradle*). The saying has been quoted in print frequently during the twentieth century.

It takes three generations to make a gentleman.   An English translation of a work entitled *The Courtier's Academy* (1598) made the first reference to this saying with "He may bee called absolutely noble, who shall have lost the memory of his ignobilitie ... during the reuolution of three generations." Some years later, the English writer Gervase Markham wrote, "Three perfit descents, do euer so conclude a perfit Gentleman of Blood," in *Five Decades of Honour* (1625). The exact wording of the modern saying was first recorded in *The Pioneers* (1823) by the American writer James Fenimore Cooper and was repeated some years later by the British prime minister Sir Robert Peel (c. 1841). Though quoted in print infrequently during the twentieth century, the saying was nevertheless adapted by W. Somerset Maugham in *Of Human Bondage* (1915) and by Michael Innes in *Comedy of Terrors* (1940).

It takes two to make a quarrel.   John Stevens's *A New Spanish and English Dictionary* (1706) recorded this saying for the first time as "When one will not, two do not Quarrel. Soon after, Thomas Fuller's *Gnomologia: Adagies and Proverbs* (1732) rendered the saying as "There must be two at least to a Quarrel," while the English reformer and founder of Methodism, John Wesley, repeated it in a letter (1765), "Two must go to a quarrel, and I declare I will not be one." The exact wording of the modern saying appeared in *Geoffrey Hamlyn* (1859) by Henry Kingsley, and was later adapted by, among others, the American playwright George S. Kaufman (1931, *Of Thee I Sing*) and the detective story writer Erle Stanley Gardner (1941, *The Case of the Empty Tin*). Earlier in this century, A. MacLaren turned the saying on itself in *Exposition Romans* (1912) to make a new and equally insightful observation, "It takes two to make peace also."

It's a great life if you don't weaken.   Although this saying appears to have originated during the twentieth century, the sentiment it expresses has a long history. The Greek dramatist Euripides wrote in *The Suppliant Women* (c. 421 B.C.), "Life is a struggle," and the Old Testament Book of Job (c. 350 B.C.) gave us the observation, "The life of man on earth is a warfare." The Roman poet Lucretius rendered perhaps the most dire assessment in *De Rerum Natura* (c. 45 B.C.) with "Life is one long struggle in the dark." The philosopher King Marcus Aurelius was more matter-of-fact in *Meditations* (c. 174) with "Life is a battle," a sentiment repeated centuries later in *Mahomet* (1741) by the French author Voltaire.

More recently, Frank W. O'Malley wrote in *Epigram* (c. 1906), "Life is just one damned thing after another," and some years later, a Chinese proverb, "Cease to struggle and you cease to live," was translated into English by S. G. Champion in *Racial Proverbs* (1938). The current saying apparently was quoted in print for the first time by Valentine Williams in *Crouching Beast, a Clubfoot Story* (1928) as "How do the smart Yankees put it? 'It's a good life if you don't weaken.' " A year later, Arlo C. Edington quoted the exact wording in *Studio Murder Mystery*. In *Big Money* (1936), the American author John Dos Passos adapted the saying to read: "New York's a great life if you don't weaken."

It's a poor heart that never rejoices.   The English writer of novels of the sea, Captain Frederick Marryat, quoted this saying for the first time in *Peter Simple* (1834) with the line, " 'Well,' continued he, 'it's a poor heart that never rejoiceth.' He then poured out half a tumbler of rum." Charles Dickens repeated the saying in *Barnaby Rudge* (1841), and again in *Martin Chuzzlewit* (1844). Saki (H. H. Munro) used the saying in *When William Come* (1914) and British Prime Minister Winston Churchill repeated it during a speech in 1943, but otherwise the saying has not been quoted frequently during the twentieth century.

It's no use crying over spilled milk.   [It's no good...] The underlying message of this popular saying can be traced back at least to 1484, when the book *Aesope* was published by William Caxton, the first English printer—"thow take no sorowe of the thynge lost whiche may not be recouered." A seventeenth-century version with wording much closer to the modern saying was recorded as "No weeping for shed milk" in James Howell's *English Proverbs* (1659) and appeared again a few years later in John Ray's *A Collection of English Proverbs* (1670). In *England's Improvement* (1681) by Andrew Yarranton, the saying is repeated as "Sir, there is no crying for shed milk, that which is past cannot be recall'd," and in the next century Jonathan Swift's *Polite Conversation* (1738) rendered it as " 'Tis folly to cry for spilt milk." In 1782, the American statesman John Jay quoted the saying in his correspondence as "It is not worth while to cry about spilt milk." Mark Twain alluded to the saying in *A Connecticut Yankee in King Arthur's Court* (1859), as did Theodore Roosevelt in *The Great Adventure* (1918). British novelist W. Somerset Maugham in *Of Human Bondage* (1915) and H. G. Wells in *You Can't Be Too Careful* (1942) both quoted the saying as "It's no good crying over spilt milk." In the 1920s, the alternate "It's no use crying..." became current, and since then both "no good" and "no use" have been quoted.

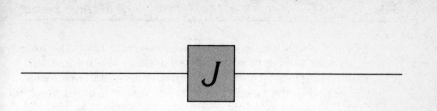

Justice is blind.   The ideal of impartiality harks back to the beginnings of civilization; a stone stele from about 2200 B.C. bore the inscription, "I am a man of justice, like the scales impartial." John Dryden rendered the considerably more modern maxim for the first time as "Justice is blind, he knows nobody," in the play *The Wild Gallant* (1663). A few years later, Samuel Butler gave the more familiar personification of justice as a woman in *Hudibras* (1678), saying, "For Justice, though she's painted blind / Is to the weaker side inclined." William Penn, a Quaker and founder of Pennsylvania, also wrote of a blind justice in *Some Fruits of Solitude* (1693): "Justice is justly represented as Blind, because she sees no Difference in the Parties concerned." While both the ideal and image of blind justice are widely known in modern times, the saying "Justice is blind" apparently has not been quoted in print frequently during the twentieth century.

King never dies, The.   *See* **Landlord never dies, The.**

King's chaff is better than other men's corn, A.   [. . . than other folk's corn; . . . is worth other men's corn.] This saying probably was known in sixteenth-century Spain, and one of the early English references to it came from Thomas Shelton's translation (1620) of *Don Quixote*, which rendered the saying as "A king's crumb is worth more than a lord's loaf." Not long after, however, *The James Carmichaell Collection of Proverbs in Scots* (c. 1628) gave it as "Kings' chaff is worth other men's corn," a version that was repeated in David Fergusson's *Scottish Proverbs* (1641) and James

Kelly's *A Complete Collection of Scotish Proverbs* (1721). The great Scottish poet Robert Burns recorded another variant in a letter of 1788: "King's caff [chaff] is better than ither folks' corn," which was repeated in the next century by Sir Walter Scott in *Rob Roy* (1818). The exact wording of the current version appeared in the *London Times* (1957), one of the few times the saying was quoted in print during the twentieth century.

Know thyself.   Attributed to Thales of Miletus (c. 600 B.C.), one of the Seven Wise Men of ancient Greece, this maxim was held in such high esteem that it was inscribed in gold on the temple of Apollo at Delphi. Plato later wrote in *Charmides* (c. 380 B.C.), "The purpose of that inscription on the temple, as it seems to me, is to serve as the god's salutation to those who enter it, instead of 'Hail!' " Similarly, the biographer Plutarch said in *To Apollonius* (A.D. c. 95), "Two of the inscriptions at Delphi are indispensable to living: 'Know thyself' and 'Avoid extremes,' for on these two hang all the rest." The earliest mention of the maxim in English appeared as "Knowe thyself," in a translation of *Higden's Polychronicon* (1387) by the translator John de Trevisa.

Almost a century later, the saying was repeated in a translation of *Reynard the Fox* (1481), published by the first English printer, William Caxton: "Late euery man knowe hym self, that is my counseyl." Roger Ascham, at one time Queen Elizabeth's tutor, explained in *Toxophilus* (1545), "That wise prouerbe of Apollo, *Know thy selfe*: that is to saye, learn to know what thou art able, fitte, and apt vnto, and folowe that." The maxim was included in Richard Taverner's *Proverbes or Adagies* (1539) and many subsequent collections, and was adapted by William Shakespeare for lines in a number of plays, including *The Merchant of Venice* (1596), *As You Like It* (1599), *Hamlet* (1600), *All's Well That Ends Well* (1602), *King Lear* (1605), *Anthony and Cleopatra* (1606), *Cymbeline* (1609), and *Henry VIII* (1612). Among the other noted writers who quoted or adapted the maxim were Rabelais in *Pantagruel* (1545), Michel de Montaigne in *Essays* (1580), Alexander Pope in *Essay on Man* (1732), Lord Edward Bulwer-Lytton in *The Caxtons* (1849, " 'Know thyself,' saith the old philosophy. 'Improve thyself,' saith the new"), and D. H. Lawrence in *Last Poems* (c. 1930).

Knowledge is power.   The Old Testament Proverbs (c. 250 B.C.) gave us an early version of the current saying with the line, "A wise man is strong; yea, a man of knowledge increaseth strength."

The first versions outside the Bible were rendered by the philosopher Francis Bacon, first in *Novum Organum* (1620) as "Knowledge and human power are synonymous," and then soon after in *De Heresibus* (c. 1626), "Knowledge itself is power."

Almost two centuries later, Lord Byron penned the exact wording of the maxim in a letter (1822): "They say that 'Knowledge is power.' I used to think so." The Scottish biographer Samuel Smiles added a note of caution in *Self Help* (1859): " 'Knowledge is power,' but . . . knowledge of itself, unless wisely directed, might merely make bad men more dangerous." As to the uses of the power, A. J. Spender observed in *Comments of Bagshot* (1925), "Women understand men . . . better than any man understands women. Since knowledge is power, woman has a control over man which man never had over her." The maxim "Knowledge is power" was also quoted by, among others, Lord Edward Bulwer-Lytton in *My Novel* (1853), George Bernard Shaw in *Mrs. Warren's Profession* (1893), Agatha Christie in *Death in the Air* (1935), and the detective story writer Erle Stanley Gardner in *Blonde Bonanza* (1962).

Landlord never dies, The. [The king never dies.] This maxim rings true enough to those of us who month-in, month-out hand over the rent (or the mortgage payment, for that matter) for a place to live. But if the landlord seems oppressive today, imagine how royal authority must have weighed on the populace in centuries past. It was in those less fortunate times that the earlier version of the current saying first appeared, in a letter written (1760) by the English historian Horace Walpole: "I had already begun to think that the lawyers for once talked sense, when they said the *King never dies*." A few years later, the jurist William Blackstone repeated the maxim in *Commentaries on the Laws of England* (1769): "Rex numquam moritur. The king never dies." *Legal Maxims* (1911) by H. Broom offered further explanation of the notion with "the king never dies . . . The sovereign always exists; the person only is changed." That was also true of landlords, however, who in many cases were not even known to their tenants. Thus the word "landlord" was at some point substituted in the older maxim, and the new version was apparently quoted for the first time in James Joyce's *Ulysses* (1922). The saying has not appeared in print frequently during the twentieth century.

Laugh and the whole world laughs with you; weep and you weep alone.　　The Roman poet Horace wrote the original version of this saying in *Ars Poetica* (c. 13 B.C.) as "Men's faces laugh on those who laugh, and correspondingly weep on those who weep." The New Testament Letter of Paul to the Romans (A.D. c. 57) voiced a similar sentiment with the passage, "Rejoice with them that do rejoice, and weep with them that weep." Chaucer gave the first English rendering in *Tale of Melibee* (c. 1387), paraphrasing the Biblical version with "Man shal rejoyse with hem that maken joye, wepen with swich folk as wepen." The current version did not appear until the nineteenth century, when it was devised by Ella Wheeler Wilcox, an American poet who for years wrote a daily poem published by a syndicate of newspapers. "Laugh and the whole world laughs ... " was included in Wilcox's poem *Solitude,* first printed in the *New York Sun* on February 23, 1883. Though a familiar saying to many today, it has not been quoted in print frequently during the twentieth century. Adaptations of the saying appeared in works by O. Henry (1907, *Trimmed Lamp*) and Saki (H. H. Munro; 1912, *Chronicle of Clovis*).

Laugh before breakfast, you'll cry before supper.　　A curious old saying probably based on some long-forgotten superstition, it was first recorded by John Palsgrave in *L'eclairissement de la langue francoyse* (1530) as "You waxe mery this morning, God gyue grace you wepe nat or nyght." The English lexicographer Randle Cotgrave rendered it in *A Dictionary of the French and English Tongues* (1611) as "Some laugh amornings who ere night shed teares," a version repeated in somewhat the same form in James Kelly's *A Complete Collection of Scotish Proverbs* (1721) with "They that laugh in the Morning may greet [weep] e'er Night." The exact wording of the current version was quoted in Vincent Lean's *Collectanea* (1902), but the saying has not been repeated in print frequently during the twentieth century.

Law has long arms, The.　　[The king has long arms.] The notion that authority can make itself felt over great distances has appeared in sayings from ancient times. The Roman poet Ovid recorded the earliest of them, "Know you not that kings have far-reaching hands?" which appeared in *Heroides* (c. 10 B.C.). Centuries later, Richard Taverner repeated that version in *Proverbes or Adagies* (1539) as "Kynges haue longe handes. They can brynge in men, they can pluck in thinges, though they be a great weye of[f]." The English writer John Lyly advised, "Kinges haue long armes and rulers large reches," in *Euphues, the Anatomy of Wit* (1579), and William Shakespeare wrote, "Great men have reaching hands," in *Henry VI, Part II* (1590). Benjamin Franklin's *Poor Richard's Almanack* (1742) gave the version, "Kings have long arms," and in the next century, Sir Walter Scott repeated the earlier "Kings have long hands," in *Peveril of the Peak* (1823). The modern "The law has long arms" apparently was first recorded by the American novelist Mary Roberts Rinehart in *The Circular Staircase* (1908).

Laws are silent amid arms.   Maxims regarding the breakdown of the rule of law during war and unrest can be traced back to ancient times. One such saying, probably already widely known, was repeated by the Roman general Gaius Marius to defend his actions during a war (101 B.C.): "The law speaks too softly to be heard amid the din of arms." Some years later, the Roman statesman Cicero repeated essentially the current saying (in Latin) in *Pro Milone* (52 B.C.) with "Laws are silent in the midst of arms." The exact wording of the saying in English did not appear until the seventeenth century, in *The Christian in Compleat Armour* (c. 1665) by William Gurnall. James Kelly's *A Complete Collection of Scotish Proverbs* (1721) rendered a somewhat more poetic version, "When drums beat laws are silent." The Latin version of "Laws are silent . . . " was quoted by the American patriot Samuel Adams in his writings (1774) and by Thomas Jefferson in his correspondence (1808). The saying has not been quoted in print frequently during the twentieth century.

Leave well enough alone.   That the urge to tamper with things often leads to more harm than good was probably known long before the Roman playwright Terence wrote in *Phormio* (161 B.C.), "Let well alone, as the saying is." A crude English version of the maxim appeared in Chaucer's *Envoy to Bukton* (c. 1386) as "Unwys [unwise] is he that kan no[t] wele [enough] endure." Later, Shakespeare warned in *King Lear* (1605), "Striving to better, oft we mar what's well," and in the next century, Thomas Fuller's *Gnomologia: Adagies and Proverbs* (1732) gave another variant: "He that is well shelter'd, is a Fool if he stir out into the

Rain." A few years later, George Cheyne rendered a variant close to the modern in *On Regimen* (1740): "I think it is his Duty ... to let Well alone." Essentially the modern version was given in Reverend Joseph B. Felt's *Annals of Salem* (1827, "Let well enough alone"), though the earlier "Let well alone" continued to be used into the twentieth century. The maxim has been quoted in print frequently during this century. *See also* **Let sleeping dogs lie.**

Lend your money and lose your friend.   Anyone who has ever lent money knows the hard feelings that can come of it, especially when friends are involved. A friend who has borrowed money owes not only the money, but also a measure of gratitude, and as often as not, that double indebtedness breeds feelings of resentment. The lender, too, is in a difficult position if the money is not repaid: Does the friend still need cash, or has the friend forgotten all about repaying it? There is no good time to ask for repayment, but if the friend is not forthcoming and the money is needed, you have no choice. The French writer Gabriel Maurier recorded an early version of the current proverb in *Tresor des Sentences* (c. 1550) as "Whoever gold or silver lends, / In losing two good things ends: / Both his money and his friends." William Shakespeare echoed the sentiment some years later in *Hamlet* (1600): "Neither a borrower nor a lender be: For loan oft loses both itself and friend, / And borrowing dulls the edge of husbandry." John Ray's *A Collection of English Proverbs* (1670) rendered the saying as "He that doth lend will lose his friend."

The exact wording of the current version was quoted not long afterward in James Kelly's *A Complete Collection of Scotish Proverbs* (1721). Kelly gave the added note, "It is not the lending of our money that loses our friend, but the demanding of it again." Benjamin Franklin gave the saying a somewhat different turn in *Poor Richard's Almanack* (1740) with "Lend money to an enemy, and thou 'lt gain him; to a friend and thou 'lt lose him." But perhaps the best advice of all for the troubling circumstance of lending to a friend appeared in Thomas Fuller's *Gnomologia: Adagies and Proverbs* (1732): "Better give a Shilling than lend and lose half a Crown." "Lend your money and lose your friend" has been quoted in print only rarely in the twentieth century.

Leopard does not change his spots, A.   The Old Testament Book of Jeremiah gave the earliest rendering of this saying as "Can the Ethiopian change his skin, or the leopard his spots?" The proverb was mentioned in English for the first time by

Bishop John Bale in *First Examination of Anne Askewe* (1546) as "Their old conditions will change when the blackamorian change his skin, and the cat a mountain [leopard] her spots." Soon after, William Shakespeare wrote, "Lions make leopards tame.—Yea, but not change his spots," in *Richard II* (1596). Giovanni Torriano's *A Common Place of Italian Proverbs and Proverbial Phrases* (1666) gave the saying as "To be like a Leopard, viz. which changeth not her spots," while Alfred Henderson gave the exact modern wording in *Latin Proverbs* (1869). The proverb has been quoted in print frequently during the twentieth century.

Less said the better, The. What do you say when you don't want to pass along stories about the past mistakes of a friend or acquaintance? Most of us will try to avoid talking about such past transgressions, and one way to deflect further questions is to invoke the current saying. "The less said the better" was apparently first rendered in the nineteenth century by Jane Austen (1811, *Sense and Sensibility*) and was repeated soon after by the English novelist Captain Frederick Marryat in *Peter Simple* (1834, "The less we say about that the better"). Charlotte Brontë also adapted the expression with the line, "Perhaps the less said on that score the better," in *Jane Eyre* (1847). The saying has not been quoted in print frequently during the twentieth century.

Let sleeping dogs lie. The idea of "let well enough alone" (don't stir up trouble unnecessarily) has been incorporated into sayings since ancient times. For example, the Greek poet Sappho advised, "Stir not the jetsam" (c. 610 B.C.), referring to the refuse found along the seashore and the distinct possibility of finding something dead and rank-smelling in it. Sophocles in *Oedipus the King* (c. 409 B.C.) gave us, " 'Twere better to leave sleeping ills at rest," and centuries later Philippus of Thessalonica gave the equally good advice in *Epigram* (c. 100), "Never rouse a sleeping wasp." A thirteenth-century French proverb noted, "He does wrong to wake a sleeping dog," and in the next century, Chaucer wrote, "It is nought good a sleping hound to wake," in *Troilus and Criseyde* (c. 1380). John Heywood's *A Dialogue Conteinyng the Number in Effect of All the Prouerbes in the Englishe Tongue* (1546) rendered the saying as "It is euyll [evil] wakyng of a sleepyng dog," and later William Shakespeare wrote, "Wake not a sleeping wolf" in *Henry IV, Part II* (1598). In *Whiggs Supplication* (1681), Samuel Colville observed, "It's best to let a sleeping mastiff rest," and over a century afterward, Sir Walter Scott wrote in *Redgauntlet*

(1824), "Take my advice, and speer as little about him as he does about you. Best to let sleeping dogs lie."

The saying in the modern form appeared in Charles Dickens's *David Copperfield* (c. 1850) in the line, "Let sleeping dogs lie— who wants to rouse 'em?" Subsequently adapted by Richard D. Blackmore (1882, *Christowell*) and D. H. Lawrence (1928, *Lady Chatterley's Lover*), among others, the saying has been quoted in print frequently during the twentieth century. *See also* **Leave well enough alone.**

Life is half spent before we know what it is.   Ask any teenager the question, "What is life?" and you will be reminded of life's baffling complexity. No one answer will do, and as the current proverb tells us, we have no choice but to experience half our lifetime (or better) to find out what life is really all about. The saying itself was first recorded by George Herbert in *Jacula Prudentum* (1640), in the current form. It appeared in such later collections as John Ray's *A Collection of English Proverbs* (1670) and Thomas Fuller's *Gnomologia: Adagies and Proverbs* (1732), but the saying has been quoted in print only very infrequently during the twentieth century.

Life is just a bowl of cherries.   Over the centuries, writers have penned a multitude of declarations about what life is. Some were depressingly bleak, as "Life is one long struggle in the dark" (Lucretius in *De Rerum Natura*, c. 45 B.C.) and "Life is a pill which none of us can bear to swallow without gilding" (attributed to Samuel Johnson). Others bordered on the ridiculous, as "What is life but a series of inspired follies?" (George Bernard Shaw in *Pygmalion*, 1912) or "Life is like a scrambled egg" (Don Marquis in *Frustration*, 1916). But from the earliest times there has also been a persistent theme that life is somehow sweet. The Greek playwright Euripides wrote in *Alcestis* (c. 438 B.C.), "I tell myself that we are long time underground, / And that life is short, but sweet." The first of such sayings in English, "The lyf is aye swete," appeared in a manuscript entitled *Patience* (c. 1350), and soon after John Gower wrote in *Confessio Amantis* (c. 1390), "The life is swete." The sixteenth-century romance writer George Pettie wrote, "Life is sweet to every one" in *A Petite Palace of Pettie His Pleasure* (1576), and the nineteenth-century writer George Borrow found sweetness everywhere in *Loavengro: The Scholar, the Gypsy, the Priest* (1851): "Life is sweet, brother . . . There's night and day, brother, both sweet things; sun, moon, and stars, brother, all sweet things; . . . Life is very sweet, brother; who would wish to die?" And what could be sweeter than a bowl of cherries? While no doubt in use for some time before, the saying was quoted in its current form in *Dark Lady* (1933), by Gavin Holt. It has become a commonly used saying in this century.

Life is not a bed of roses.   Though this saying apparently originated in the nineteenth century, the use of "bed of roses" as a metaphor for luxurious or otherwise desirable circumstances first appeared in the seventeenth century. The English poet Francis Quarles first used it in *Emblems* (1635): "And he repents in thorns, that sleeps in beds of roses." In the next century, the metaphorical "bed of roses" was mentioned by the American statesman John Jay (1786, in correspondence) with the line, "Though patriots seldom rest on beds of roses." Charles Dickens rendered the earliest version of the current saying in *Oliver Twist* (1838): "A parochial life is not a bed of roses." Though probably in use well before then, the more generalized saying was quoted in 1928 as "Her life is not . . . a bed of roses," in *Fatal Kiss Mystery* by Rufus King. *See also* **Life is just a bowl of cherries.**

Life without a friend is death without a witness.   This old proverb seems every bit as morose as life really can be when you miss the company of friends. The Jewish poet and philosopher Ibn Gabirol recorded a similar, if less dire, saying in *Choice of Pearls* (c. 1050): "A friendless man is like a left hand without a right hand." The current saying, however, came from a Spanish proverb, which was first translated into English (using the modern wording) by George Herbert in *Jacula Prudentum* (1640). John Ray's *A Collection of English Proverbs* (1670) rendered a slightly different version: "Life without a friend is death with a witness," as did Thomas Fuller in *Gnomologia: Adagies and Proverbs* (1732): "Life without a Friend, is Death with a Vengeance." The proverb has been little used since the eighteenth century.

Lightning never strikes twice in the same place.   Now a familiar (and patently untrue) superstition, this saying was apparently first recorded in print by Hamilton Myers in *Thrilling Adventures of the Prisoner of the Border* (1857). Repeated frequently during the twentieth century, it was adapted by, among others, the American novelist Mary Roberts Rinehart (1909, *Man in Lower Ten*) and the English writer P. G. Wodehouse (1914, *Little Nugget*). For those who think there might be a little truth to the saying, one Virginia park ranger provided unquestionable proof that lightning does in fact strike twice—and more. The "same place" was Shenandoah Park ranger Roy C. Sullivan, who was struck by lightning an incredible seven different times between 1942 and 1977. He lived to tell about every one of the seven (a world's record), and his scorched park ranger hats were put on exhibition.

Like attracts like.   [Like will to like.] The Greek poet Homer wrote in the *Odyssey* (c. 850 B.C.), "As ever, the god is bringing like and like together." This notion of likes coming together was repeated often during ancient times, as in Plato's "Like and like together strike" (c. 380 B.C., *Symposium*), Aristotle's "Like is dear to like" (c. 335 B.C., *Nicomachean Ethics*), and Jesus Ben Sirach's "All flesh consorteth according to kind" (c. 190 B.C., *Book of Wisdom*). Centuries later, a manuscript titled *Scottish Legends of the Saints* (c. 1375) gave an early version of the saying as "Lyk to lyk accordis wele [well]," and Sir Thomas Malory's *Le Morte d'Arthur* (c. 1480) rendered it, "Lyke will drawe to lyke." John Heywood shortened that to "Like will to like" in his *A Dialogue Conteinyng the Number in Effect of All the Prouerbes in the Englishe Tongue* (1546). This became the common form of the saying until the twentieth century and was repeated by the English poet John Lyly in *Euphues, the Anatomy of Wit* (1579) and by Sir Walter Scott in *Peveril of the Peak* (1822). The current wording, "Like attracts like," was apparently first quoted in A. E. Apple's *Mr. Chang's Crime Ray* (1928). The saying has been quoted in print only infrequently during the twentieth century.

Like cures like.   The remnant of an apparently ineffectual but once-popular medical theory, this maxim was devised by C. F. Samuel Hahnemann, a German physician who founded the short-lived homoeophathic school of medicine in 1796. Hahnemann formulated homoeopathy after noticing that quinine, when given to a healthy person, produced symptoms like those of malaria, which the drug helped to cure. Hahnemann claimed he based his motto "Like cures like" on a similar observation recorded by Hippocrates and began cataloging effects of drugs on healthy individuals. But Hahnemann's new technique called for administering drugs in very small doses, an approach that threatened the livelihood of local apothecaries and resulted in their driving him out of Leipzig in 1821. The apothecaries' ire notwithstanding, homoepathy enjoyed widespread popularity for a time in the nineteenth century, until modern medical techniques superseded it. The motto "Like cures like" continues to appear in collections of proverbs but has not been quoted frequently outside them during the twentieth century.

Like father, like son.   The many variants of this maxim include an English saying, "As the old cock crows, so the young one chirrups," and one from Persia, "The son of a tyrant will be a tyrant, as the broken sword becomes a dagger." Perhaps the earliest version, however, was the more generalized, "From good parents comes a good son," recorded by Aristotle in *Politics* (c. 330 B.C.). Centuries later, the Middle English poem *Piers Plowman* (c. 1362) rendered a version that read, "Such as the father is, such is the son; a good tree brings forth good fruit." About the same time, Chaucer wrote, "As doth the fox Renard, [so doth] the foxes sone," in *The Legend of Good Women* (c. 1386). The clergyman Alexander Barclay gave the saying in *The Shyp of Folys* (1509) as "An olde prouerbe hath longe agone be sayde That oft the sone in maner lyke wyll be Vnto the Father," and the English historian William Camden rendered it as "Such a Father, such a Son," in *Remaines Concerning Britaine* (1614).

The exact wording of the modern version first appeared in Thomas Draxe's *Bibliotheca Scholastica Instructissima, or A Treasurie of Ancient Adages* (1616). The saying was later repeated by, among others, the English novelist George Meredith (1860, *Evan Harrington*), the American writer Henry Miller (1939, *Tropic of Capricorn*), and the detective story writer Ellery Queen (1968, *The House of Brass*).

Little leak will sink a great ship, A.   Here is a proverb that is the reverse side to "*Little strokes fell great oaks.*" While "Little strokes..." speaks of the great achievements coming from doing things a little bit at a time, "A little leak..." reminds us that leaving little things unattended may lead to great disasters. The earliest mention of the saying was recorded in Thomas Adams's *Three Divine Sisters* (1616): "It is a little leake that drowneth a shippe," and soon afterward Thomas Fuller rendered a somewhat different thought, "Many little leaks may sink a ship," in *The Holy State and the Profane State* (1642). Almost a century later, a different Thomas Fuller gave us "A small leak will sink a great ship," in *Gnomologia: Adagies and Proverbs* (1732). Benjamin Franklin repeated that version in *Poor Richard's Almanack* (1745) and *The Way to Wealth* (1758) with the advice, "Beware of little

Expences: a small leak will sink a great ship." The exact wording of the modern saying appeared in W. Carew Hazlitt's *English Proverbs and Proverbial Phrases* (1907), but the saying has appeared in print only infrequently during the twentieth century. *See also* **Little strokes fell great oaks**.

Little learning is a dangerous thing, A.   The English poet Alexander Pope rendered this saying in the current form in a line from *An Essay on Criticism* (1709). The dramatist George Colman, Jr., expanded on that thought in *Random Recollections* (1830) with " 'A little learning is a dangerous thing';—and a great deal cannot be hammer'd into the heads of vulgar men." But the English novelist Thomas Huxley, grandfather of Aldous Huxley, posed the more difficult question of just how much learning is enough. In *Science and Culture* (1881), he wrote: "If a little knowledge is dangerous, where is the man who has so much as to be out of danger?" Though the saying has not been quoted in print frequently during the twentieth century, a variant of it did appear in Agatha Christie's *Easy to Kill* (1939, "A little science might be . . . ").

Little pot is soon hot, A.   This amusing rhyme was first recorded as "Little potte soone whot," in John Heywood's *A Dialogue Conteinyng the Nomber in Effect of All the Prouerbes in the Englishe Tongue* (1546). Some years later, Shakespeare adapted it for a passage in *The Taming of the Shrew* (1594), which read: "Now were not I a little pot and soon hot, my very lips might freeze to my teeth." The modern wording appeared years later in the lines, "A little pot's soon hot. Little persons are commonly choleric," from John Ray's *A Collection of English Proverbs* (1670). The saying was repeated in Washington Irving's *Knickerbocker's History of New York* (1809) and adapted by Henry Wadsworth Longfellow in *The Courtship of Miles Standish* (1858, "He was a little chimney heated hot in a moment"). Apparently the saying has not been quoted in print outside collections of proverbs during the twentieth century.

Little strokes fell great oaks.   Seemingly impossible tasks can be accomplished by persistently chipping away at them, according to this saying. In its earliest form, the proverb appeared in Richard Taverner's *Proverbes or Adagies* (1539) as "Wyth many strokes is an oke ouerthrowen," followed by the additional explanation, "Nothyng is so stronge but by lyttell and lyttell maye be brought downe. Wherefore yonge men ought not to be discouraged by the greatnesse of an enterpryse." William Shakespeare wrote in *Henry VI, Part III* (1591), "Many strokes, though with little axe, / Hew down, and fell the hardest-timber'd oak," and the dramatist Thomas Kyd noted in *The Spanish Tragedy* (1592), "In time small wedges cleave the hardest oak." John Ray's *A Collection of English Proverbs* (1670) rendered nearly the modern saying: "Many strokes fell great oaks. Assiduity overcometh all difficulty." The exact wording apparently first appeared in Benjamin Franklin's *Poor Richard's Almanack* (1750), and was repeated in Franklin's *The Way to Wealth* (1758). The saying has not been quoted in print frequently during the twentieth century.

Live and learn.   The Roman playwright Seneca wrote in *Ad Lucilium* (A.D. c. 64), "We learn not in the school, but in life," and this notion of learning from experience eventually became the basis for the maxim "Live and learn." The English poet George Gascoigne apparently gave the earliest rendering of the current saying as "We live to learne," in *A Glass of Government* (1575), and some years later, John Clarke's *Paroemiologia Anglo-Latina* (1639) quoted the exact wording of the maxim. James Howell's *Proverbs in English, Italian, French and Spanish* (1659) later repeated the saying with an amusing footnote: "One may live and learn, and be hang'd and forget all." The maxim was subsequently included in collections of sayings and was quoted by, among others, the English satirist Jonathan Swift (1738, *Polite Conversation*), Thomas Haliburton (1840, *The Clockmaker, or Sayings and Doings of Sam Slick*), Charles Dickens (1837, *Pickwick Papers*), Mark Twain (1885, in correspondence), the English statesman Lord Avebury (1894, *Use of Life*), Jack London (1909, in correspondence), D. H. Lawrence (1928, *Lady Chatterley's Lover*), and the American novelist J. P. Marquand (1957, *Life at Happy Knoll*).

Live and let live.   Originally a Dutch saying, this maxim first appeared in Gerard de Malynes's *Consuetudo vel Lex Mercatoria* (1622) as "To liue and let other liue." David Fergusson's *Scottish Proverbs From the Original Print of 1641* gave the current wording, which also appeared in John Ray's *A Collection of English Proverbs* (1670) and subsequent books of proverbs. Among those who repeated the saying were the English novelist Tobias Smollett (1762, *Sir Launcelot Greaves*), the American statesman John Adams (1785, in his writings), George Washington (1799, in his writings), James Fenimore Cooper (1832, in correspondence), the English novelist Robert Surtees (1843, *Handley Cross*), Charles

Dickens (1852, *Bleak House*), and, more recently, the American detective story writer Erle Stanley Gardner (1952, *Case of the Grinning Gorilla*). Spy adventure novelist Ian Fleming adapted the saying for his James Bond story *Live and Let Die* (1954), which later was made into a motion picture.

Look before you leap.   Never act too hastily or without due thought, this familiar saying tells us. Apparently first recorded in a fourteenth-century manuscript as "First loke and aftirward lepe," the saying was shortened to "Look ere thou leap" by the English theologian William Tyndale in *The Obedience of Christian Man* (1528). John Heywood's *A Dialogue Conteinyng the Number in Effect of All the Prouerbes in the Englishe Tongue* (1546) warned against matrimonial haste with "In weddyng and al thing, to looke or ye leape," and the poet John Lyly noted in *Euphues, the Anatomy of Wit* (1579), "In things of great importance, we commonly look before we leape." The exact wording of the modern version appeared in Robert Burton's *The Anatomy of Melancholy* (1621). The saying was subsequently quoted or adapted by, among others, the English poet Samuel Butler (1664, *Hudibras*), the playwright Richard Steele (1705, *The Tender Husband*), the satirist Jonathan Swift (1738, *Polite Conversation*), George Washington (1779, 1788, in his writings), Henry David Thoreau (1857, in his journal), and, more recently, the American novelist James T. Farrell (1934, *Young Manhood of Studs Lonigan*). In her novel *Shirley* (1849), Charlotte Brontë created a special version to warn off a character contemplating marriage: "When you feel tempted to marry, think of our four sons and two daughters, and look twice before you leap."

Love and a cough cannot be hid.   Try as you might to stifle a cough in public, when that unrelenting tickle begins in your throat, the best you can ever do is cover your mouth and hack away. And according to this amusing old saying, the look of someone in love, full of joy and happy prospects, is just as hard to keep secret as a cough. An early version of the saying, which appeared in James Sanford's *Houres of Recreation* (1572), included a longer list of things that cannot be concealed: "Foure thinge cannot be kept close, Loue, the cough, fyre [fear] and sorowe." The modern wording was quoted soon afterward in Randle Cotgrave's *Dictionary* (1611) and in George Herbert's collected proverbs, *Jacula Prudentum* (1640). A number of other interesting variations on the saying were quoted at one time or another, including: "Love and light cannot be hid," by James Kelly in *A Complete Collection of Scotish Proverbs* (1721); "Love, the Itch, and a Cough cannot be hid," by Thomas Fuller in *Gnomologia: Adagies and Proverbs* (1732); and "Love, cough, and smoke, can't well be hid," by Benjamin Franklin in *Poor Richard's Almanack* (1737). But by far the most eclectic list of the unconcealable was presented by the English lexicographer John Florio in *Firste Fruites* (1578): "Six things can neuer hide them selues, A scabbe in a hande, a cough at a feaste, an awle in a bagge, a strumpette in a wyndowe, pouertye in pride, and wantonness in lust."

Love and pease pottage are two dangerous things.   Nothing is quite so miserable as losing at love, but apparently pease pottage—a pot full of peas cooked until soft—can produce effects nearly as disagreeable. In *Pleasant Notes Upon Don Quixote* (1654), Edmund Gayton observed, "Love and Pease-pottage are a dangerous surfet," and a laughable explanation, "One breaks the heart, the other the belly," was included along with the saying in James Howell's *Proverbs in English, Italian, French and Spanish* (1659). Yet another version, "Sad are the effects of love and pease porridge," was included in *The English Rogue* (1671) by Richard Head and Francis Kirkman. A few years later, James Kelly rendered the saying as "Love, and raw pease, are two ill things, the one breaks the heart, and the other bursts the belly" in *A Complete Collection of Scotish Proverbs* (1721). Meanwhile, Thomas Fuller's *Gnomologia: Adagies and Proverbs* (1732) passed along a sample of eighteenth-century rustic folk humor with this variant: "Love and Pease will make a Man speak at both ends." The exact wording of the current version also appeared about this time, in Jonathan Swift's *Polite Conversation* (1738). Though included in recent collections of proverbs, the saying apparently has not been quoted in print outside them during the twentieth century.

Love comes in at the window and goes out at the door.   Here is a curious seventeenth-century proverb that speaks metaphorically of feelings that come with winning and losing love. Like the reverie of new love itself, there is something whimsical and romantic about the idea of love flying in through the window of a house. Not so with the unceremonious going out at the door, which hints at some of that vaguely insulted feeling lost love brings—it feels strangely akin to being unceremoniously booted out the front door. The saying itself appeared in essentially its current form as "Love cometh in at the window and goeth out at the door" in William Camden's *Remaines Concerning Britaine* (1614). A short time later, John Ray's *A Collection of English Proverbs* (1670) repeated the saying as "Love comes in at the windows, and goes out at the doors," and Thomas Fuller's *Gnomologia: Adagies and Proverbs* (1732) rendered it as "Love comes in at the Window, and flies out at the Door." The proverb has apparently been quoted in print only rarely during subsequent centuries.

Love conquers all.   This familiar maxim arose in Cleopatra's time, an altogether appropriate coincidence considering the triumphs of her charms over Caesar and Antony. In *Ciris* (c. 50 B.C.), the Roman poet Virgil rendered the line, "Love conquered all; for what could Love not conquer?" Later, in *Eclogues* (37 B.C.), he wrote the Latin version of the modern saying, "*Omnia vincit Amor.*" Centuries later, Chaucer repeated the Latin phrase in *Canterbury Tales* (c. 1387), and the lexicographer John Florio gave it in English as "Loue conquereth al" in *Firste Fruites* (1578). The English playwright Thomas Heywood repeated the saying as "Love oercomes all" in *Fair Maid Exchange* (1607).

More recently, in *Locksley Hall Sixty Years After* (1886), the English poet laureate Lord Tennyson wrote, "Love will conquer at the last." The current "Love conquers all" appeared in print at least as early as 1929 and has been used widely during this century. *See also* **Love laughs at locksmiths** and **Love will find a way.**

Love is blind.   On the self-deceptions wrought by love, the Spanish novelist Miguel de Cervantes wrote in *Don Quixote* (1615), "Love looks through spectacles which make copper appear gold, riches poverty, and weak eyes distil pearls." Similarly, Benjamin Franklin noted "There are no ugly loves, nor handsome prisons," in *Poor Richard's Almanack* (1737). The saying "Love is blind" is far older yet, with Plato rendering it for the first time in *Laws* (c. 375 B.C.) as "Love is blind as regards the beloved." The Roman playwright Plautus recorded the Latin version of the modern saying in *Miles Gloriosus* (c. 200 B.C.), and later Chaucer gave the earliest English rendering in *Canterbury Tales* (c. 1386) as "Love is blind al day, and may nat see." The exact wording of the current proverb was recorded a century later in a manuscript titled *Partonope* (c. 1490). Shakespeare wrote, "If you love her, you cannot see her . . . Because love is blind," in *The Two Gentlemen of Verona* (1594), and repeated the saying in *Romeo and Juliet* (1595), *The Merchant of Venice* (1597), and *Henry V* (1599). The

saying was also used by the English churchman Robert Burton
(1621, *The Anatomy of Melancholy*), Charles Dickens (1837, *Pickwick
Papers*), and the American adventure story writer Edgar Rice
Burroughs (1919, *The Warlord of Mars*). "Love is blind" has been
quoted in print frequently during the twentieth century.

Love laughs at locksmiths.   One of the proverbial testaments
to love's power for overcoming obstacles, this earliest version of
the saying was rendered in William Shakespeare's poem *Venus
and Adonis* (1593) as "Were beauty under twenty locks kept fast,
/ Yet love breaks through and pickes them all at last." The exact
wording of the saying appeared just over two centuries later as
the title of a play written (1803) by the English dramatist George
Colman, Jr. Subsequently, it was quoted in such collections of
proverbs as Burton Stevenson's *Home Book of Proverbs, Maxims,
and Famous Phrases* (1948) and *The Oxford Dictionary of English
Proverbs* (1970), and was repeated by, among others, the English
writer Thomas C. Haliburton (1855, in *Nature and Human Nature*)
and by James Joyce in *Ulysses* (1922). *See also* **Love conquers all**
and **Love will find a way.**

Love makes the world go 'round.   This saying puts love on a
par with primal forces—it makes the world go 'round. Possibly
an adaptation of the Latin proverb, "Love made the world," the
saying first appeared in the French work *C'est l'Amour* (c. 1700)
as " 'Tis love, love, that makes the world go 'round."

Charles Dickens quoted it as " 'Tis love that makes the world
go 'round," in *Our Mutual Friend* (1865), a version repeated by
Lewis Carroll (1865, *Alice's Adventures in Wonderland*), Joaquin
Miller (1877, *The Danites*), and William S. Gilbert (1882, *Iolanthe*).
The American short story writer O. Henry rendered the current
wording, nested in a humorous passage doubting the truth of
the proverb. Writing in *Cupid a la Carte* (1907), O. Henry explained, "It's said that love makes the world go 'round—the an-
nouncement lacks verification. It's wind from the dinner horn
that does it." The saying was adapted more recently by the English writer P. G. Wodehouse (1937, *Crime Wave at Blandings*),
among others.

Love of money is the root of all evil, The.   In *Apothegm* (c. 350
B.C.), the Greek philosopher Diogenes recorded one of the earliest versions of this saying as "The love of money is the mother-
city of all evils," but it was the New Testament Letter to Timothy

I (A.D. c. 62) that first gave us the current form. Early English versions usually substituted "covetousness" or "riches" for the word "money," though the fifteenth-century *Repressor of Over Much Blaming of the Clergy* (c. 1449) by Reginald Pecock used it in "Loue to money . . . is worthi to be forborn . . . as Poul seith, it is 'the roote of al yuel.'" The current "The love of money . . ." appeared regularly (outside the Bible) in correspondence and other writings in colonial America from about 1700 onward, and in 1788, the American Thomas Paine included in *Politician* what has become a commonly used shortened version: "Money is the root of all evil," as distinct from "love of money." Among the writers who subsequently quoted or adapted the saying were the American novelist James Fenimore Cooper (1846, *Redskins*), Herman Melville (1846, *Typee: A Peep at Polynesian Life*; 1851, *Moby-Dick, or The Whale*), and the English novelist Anthony Trollope (1854, *Dr. Thorne*). Not surprisingly, the saying has been quoted in print frequently during the twentieth century.

Love will find a way.   Like water seeping into a basement, or dust collecting beneath the bed, if there is a way for love to get in, this proverb tells us it will surely find a way. Probably the earliest words written in this vein were those of the English balladeer Thomas Deloney, who said in *The Gentle Craft* (1597): "Thus loue you see, can find a way To make both men and maids obey." Later, the *Roxbury Ballads* (c. 1600) gave nearly the modern wording, "Love will find out the way," and the English philosopher Francis Bacon further expanded on the idea in his essay *Of Love* (1625): "Love can finde entrance, not only into an open Heart; but also into a Heart well fortified; if watch be not well kept." In *The Giaour* (1844), Lord Byron rendered the romantically more daring, "Love will find its way / Through paths where wolves would fear to prey," but it was apparently not until 1930 that the modern wording first appeared in print in Mrs. Dorothy Ogburn's *Ra-ta-plan!* *See also* **Love conquers all** and **Love laughs at locksmiths.**

M

Maid that laughs is half taken, A.   Good news for single men: According to this old proverb, single women (today's term for "maid") like men who make them laugh. Although the observation may never be glorified by a "scientific" study like those we read about in newspapers, it certainly does seem to be true. Robert Codrington's *A Collection of Many Select and Excellent Proverbs Out of Severall Languages* (1664), compiled back in the days when women were maids, quoted the exact wording of the proverb for the first time, and soon after, it was repeated in John Ray's *A Collection of English Proverbs* (1670). Though the saying has been included in collections of proverbs up to modern times, it has rarely appeared in print outside them. Perhaps it was just a closely guarded secret.

Make hay while the sun shines.   The Scottish priest Alexander Barclay wrote what was probably the earliest version of this familiar saying in *Shyp of Folys* (1508): "Who that in July whyle Phebus is shynynge About his hay is nat besy labourynge . . . Shall in the wynter his negligence bewayle." Soon afterward, John Heywood's *A Dialogue Conteinyng the Nomber in Effect of All the Prouerbes in the Englishe Tongue* (1546) repeated that theme: "Whan the sunne shinth make hay: whiche is to say, / Take time whan time comth, lest time steale awaie." The exact wording of the modern version appeared later that century in Brian Melbancke's *Philotimus: The Warre Betwixt Nature and Fortune* (1583), in the lines, "Yt is well, therefore, to make hay while the sunne shines, when winde is at will to hoist up saile." The saying was subsequently quoted or adapted by, among others, William Shakespeare (1591, *Henry VI, Part III*), Charles Dickens (1844, *Martin Chuzzlewit*), and more recently James Joyce (1922, *Ulysses*), the English poet A. E. Housman (1926, in correspondence), and e. e. cummings (1933, *Eimi*).

Man does not live by bread alone.   A declaration that one must have more than the bare necessities in order to live a full life, this proverb first appeared in the Old Testament Book of Deuteronomy (c. 650 B.C.) as "Man doth not live by bread alone," and in the New Testament Gospel According to Matthew (A.D. c. 65) as "Man shall not live by bread alone." The American essayist Ralph Waldo Emerson expanded on that theme in *The Sovereignty of Ethics* (1875) with "Man does not live by bread alone, but by faith, by admiration, and by sympathy." Robert Louis Stevenson, on the other hand, gave the saying a witty turn in *Virginibus Puerisque* (1881) with "Man is a creature who lives not by bread alone, but principally by catch-words." John Buchan's *Witch Wood* (1927), meanwhile, provided a somewhat more conservative perspective, observing, "Man canna live by bread alone, but he assuredly canna live without it."

Man is known by the company he keeps, A.   The Swiss reformer Heinrich Bullinger recorded what was probably the earliest version of this saying with the line, "For a man is for the moost parte condicioned euen lyke vnto them that he kepeth company wythe all." The line appeared in the original edition of *Christian State of Matrimony* (1541) and in English translation just two years later. The English Puritan leader Arthur Dent rendered the straightforward "As a man is, so is his company" in *The Plaine Man's Path-way to Heaven* (1601), and Miguel de Cervantes observed with equal forthrightness in *Don Quixote* (1615), "Tell me what company you keep, and I'll tell you what you are." Variants similar to that recorded by Cervantes also appeared in a letter written by Lord Chesterfield (1747) and in *Spruche in Prosa* (1819) by Johann Wolfgang von Goethe. The English dramatist William Wycherley quoted a version closer to the modern in *Love in a Wood* (1672, "You may know a man by his company") as did the novelist Samuel Richardson in *Clarissa* (1748, "Men are known by their companions").

Virtually the current wording was recorded by the American novelist James Fenimore Cooper in *The Prairie* (1827) with "A man can be known by the company he keeps," and the exact wording finally appeared in Elbert Hubbard's monthly magazine *The Philistine* (1901). Hubbard, incidentally, called it "the motto of a prig," and went on to say, "Little men with foot rules six inches long, applied their measuring sticks in this way." The saying has been quoted in print frequently during the twentieth century and was repeated by, among others, Saki (H. H. Munro) in *Chronicles of Clovis* (1927) and e. e. cummings in *Eimi* (1933).

Manners make the man.   A fourteenth-century manuscript by an unknown author recorded the earliest version of this saying as "Maner mayks man." The English nobleman William of Wykeham adopted "Manners makyth man" as his personal motto and had it inscribed on New College, which he founded at Oxford in 1380, as well as on other structures he built. The Scottish clergyman Alexander Barclay wrote that "good lyfe and maners maketh man," in *Shyp of Folys* (1509), and essentially the modern wording appeared a century later, in the lines of a play titled *London Prodigal* (1605): "Be he borne in barne or hall, / 'Tis maners makes the man and all." The exact wording was rendered some years later in *Don Quixote* (1659) by the songwriter and playwright Thomas D'Urfey, and was repeated by, among others, Daniel Defoe (1701, *The True-Born Englishman*; 1729, *The Compleat English Gentleman*), Benjamin Franklin (1742, *Poor Richard's Almanack*), and, more recently, by P. G. Wodehouse (1957, *Over Seventy*, "Manners makyth Man"). The English poet Lord Byron also adapted the saying in *Don Juan* (1824), observing, "The difference is, that in the days of old, Men made the manners; manners now make men."

Many a true word is spoken in jest.   Some truths, too painful or too likely to provoke, can be spoken only when the listener has been disarmed by laughter. A proverbial truth known for centuries, this notion was apparently first recorded by Chaucer with the line, "A man may seye full sooth [truth] in game and pley," from *Canterbury Tales* (c. 1387). In *King Lear* (1605), William Shakespeare wrote, "Jesters do oft prove prophets," and some years later, essentially the modern version was rendered in the *Roxburghe Ballad* (c. 1665): "Many a true word hath been spoken in jest." Jonathan Swift's *Polite Conversation* (1738) gave the modern version, and among other writers who subsequently quoted or adapted the saying were the English writer Thomas C. Haliburton (1837, *The Clockmaker, or The Sayings and Doings of Samuel Slick of Slickville*), George Bernard Shaw (1892, *Widowers' Houses*; 1905, *John Bull's Other Island*), James Joyce (1922, *Ulysses*), and D. H. Lawrence (1928, in correspondence).

Many hands make light work.   The idea of dividing up work among "many hands" was probably first recorded by the Greek poet Hesiod: "More hands mean more work and more increase," in *Works and Days* (c. 800 B.C.). Centuries later, the Latin epigrammatist Martial observed in *Epigrams* (A.D. c. 90), "Work divided is in that way shortened." The modern wording—but certainly not the modern spelling—appeared in a manuscript dating from about 1350, which gave the saying as "Many hondys [hands] makyn lyght worke." Almost two centuries later, Richard Taverner's *Proverbes or Adagies* (1539) rendered a variant, "Many handes make a lyghte burthen," but from the publication of John Heywood's *A Dialogue Conteinyng the Number in Effect of All the Prouerbes in the Englishe Tongue* (1546) onward, the current form of the saying was listed in collections of proverbs. Among others who have quoted or adapted the saying were the English poet Samuel Butler (1678, *Hudibras*) and, in much more recent times, the American novelist Kurt Vonnegut (1963, *Cat's Cradle*).

March comes in like a lion and goes out like a lamb.   The month of March usually marks the transition from winter to early spring, and as this familiar proverb says, often starts with cold blustery weather that changes to warm and springlike by month's end. The English playwright John Fletcher rendered an early version of the saying in *A Wife for a Month* (1624) with the lines, "I would chuse March for I would come in like a Lion . . . But you'd go out like a Lamb, when you went to hanging." Essentially the modern wording appeared some years later in John Ray's *A Collection of English Proverbs* (1670), which rendered the saying as "March hack ham / Comes in like a lion, goes out like a lamb." The saying was repeated in Thomas Fuller's *Gnomologia: Adagies and Proverbs* (1732, "March balkham . . . ") and adapted by Lord North (1740, *Lives of the Norths*), John Quincy Adams (1788, in his diary), Charlotte Brontë (1849, *Shirley*), and, more recently, by J. B. Priestley (1929, *Good Companions*). "March comes in . . ." has been quoted in print frequently during the twentieth century.

Marriage is the only adventure open to the cowardly.   This bit of cynical witticism was penned by the French writer Voltaire in *Pensees d'un Philosophe* (c. 1778). While love may in fact sometimes smile upon the cowardly, it seems likely that surviving the adventure of marriage breeds courage (as well as children). In *Rocket to the Moon* (1938) for example, the American writer Clifford Odets disagreed with Voltaire's barb, saying that Voltaire "made a mistake; you have to be a hero to face the pains and disappointments." Right or wrong, Voltaire's saying has been quoted in print only rarely in the twentieth century.

Might makes right.   [Might is right; Might overcomes right.] Still a familiar maxim today, this saying was rendered first in Plato's *The Republic* (c. 375 B.C.) with the line, "I affirm that might is right, justice the interest of the stronger." The exact wording of the modern form appeared in the early English text *Political Songs* (c. 1327), nested in the line, "For miht is right, the lond is lawless," though it apparently was not repeated again for some centuries. Instead, the established version became "Might overcomes right," which appeared for the first time in John Heywood's *A Dialogue Conteinyng the Number in Effect of All the Prouerbes in the Englishe Tongue* (1546). William Shakespeare wrote in *Henry IV, Part II* (1598), "O God, that right should thus overcome might!" and a few years later, Sir Walter Raleigh noted, "It is an old country proverb that Might overcomes Right," in *Prerogative of Parliament* (1616).

The modern version apparently remained out of use until the nineteenth century, when it was repeated by the American novelist James Fenimore Cooper in *The Pioneers* (1823) and by Ralph Waldo Emerson in his journal for 1866. The saying, of course, has found its way into other languages as well, two grimly witty German variants being among the most interesting: "A handful of might is better than a sackful of right," and "There is no argument like that of the stick."

Misery loves company.   The Roman playwright and philosopher Seneca wrote in *Ad Marciam de Consolatione* (A.D. c. 54), "A crowd of fellow sufferers is a kind of comfort in misery." Centuries later, that observation was echoed by the English hermit and mystic Richard Rolle of Hampole, who recorded the earliest English version in *Meditations on the Passion* (c. 1349): "It is solace to haue companie in peyne." Chaucer repeated a similar version in *Troilus and Criseyde* (c. 1385), and the English poet John Lyly penned a version closer to the modern in *Euphues, the Anatomy of Wit* (1579): "In misery it is great comfort to haue a companion." Other variants were rendered by both William Shakespeare (1594, *The Rape of Lucrece*) and Miguel de Cervantes (1615, *Don Quixote*). The modern wording appeared for the first time (1775) in a letter written during the American Revolution, and was later repeated or adapted by John Quincy Adams (1817, in his writings), Henry David Thoreau (1851, in his journal), Mark Twain (1872, *Roughing It*), O. Henry (1911, *The Day We Celebrate*), and, more recently, the American detective story writer Ellery Queen

(1948, *Ten Days' Wonder*). The saying has appeared in print frequently during the twentieth century.

Misfortunes never come singly.   The Greek historian Herodotus observed in his *History* (c. 445 B.C.), "Misfortune is piled upon misfortune," and the inevitability of calamities following one another has probably been a common superstition from ancient times to the present day. The earliest version of the current proverb in English appeared in a medieval manuscript titled *Kyng Alisaunder* (c. 1300): "The qued [misfortune] commth nowher alone." The French writer Rabelais rendered the saying in *Pantagruel* (1532) as "Misfortune never comes alone," and the poet John Dryden gave it as "Ill fortune seldom comes alone," in *Cymon and Iphigenia* (1700). Joseph Addison, in a contribution to *The Spectator* (1711), quoted nearly the modern version with "Misfortunes never come single," and the exact wording was first used by Aaron Burr's daughter, Theodosia, in a letter dated 1791. Coincidentally, Aaron Burr himself wrote a prophetic passage on the subject a few years later in a letter to Theodosia: "That good and ill fortune never come in single strokes, but in sequences, you have heard since you were four years old." The very next year Burr killed Alexander Hamilton, after this political foe had cost him election to the New York governorship and then reelection to the vice presidency of the United States. Three years later, Burr was tried for treason and acquitted under a cloud of suspicion. But that was not all; tragedy again struck Burr in 1813 when his daughter Theodosia was lost at sea. "Misfortunes never come singly" has been quoted in print frequently during the twentieth century. *See also* **All things come in threes.**

Miss is as good as a mile, A.   This saying in its original longer form is less confusing: "An inch in a miss is as good as an ell [about 42 inches]," which is to say that when you miss the mark, it is still a miss no matter how wide of the target you are. "An inch in a miss..." first appeared in William Camden's *Remaines Concerning Britaine* (1611) and was subsequently included in collections of English proverbs. The modern "A miss is as good as a mile" apparently became current in America during the eighteenth century, however. An American soldier at Lexington reportedly shouted those very words in 1775 during the opening skirmish of the American Revolution, when a poorly aimed bullet passed harmlessly through his cap. The saying appeared in written form in the United States from 1788. During the nineteenth century, the saying became more widely used and was quoted by, among others, the American novelist James Fenimore Cooper (1821, *The Spy*; 1840, *The Pathfinder*), the English novelist Sir Walter Scott (1825, in his journal), the American novelist Richard Henry Dana (1840, *Two Years Before the Mast*), and the English playwright George Bernard Shaw (1894, *Arms and the Man*). More recently, the saying was repeated by e. e. cummings (1933, *Eimi*).

Moderation in all things.   Thinkers of ancient Greece held the notion of moderation in high esteem. As early as the ninth century B.C., the historian Hesiod wrote in *Works and Days*, "Observe due measure, moderation is best in all things." The Greek playwright Euripides echoed that sentiment in *Medea* (c. 431 B.C.) with "Moderation, the noblest gift of heaven," and after him the philosopher Plato advised in *Gorgias* (c. 375 B.C.), "We should pursue and practice moderation." Centuries later, Chaucer first rendered a similar English saying in *Troilus and Criseyde* (c. 1385) with "In every thyng, I woot, there lith mesure [moderation or proportion]. In *The Shyp of Folys* (1508), Alexander Barclay wrote, "There is a measure in all things," while the English satirist Thomas Nashe quoted the saying with slightly different wording in *The Unfortunate Traveller, or The Life of Jack Wilton* (1594): "There is a moderation in all things." Over two centuries later, Herman Melville in *Mardi and a Voyage Thither* (1849) wrote, "All things in moderation are good." William H. G. Kingston gave the exact wording of the modern version in his translation of *Swiss Family Robinson* (1877). The saying has not been quoted in print frequently during the twentieth century.

Money does not grow on trees.   Would that it were only so, but as this maxim says, money is harder to come by than that. An earlier version of the saying, with gold instead of money growing on the proverbial tree, was recorded in colonial America in a miscellaneous writing dated 1750: "Africa, where 'tis so falsly said, that Gold grows on the Trees." A few years later in 1787, an overly optimistic American colonial rendered the earliest version using the word "money": "When the new government is established, 'money will grow upon the trees.' " Though probably in use much earlier, the exact wording of the current version appeared in John S. Strange's *Night of Reckoning* (1958).

Morning dreams come true.   An old superstition that may or may not be true, this saying can be traced back to Roman times. The poet Horace wrote the line, "After midnight, when dreams come true," in *Satires* (35 B.C.), while Ovid rendered the more explicit "Those dreams are true which we have in the morning," in *Heroides* (c. 10 B.C.). The Hebrew Biblical commentaries known as the *Midrash* (seventh century) observed, "The dream toward morning is likely to be fulfilled." The English grammarian John Palsgrave gave the earliest known English version in *Acolastus* (1540): "After mydnyght men saye, that dreams be true," and the venerable Ben Jonson wrote a version closer to the modern in *Love Restored* (1611): "And all the morning dreams are true." The notion also appeared in lines from John Dryden's *The Spanish Fryar* (1681) and John Gay's *The Wife of Bath* (1713). The English playwright William Barnes Rhodes recorded the exact wording of the modern version in *Bombastes Furioso* (1810). The saying has been little used during the twentieth century.

Morning has gold in its mouth, The.   The seemingly quixotic imagery of this proverb is far less puzzling when you know its French cousin, "Work in the morning brings in the gold." The current saying originated in Germany, probably in the eighteenth century, and first appeared in R. C. Trench's *On the Lessons of Proverbs* (1853), with the further explanation that work in the morning hours tends to be more productive than work later in the day. The saying was included in Burton Stevenson's *Home Book of Proverbs* (1948) and was quoted by the Canadian writer Stephen Leacock in *Iron Man and the Tin Woman* (1929, "The morning hour ... "), but otherwise has been little used in the twentieth century.

Mother knows best.   [Father knows best.] A maxim familiar in both its forms today, the saying "Mother knows best" probably appeared first. There were earlier proverbs expressing such similar sentiments as "God could not be everywhere and therefore he made mothers" (an old Hebrew proverb), and "The mother's heart is the child's schoolroom" (*Proverbs From Plymouth Pulpit*, 1887, by Henry Ward Beecher). But the saying "Mother knows best" did not appear in print until 1927, when the American writer Edna Ferber used it as a story title. Probably in use for some time before the 1920s, the saying was quoted in print again a few years later by Carolyn Wells in *Horror House* (1931) and, somewhat prematurely, a citation in 1953 referred to it as an old-fashioned saying. "Father knows best" may well have come into use years earlier, but the popular television situation comedy "Father Knows Best" (aired 1954–63) gave widespread currency to the maxim (and to the impression that mother often knew better). "Mother knows best" has been quoted infrequently in print during the twentieth century, though it was repeated by the mystery writer Agatha Christie in *Ordeal by Innocence* (1958).

Murder will out.   *See* **Truth will out.**

Mutton is meat for a glutton.   The earliest reference to this amusing old saying was made by Randle Cotgrave, who explained in *A Dictionary of the French and English Tongues* (1611), "Flesh of Mutton is food for a glutton; (or was held so in old time, when Beefe and Bacon were your onely dainties)." The exact wording of the current version appeared soon after in Giovanni Torriano's *A Common Place of Italian Proverbs and Proverbial Phrases* (1666). Though the saying has not been repeated frequently in print since then, a variant, "Mustard with mutton is the sign of a glutton," was recently recorded in *Life Is a Four Letter Word* (1966) by Nicholas Monsarrat. Incidentally, some other sayings from the sixteenth century referred to "laced mutton," but that term was an old euphemism for a prostitute.

My son is my son till he gets him a wife, but my daughter is my daughter all the days of her life.   Though it undoubtedly was in use before then, this proverb on the filial fortunes of sons and daughters first appeared in John Ray's *A Collection of English Proverbs* (1670). From that time forward, it remained in regular use and was quoted in major collections of proverbs, including James Kelly's *A Complete Collection of Scotish Proverbs* (1721), Thomas Fuller's *Gnomologia* (1732), W. Carew Hazlitt's *English Proverbs and Proverbial Phrases* (1907 edition), and *The Oxford Dictionary of English Proverbs* (1970).

Necessity is the mother of invention.   Needs—simple, basic, and unavoidable—sometimes drive people to accomplish far more than they think possible, only because they have to. In

Vulgaria (1519), William Horman noted, "Nede taught hym wytte," and a few years later, Queen Elizabeth's tutor, Roger Ascham, wrote, "Necessitie, the inuentour of all goodnesse (as all authours in a maner, doo saye)." The French writer Rabelais called necessity "the mother of eloquence" in *Pantagruel* (1548), and a century later, the exact wording of the current version was quoted in Richard Franck's *Northern Memoirs* (1658). The saying was subsequently repeated or adapted by, among others, the English dramatist William Wycherly (1672, *Love in a Wood*), the satirist Jonathan Swift (1726, *Gulliver's Travels*), Sir Walter Scott (1822, *Peveril of the Peak*; 1830, in his journal), the American novelist Richard Henry Dana (1840, *Two Years Before the Mast*), Louisa May Alcott (1868, *Little Women*), Mark Twain (1872, *Roughing It*). "Necessity is the mother..." has been repeated frequently during the twentieth century.

Neither a borrower nor a lender be.   *See* **Lend your money and lose your friend.**

Never judge a book by its cover.   While this familiar adage is surprisingly recent, the notion of not judging by appearances can be traced back to ancient times. The New Testament Gospel According to John (c. 100) included the warning, "Judge not according to the appearance," and centuries later, the French writer Jean de la Fontaine wrote in *Fables* (1678), "Never judge people by their appearance." Benjamin Franklin's *Poor Richard's Almanack* (1751) gave a more particular caution with "Don't judge of Men's Wealth or Piety by their Sunday Appearances," and the line, "Never to judge a person's character by external appearance," appeared somewhat later in Timothy Alden's *A Collection of American Epitaphs and Inscriptions* (1814). The current version based on the deceptive book cover (usually a metaphor, but at times used literally) did not appear until the twentieth century. The earliest citation, "You can't judge a book by its binding," was recorded in *American Speech* (1929). Some years later, Edwin Rolfe used a closer version, "You can never tell a book by its cover," in *Glass Room* (1946), and the exact wording of the current version was quoted about the same time by Heather Gardiner in *Murder in Haste* (1954).

Never look a gift horse in the mouth.   A much-used saying, it is often attributed to Saint Jerome, whose preface to *Commentary on the Epistle to the Ephesians* (420) contained the saying (in Latin):

"Do not, as the common proverb says, inspect the teeth of a gift horse." Medieval monks repeated the saying as a Latin jingle, "If somebody gives you a horse, don't seek its age in its teeth," and in *Adagia* (1508), the Dutch scholar Desiderius Erasmus included a version of the Latin saying, "One ought not to inspect the teeth of a gift horse." John Stanbridge wrote in *Vulgaria* (1536), "A gyuen hors may not [be] loked in the mouth," a version repeated soon after by Richard Taverner in his translation of Erasmus's *Adagia* in 1539 and by John Heywood in *A Dialogue Conteinyng the Number in Effect of all the Prouerbes in the Englishe Tongue* (1546). Thomas Shelton's translation of *Don Quixote* (1620) contained essentially the modern wording: "Look not a given horse in the mouth," and in 1663, the English poet Samuel Butler wrote in his satire *Hudibras*, "To look a gift-horse in the mouth." The version "Look not..." appeared in John Ray's *A Collection of English Proverbs* (1670) and was used regularly in subsequent centuries. The version "Never...," which along with other variants is in use today, appeared in S. Palmer's *Moral Essays on Some of the Most Curious and Significant English, Scotch, and Foreign Proverbs* (1710). The saying has been quoted or adapted by such writers as Charles Lamb (1826, *Popular Fallacies*), George Eliot (1871, *Middlemarch*), P. G. Wodehouse (1915, *Something New*), and Ellery Queen (1965, *Queens Full*).

Never put off until tomorrow what you can do today. The bane of proscrastinators everywhere, this familiar proverb was first rendered by the Greek poet Hesiod in *Works and Days* (c. 800 B.C.) as "Do not put off work till tomorrow and the day after." Several centuries afterward, the Greek biographer Plutarch noted that the proverb was common in his time (second century B.C.), and during the late Roman empire, Saint John Chrysostom wrote another version in *Adagia* (c. 390), "Put not off till tomorrow; for the morrow never comes to completion." Chaucer gave us the first English version in the *Tale of Melibee* (c. 1387) with the passage, "The goodnesse that thou mayst do this day, do it; and abyde nat ne delaye it nat till to-morrow." Thomas Draxe rendered the straightforward, "Deferre not vntil to morrow, if thou canst do it to day," in *Bibliotheca Scholastica Instructissima, or A Treasurie of Ancient Adages* (1616), and in the next century the poet Joseph Addison wrote in a contribution to *The Spectator* (1712) that it "should be inviolable with a man in office, never to think of doing that tomorrow which may be done to-day." The modern wording was first quoted some years later by Lord Chesterfield in letters dating from 1749 and 1750. The proverb was repeated by George Washington in his writings (1793, 1796), and was a special favorite of Thomas Jefferson (1797, 1811, 1812, 1817, 1823, in his writings)—he once included it among his ten canons of conduct. Aaron Burr, on the other hand, invoked the contrary, saying the original maxim was one "for sluggards." "A better reading of the maxim is," he wrote in *Maxim* (c. 1785), "Never do to-day what you can do to-morrow, because something may occur to make you regret your premature action."

In *Letters and Social Aims: Quotation and Originality* (1875), Ralph Waldo Emerson noted just such a proclivity in the great American statesman Senator Daniel Webster, citing Webster's three rules: "First, never do to-day what he could defer till to-morrow; secondly, never to do himself what he could make another do for him; and, thirdly, never to pay any debt to-day." The saying was also repeated in one form or another by, among others, Benjamin Franklin (1742, *Poor Richard's Almanack*); Abraham Lincoln (1850, *Notes for a Law Lecture*), Charles Dickens (1850, *David Copperfield*), James Joyce (1922, *Ulysses*), and Robert A. Heinlein (1962, *6XH*). A familiar proverb in modern times, it has been quoted in print frequently during the twentieth century.

Never too late to learn. [Never too old to learn.]   The Roman playwright Seneca declared in *Ad Lucilium* (A.D. 64), "You should keep learning as long as there is anything you do not know; if we may believe the proverb, as long as you live." That sentiment was first recorded in English by the clergyman Alexander Barclay in *Eclogues* (c. 1530): "Coridon thou art not to olde for to lere [learn]." Later that century, Shakespeare wrote in *The Merchant of Venice* (1596), "Happy in this, she is not yet so old But she may learn," a thought echoed by his contemporary Thomas Middleton in *Michaelmas Terme* (1607) with the line, "There's no woman so old but she may learn." About two decades later, in *The Mayor of Quinborough* (c. 1627), Middleton said the same of men: "A man is never too old to learn." The version "Never too old to learn" was quoted in John Ray's *A Collection of English Proverbs* (1670) and remained in use thereafter.

The current "Never too late to learn" was apparently first recorded by the English writer Sir Roger L'Estrange in *Seneca's Epistles* (c. 1680) and was repeated in James Kelly's *A Complete Collection of Scotish Proverbs* (1721). The English novelist Henry Fielding adapted the saying in *Covent Garden Journal* (1752), as did Anthony Trollope in *Doctor Thorne* (1858). The saying has continued in use up to the present day.

Never trouble trouble till trouble troubles you. Good advice couched in an amusing rhyme, this proverb tells us not to go looking for troubles, either by deliberately provoking them or by anticipating those that may never come. Shakespeare wrote of such sentiments in *Much Ado About Nothing* (1598) with the line, "Are you come to meet your trouble? The fashion of the world is to avoid cost, and you encounter it." Over a century later, Thomas Fuller's *Gnomologia: Adagies and Proverbs* (1732) warned, "Let your Trouble tarry till its own Day comes," and the American statesman Charles Carroll noted in a letter dated 1824, "This proves that it is wrong to anticipate evils which may never happen." "Never trouble trouble..." appeared in its current form in an 1884 edition of the *Folk-Lore Journal*, and though the saying is not among the more familiar, it has appeared in print during the twentieth century.

New brooms sweep clean. The "new broom" of this saying is really a metaphor originally applied to, among others, new household servants who clean diligently only for the first few days after being hired. Public officials and clergy who take office with a flourish of housecleaning reforms or strict application of rules are also among the "new brooms" of this proverb. According-ing to a naval tradition, the saying came about in the 1600s after a Dutch admiral signaled his determination to "sweep" the British navy from the high seas by tying a broom to his ship's mast (the British response was a horsewhip tied to the mast of their ad-miral's flagship). Such colorful traditions notwithstanding, the earliest published version of the proverb was recorded in the 1500s as "The greene new brome swepith clean," in John Hey-wood's *A Dialogue Conteinyng the Nomber in Effect of All the Prouerbes in the Englishe Tongue* (1546). Soon afterward, the English writer George Pettie noted that "the common errour of servauntes, who like a new broome which sweepeth the house cleane, serve dili-gentlye at the first, but after growe slothfull," in *Civil Conversation of M. Stephen Guazzo* (1581). William Shakespeare wrote in *Henry IV, Part II* (1590), "I am the besom [broom] that must sweep the court clean," and the English clergyman Thomas Fuller com-plained in *Church History of Britain* (1655), "Though they [the monks] swept clean at the first, as new besoms, yet afterwards left more dust behind them of their own bringing in than their predecessors had done." In the next century, James Kelly's *A Complete Collection of Scotish Proverbs* (1721) quoted the saying with an additional explanation, "Spoken of new servants, who are commonly very diligent; and new officers, who are commonly very severe." The modern wording first appeared in John Withal's *A Short Dictionary Most Profitable for Young Beginners* (1616) as "New broomes sweepe cleane," and the saying was later repeated or adapted by, among others, Sir Walter Scott (1815, *Guy Mannering*), James Fenimore Cooper (1845, in correspondence), and Louisa May Alcott (1868, *Little Women*). The proverb has been quoted in print frequently during the twentieth century.

No fool like an old fool.   An old fool seems far worse than a young one, probably because the rest of us expect an older person to have gained something from added years of experience. The saying itself was first recorded as "There is no foole to [like] the olde foole," in John Heywood's *A Dialogue Conteinyng the Number in Effect of All the Prouerbes in the Englishe Tongue* (1546). A century later, the French writer Duc François de La Rochefoucauld included the version, "Old fools are greater fools than young ones," in *The Maximes* (1665), a sentiment echoed by the English poet and playwright John Gay (1712, *The Mohawks*). The wording of the current version was rendered by the English playwright James R. Planche in the line, "In love there's no fool...like an old fool." The proverb was later repeated in one form or another by Sir Walter Scott (1814, *Waverly*), Alfred Tennyson (1859, *The Grandmother*), Mark Twain (1876, *The Adventures of Tom Sawyer*), Rudyard Kipling (1910, *Rewards and Fairies*), Agatha Christie (1920, *Mysterious Affair at Styles*), and James Joyce (1922, *Ulysses*).

No man is a hero to his valet.   Besides the valets, few know the truth of this saying better than those who are worshiped as heroes (and who have not been overwhelmed by the experience). As long ago as about 300 B.C., the Macedonian King Antigonus was said to have responded to being called a god with "The slave who looks after my chamber-pot does not consider me a god." Centuries later, the French moralist Michel de Montaigne wrote in *Essays* (1595), "Few men have been admired by their servants." Almost a century after that, a French woman named Madame Cornuel rendered the current version (in French) in her correspondence (c. 1670). Samuel Johnson noted in a contribution to the *Idler* (1759), "If it be true...'that no man was a hero to the servants of his chamber,' it is equally true, that every man is yet less a hero to himself." The modern wording in English finally appeared in Sir James Prior's *Life of Burke* (1824). One version or another of the saying was adapted by, among others, Johann Wolfgang von Goethe (1809, *Wahlverwandtschaften*; c. 1820, *Spruche in Prosa*), Lord Byron (1817, *Beppo*), Thomas Carlyle (1840, *On Heroes and Hero-Worship*), and, more recently, by O. Henry (1910, *A Dinner at———*; 1911, *The Last of the Troubadours*), Saki (H. H. Munro, 1914, *Beasts and Super-beasts*), and Agatha Christie (1941, *Patriotic Murders*; 1967, *Endless Night*).

No news is good news.   The earliest version of this familiar saying was attributed to the English King James I, who wrote in 1616, "No newis is bettir than evill newis." Virtually the modern saying appeared some years later in James Howell's *Familiar Letters* (c. 1645) with the line, "I am of the Italians mind that said . . . no news, good news." The exact wording was recorded by Samuel Johnson, first president of King's College (now Columbia University), in his writings of 1754. The saying was subsequently repeated or adapted by, among others, the English dramatist George Colman (1776, *The Spleen*), Thomas Jefferson (1788, 1798, in correspondence), George Washington (1788, in correspondence), Charles Dickens (1850, *David Copperfield*), and, more recently, the English playwright Noel Coward (1931, *Cavalcade*), the English poet A. E. Housman (1933, in correspondence), the American poet Edna St. Vincent Millay (1941, in correspondence), and the English novelist Christopher Isherwood (1954, *World in the Evening*). "No news . . ." has been quoted in print frequently during the twentieth century.

No pain, no gain.   From athletes to joggers and would-be weight losers, this maxim may well be etched in the minds of all who have endured the breathless exhaustion and stinging muscles of a tough physical workout. Although it has become common currency in the world of exercise today, the saying originally was used in a broader sense, and the earliest version would be unrecognizable To today's exercise buffs: "Who will the fruyte that haruest yeeldes, must take the payne." Not what you would expect to hear in aerobics class, but the writer, John Grange, had other things in mind when he included the saying in *The Golden Aphroditis* (1577). A shortened version, "No gaine without pain," appeared not long after, however, in *Display of Dutie* (1589) by Leonard Wright. In the next century, the English poet Robert Herrick shortened the maxim still further to *No Paines, No Gaines,* the title of his book (1648), in which he observed, "Mans fortunes are according to his paines." John Ray's *A Collection of English Proverbs* (1670) rendered the saying as "Without pains, no gains," and Benjamin Franklin reversed the wording in *Poor Richard's Almanack* (1745) to "No gains without pains."

The nineteenth-century writer R. C. Trench probably came closest to the modern usage in *On the Lessons in Proverbs* (1852) with "the law of labour, *No pains, no gains, no sweat, no sweet.*" While "No pains, no gains" and other earlier variants are quoted in contemporary books of proverbs, the saying has rarely appeared in print during the twentieth century. The current "No pain, no gain" has been in use at least since the 1980s and possibly earlier.

None so blind as those who will not see.   Probably the earliest version of this proverb, "Who is so deafe, or so blynde as is hee / That wilfully will nother here [hear] or see," was recorded in John Heywood's *A Dialogue Conteinyng the Nomber in Effect of All the Prouerbes in the Englishe Tongue* (1546), while a year later the still closer version, "Who is blynder than he yt wyl nat se," appeared in Andrew Boorde's *Breviary of Healthe* (1547). The English church historian Peter Heylyn quoted the exact wording of the modern version in *Animadversions* (1659) in the next century, and the saying was subsequently repeated in one form or another in John Ray's *A Collection of English Proverbs* (1670), Jonathan Swift's *Polite Conversation* (1738), Thomas C. Haliburton's *The Clockmaker, or The Sayings and Doings of Samuel Slick of Slickville* (1837), Edward Fitzgerald's *Polonius: A Collection of Wise Saws and Modern Instances* (1852), and James Joyce's *Ulysses* (1922). *See also* **None so deaf as those who will not hear**.

None so deaf as those who will not hear.   As in the above proverb, John Heywood's *A Dialogue Conteinyng the Nomber in Effect of All the Prouerbes in the Englishe Tongue* (1546) recorded the earliest version of this proverb, rendering it as "Who is so deafe, or so blynde as is hee / That wilfully will nother here [hear] or see." A few years later, essentially the modern wording appeared in Thomas Ingeland's *Disobedient Child* (c. 1570) as "None is so deaf as who will not hear." In the next century, George Herbert quoted the saying in *Jacula Prudentum* (1640) as "Who is so deaf as he that will not hear," and in the eighteenth century, a letter written to Benjamin Franklin in 1766 contained the exact wording of the current version. Among those who quoted or adapted the saying were Jeremy Bentham in *Book of Fallacies* (1824) and Agatha Christie in *Easy to Kill* (1939). "None so deaf . . ." has been quoted in print only infrequently during the twentieth century.

Nothing succeeds like success.   The French moralist Jean de La Bruyere once observed somewhat cynically, "There are only two ways of getting on in the world: by one's own industry, or by the stupidity of others." But as the current saying declares, once you have become successful, your very success breeds even greater rewards. The French apparently originated the saying— it was recorded by Alexandre Dumas in *Ange Pitou* (1854)—and the first English rendering appeared in Sir Arthur Helps's *Realmah* (1868), where the saying was given in the current form. Some years later, the *Pall Mall Gazette* (1884) noted with some annoyance, "the new and great commandment that nothing succeeds like success." Among those who subsequently repeated or adapted the saying were the Anglican scholar William Inge (1919, *Outspoken Essays*) and, more recently, the American detective story writer Erle Stanley Gardner (1962, *The Case of the Ice-Cold Hands*). The saying has been quoted in print frequently during the twentieth century.

Nothing ventured nothing gained. [Nothing ventured, nothing have; Nothing ventured, nothing win.]   Chaucer rendered the earliest known version of this familiar saying in *Troilus and Criseyde* (1385): "He which that no-thing under-taketh, No thing ne acheveth." Soon after, Chaucer's friend John Gower echoed that notion in *Confessio Amantis* (c. 1390) with the lines, "Who that nought dare undertake, By ryght he shall no profit take." The French writer Rabelais observed in *Gargantua* (1534), "He that nothing ventures, hath neither horse nor mule," and that same century, John Heywood's *A Dialogue Conteinyng the Number in Effect of All the Prouerbes in the Englishe Tongue* (1546) gave the early form of one version that has been repeated up to the present day: "Nothing venter, nought have." The exact wording of another common version was first recorded by the English dramatist Sir Charles Sedley in *The Mulberry Garden* (1668) with "Who ever caught anything with a naked hook? Nothing venture, nothing win." "Nothing venture, nothing win" was subsequently repeated by James Boswell (1791, *Life of Samuel Johnson*), Lord Edward Bulwer-Lytton (1840, *Money*; 1852, *My Novel*), the English novelist Richard Blackmore (1876, *Cripps the Carrier*), D. H. Lawrence (1928, *Lady Chatterley's Lover*), and T. H. White (1957, *Master*). The current "Nothing ventured, nothing gained" apparently was first recorded by the American writer Thorne Smith in *Topper Takes a Trip* (1932).

Of two evils, choose the lesser.   The Greek philosopher Plato advised in *Protagoras* (c. 389 B.C.), "When compelled to choose one of two evils, nobody will choose the greater when he may choose the lesser," a sentiment rendered more succinctly by the Roman statesman Cicero in *De Officiis* (c. 45 B.C.), "Of evils choose the least." The medieval Frenchman Milon d'Amiens rendered the French equivalent of the modern version in *Du Prestre et du Chevalier* (c. 1250), and over a century later, Chaucer gave the earliest English version, "Of harmes two, the lesse is for to chese," in *Troilus and Criseyde* (c. 1385). In the sixteenth century, John Heywood's *A Dialogue Conteinyng the Number in Effect of All the Prouerbes in the Englishe Tongue* (1546) quoted the saying as "Of two yls, choose the least."

Virtually the exact modern wording—"Of two evils choose the least"—appeared in correspondence received (1714) by the Winthrops, a prominent New England family in colonial times, and was repeated by the American clergyman Cotton Mather in a letter dated 1723. This version was repeated by Thomas Paine in *Common Sense* (1776), although the word "lesser" began to replace "least" in versions of the saying recorded during that century. George Washington, who made fairly frequent use of the saying in his writings (1779, 1786, 1793, 1797, 1799), at times repeated, "Of two evils choose the least" and at others adapted the saying using the word "lesser." Thomas Jefferson also adapted the saying in his writings, apparently preferring "lesser" to "least" (1785; 1808; 1817, "less degree of..."; 1825). The English writer Henry Fielding gave it as "The lesser evil of the two," in *The Temple Beau* (1730), and the satirist Jonathan Swift quoted the saying in *Polite Conversation* (1738) as "Of all evils we ought to choose the least." More recently, the English writer John Galsworthy wrote, "Of two evils . . . choose the least," in his play *The Fugitive* (1913), and the adventure writer Edgar Rice Burroughs used "the lesser of two evils" in *Swords of Mars* (1936).

Offense is the best defense. The American revolutionary leader William H. Drayton recorded this saying for the first time as "It is a maxim, that it is better to attack than to receive one" (1775, in his writings). Another American, H. H. Brackenridge, shortened that to "the best defence is offence" (c. 1790), and George Washington explained, "Offensive operations often times, is the surest, if not the only . . . means of defence." In the twentieth century, the saying was rendered as "Offensive is the best defensive" by Ernst A. Lehmann in *Zeppelins* (1928), and the exact wording of the current version appeared in James Reach's *Late Last Night* (1949).

Old soldiers never die, they just fade away. A shortened version of this sentimental adage was first recorded as the title of the 1920 song "Old Soldiers Never Die," written by J. Foley. A decade later, the exact wording of the current version appeared in *Songs and Slang of the British Soldier* (1931), by John Brophy and Eric Partridge. The saying has since become familiar, being quoted or adapted with an interesting regularity in newspapers and magazines over the years. A writer in the *New Yorker* (1957), for example, complained, "Old soldiers never die; they simply keep on arguing," and more recently, the British newspaper the *Daily Telegraph* (1979) reported a union objection to government policy with the words, "Old soldiers never die, but are given jobs in the Civil Service."

Once bitten, twice shy. William Caxton, the first English printer, gave the earliest version of this saying in *Aesope* (1484), his translation of Aesop's fables: "He that hath ben ones begyled by somme other ought to kepe hym wel fro[m] the same." Centuries later, the English novelist Robert Surtees referred to the saying in *Mr. Sponge's Sporting Tour* (1853) with "[He] had been bit once, and he was not going to give Mr. Sponge a second chance." The exact wording of the saying was recorded later that century in *Folk Phrases of Four Counties* (1894) by G. G. Northall and was repeated by, among others, the English novelist Joseph Conrad (1920, *The Rescue*), the novelist Aldous Huxley (1928, *Point Counter Point*), and the novelist Wyndham Lewis (1930, *The*

Apes of God). "Once bitten, twice shy" has been a familiar saying in the twentieth century.

One good turn deserves another.   The medieval manuscript titled *Bulletin of the John Rylands Library* (c. 1400) gave the earliest version of this familiar maxim as "O good turne asket another." Another version, "One good tourne askth an other," appeared in John Heywood's *A Dialogue Conteinyng the Number in Effect of All the Prouerbes in the Englishe Tongue* (1546), and almost a century later, the English dramatist Thomas Randolph recorded the exact wording of the modern version in his pastoral drama *Amyntas* (1638). The saying was subsequently repeated by, among others, Thomas Paine (1796, in correspondence), Johann Wolfgang von Goethe (1806, *Faust*), Sir Walter Scott (1818, *Heart of the Midlothian*; 1824, *St. Roman's Well*), Robert Louis Stevenson (1894, *St. Ives*), James Joyce (1922, *Ulysses*), and the English fantasy writer J. R. R. Tolkien (1956, *The Return of the King*). "One good turn . . . " has been quoted in print frequently during the twentieth century.

One hand washes the other.   In politics, they call it patronage, in business, networking, and out in rural America, they say it is "being neighborly." The idea of friends and acquaintances helping one another is probably as old as civilization itself, and the proverbial metaphor for it, "One hand washes the other," can be traced back at least as far as ancient Greek times. Epicharmus, the Sicilian writer of Greek comic poetry, recorded the Greek saying, "One hand washes the other," in the sixth century B.C. It was later repeated by Plato (*Axiochus*), the Roman philosopher Seneca (A.D. c. 55, *Apocolocyntosis*), and the Roman writer Petronius (before A.D. 66, *Satyricon*). Bishop John Jewel recorded the earliest English version in *Defence of the Apology* (1567), "One hand claweth another," and James Sanford's *The Garden of Pleasure* (1573) rendered the version, "One hand washeth an other, and both wash the face." The poet John Lyly repeated the latter version in *Euphues and His England* (1580), and a few years later, Edmund Spenser rendered it, "The left hand rubs the right," in *The Faerie Queene* (1596).

The exact wording of the current version first appeared soon after in Randle Cotgrave's *A Dictionary of the French and English Tongues* (1611) and was repeated in Giovanni Torriano's *A Common Place of Italian Proverbs and Proverbial Phrases* (1666). James Kelly's *A Complete Collection of Scotish Proverbs* (1721) gave the saying a clever turn with "One hand will not wash the other for nothing." During the twentieth century, the proverb was repeated by, among others, the English poet and novelist Robert Graves (1935, *Claudius, the God, and His Wife Messalina*) and the American novelist Gore Vidal (1964, *Julian*).

One hour's sleep before midnight is worth two afterward.

Ever wonder why getting to bed late leaves you feeling tired, even though you sleep late the next morning? This old proverb may well have the answer, depending, of course, on what kept you up (a night of celebrating can be wearing all by itself). At any rate, the saying first appeared in virtually its modern form in George Herbert's *Jacula Prudentum* (1640) as "One hour's sleep before midnight is worth three after," while the version with "two hours" was recorded soon after in John Ray's *A Collection of English Proverbs* (1670) and Thomas Fuller's *Gnomologia: Adagies and Proverbs* (1732). The Englishman William Cobbett repeated the saying in *Advice to Young Men* (1830), but the proverb was apparently little used during the rest of the nineteenth century and the twentieth century.

One man's loss is another man's gain.

In *Sententiae* (c. 43 B.C.), the Latin writer Pubilius Syrus rendered what was probably the earliest version of this saying, "Gain cannot be made without another's loss." The Latin equivalent of the modern version appeared later, and the saying was first rendered in English by T. Berthelet in *Erasmus' Sayings of Wise Men* (c. 1527) as "Lyghtly whan one wynneth, an other loseth." William Shakespeare adapted the saying in *Macbeth* (c. 1606) with the line, "What he hath lost noble Macbeth hath won," and some years afterward, the English philosopher Francis Bacon gave the proverb as "Whatsoever is some where gotten is some where lost," in his essay *Of Seditions and Troubles* (1625). A letter received by the English satirist Jonathan Swift in 1733 included a version close to the modern—"Your loss will be our gain"—and the exact wording was recorded about a century later in Sir Walter Scott's *The Pirate* (1822). The proverb was adapted by, among others, D. H. Lawrence (1918, in correspondence) and the detective story writer Freeman W. Crofts (1939, *Fatal Venture*).

One rotten apple can spoil the whole barrel.

The earliest version of this saying was recorded in the *Ayenbite of Inwyt* (1340) by Dan Michel of Northgate: "A roted eppel amang the holen maketh rotie they yzounde." Soon after, Chaucer rendered the saying in *Canterbury Tales* (c. 1386) as "Wel bet is roten appel out of hord / Than that it rotie al the remenaunt." Almost two centuries later, John Northbrooke's *Treatise Against Dicing* (1577) gave the proverb as "A rotten apple layd among sounde apples, which will rot all the rest." James Howell's *Proverbs in English, Italian, French and Spanish* (1659) cautioned, "The rotten apple spoils his companions," a form of the saying repeated in Benjamin Franklin's *Poor Richard's Almanack* (1736). The idea of spoiling "the whole barrel" apparently did not appear until the 1900s, when variants like "A rotten officer is like a rotten apple; he spoils the whole barrel" (1937, *Here's to Crime* by Courtney R. Cooper) and "It would take but one rotten apple to spoil the whole barrel" (1960, *Bullet Proof* by Amber Dean). Although a reference using the exact wording of the current version did not appear in sources until 1979 (*Raven Feathers His Nest* by Donald MacKenzie), other close variants were quoted in print frequently during the twentieth century.

One swallow does not make a summer. One of Aesop's *Fables* (sixth century B.C.) told of a young rake who, having squandered all his inheritance but a winter cloak, spied a single swallow that had arrived during a warm day in late winter. Deciding that summer weather was at hand, the rake quickly sold his cloak and spent the money. The winter frosts returned soon after, proving the truth of the current saying. The proverb was well-known in ancient Greece as "One swallow will not make spring," and was repeated in essentially that form by the philosopher Aristotle in *Nicomachean Ethics* (c. 335 B.C.). Centuries later, the Dutch scholar Erasmus included the Latin version in his *Adagia* (c. 1500), while Richard Taverner's *Proverbes or Adagies* (1539) gave the earliest English rendering as "It is not one swalowe that bryngeth in somer." John Heywood rendered the saying as "One swalowe maketh not summer," in *A Dialogue Conteinyng the Number in Effect of All the Prouerbes in the Englishe Tongue* (1546). In the next century, Miguel de Cervantes rendered a Spanish version of the saying in *Don Quixote* (1605), and essentially the modern version appeared in James Howell's *Proverbs in English, Italian, French and Spanish* (1659) as "One Swallow doth not make a Summer."

   The exact wording of the current version was recorded in 1789 by the U.S. Senator William Maclay in his journal. The saying was later adapted by, among others, Sir Walter Scott (1823, *Kenilworth*), Charles Dickens (1844, *Martin Chuzzlewit*), the American novelist James Fenimore Cooper (1850, in correspondence), and Herman Melville (1856, *The Piazza Tales*). The saying has been quoted in print frequently during the twentieth century.

One thing at a time and that done well.   Though the saying was probably known well beforehand, the earliest recorded version—"One thing at a time"—appeared in the correspondence (1702) of William Penn, founder of the colony of Pennsylvania. Toward the end of the eighteenth century, the American novelist Hugh H. Brackenridge rendered the saying as "One thing at once, is the best maxim that ever came into the mind of man," which he included in the manuscript of *Modern Chivalry* (1792–1815). The proverb appeared next as a complaint in an 1825 edition of the *Edinburgh Review*: "Snail's Pace Argument—One thing at a time!" The English detective story writer Wilkie Collins repeated the shortened version in *The Moonstone* (1868) with the line, " 'One thing at a time,' said the Sergeant," and the English novelist David C. Murray gave the exact wording of the full version in *Rainbow Gold* (1885). Adapted by Mark Twain in *A Connecticut Yankee in King Arthur's Court* (1889), the proverb has been repeated frequently during the twentieth century.

One wedding brings another.   This old belief persists even today, symbolically in the throwing of the bride's bouquet, as well as by oral repetition of the proverb. First recorded in the *Roxburghe Ballads* (c. 1634) as "One wedding produces another," the proverb was later rendered by the English poet and playwright John Gay in *The Wife of Bath* (1713) as "One wedding...begets another." Over a century later, the papers of an American named Thomas Ruffin (1832) gave the version, "One marriage always brings about another," and Charles Dickens penned the straightforward, "One wedding makes many," in *Dombey and Son* (1848). The exact wording of the modern version appeared some years later in Sylvia T. Warner's *True Heart* (1929).

Only dogs and Englishmen walk in the sun.   Originally this was a South American saying, and the earliest known English version was recorded in H. M. Brackenridge's *Voyage to South America* (1819) as "It was formerly a saying, that during the siesta, none but dogs and foreigners were to be seen in the street." Quoted in print only rarely thereafter, the exact wording of the saying appeared in *And Then...One Dark Night* (1933) by Edmund Snell. The Noel Coward song titled "Mad Dogs and Englishmen" (1931) brought the saying before a wide English-speaking audience for the first time.

Open confession is good for the soul.   *See* **Confession is good for the soul.**

Opportunity knocks but once.   In *Epigrams* (c. 370), the Roman scholar Ausonius recounted an amusing description of the goddess Opportunity, who was said to be hairy in front and bald behind: "I am a goddess seldom found and known to few...I am ever flying. I am bald behind that none may catch me [by the hair] as I flee. Remorse bears me company. When I have flown away, she is retained by those who did not grasp me as I passed." The idea of the missed opportunity is much older still, of course, and the saying, "Opportunity is seldom presented, easily lost," appeared in *Sententiae* (c. 43 B.C.) by the Latin writer Pubilius Syrus. The politician and writer Sir Geoffrey Fenton gave an early English version in *Bandello* (1567), "Fortune once in the course of our life dothe put into our handes the offer of a good torne," while Thomas Shelton's translation of *Don Quixote* (1620) advised, "It is not fit that whilst good lucke is knocking at our doore, we shut it." The founder of the Pennsylvania colony, William Penn, likewise warned, "Opportunities should never be lost, because they can hardly be regained," in *Some Fruits of Solitude* (1693).

   A saying closer to the current version, "Fortune knocks once, at least, at every man's door," was recorded in *The Port Folio* (1809), and the exact wording of the modern saying appeared over a century later in John Dos Passos's novel *The 42d Parallel* (1930). The saying, repeated or adapted in print frequently during the twentieth century, rightly urges us to be quick to take advantage of opportunities that present themselves. But another saying, from Francis Bacon's *Essays* (1597), is also worth remembering: "A wise man will make more opportunities than he finds."

Ounce of prevention is worth a pound of cure, An.   The Roman poet Persius recorded an early version of this proverb in *Satires* (A.D. c. 58) as, "Meet the malady on its way," and the first English version, "Preuention is so much better than healing, because it saues the labour of being sicke," was quoted in Thomas Adams's *Works* (1630). Thomas Fuller's *Gnomologia: Adagies and Proverbs* (1732) rendered the saying as "Prevention is much preferable to Cure." The exact wording of the modern version ap-

peared just three years later in Benjamin Franklin's personal
papers. Franklin repeated the proverb in his papers again in
1750 and 1784, and his contemporary George Washington became fond of using the notion that prevention is better than
cure, if not the exact wording (1785, 1786, 1792, 1798, in his
writings). The English satirist Thomas C. Haliburton repeated
the current version (1837, *The Clockmaker, or The Sayings and
Doings of Samuel Slick of Slickville*), as did the American detective
story writer Erle Stanley Gardner (1941, *Case of The Turning Tide*).

Out of sight, out of mind. Still familiar today, this saying was
first recorded by the Greek poet Homer in his epic *Odyssey* (ninth
century B.C.) as "Out of sight, out of remembrance." The Roman
emperor and philosopher Marcus Aurelius repeated the sentiment centuries later in his *Meditations* (c. 174) with the lines, "As
soon as the breath is out of their bodies, it is 'Out of sight, out of
mind.' " The earliest English version appeared in *Proverbs of Alfred*
(c. 1275) as "For he that is ute bi-loken [absent] he is inne sone
[soon] for-geten." Over a century later, the English translation of
De Imitatione Christi (c. 1450) rendered the saying as "Whan man is
out of sight, sone he passeth oute of mynde." The exact wording
of the current version was first quoted in Richard Taverner's
translation of *Eramus's Adagies* (1545), and a year later it was repeated in John Heywood's *A Dialogue Conteinyng the Number in Effect of All the Prouerbes in the Englishe Tongue* (1546). Among those
who subsequently repeated or adapted the saying were George
Washington (1750, in his writings), the American statesman John
Jay (1781, in correspondence), Johann Wolfgang von Goethe
(1806, *Faust*), Harriet Beecher Stowe (1852, *Uncle Tom's Cabin, or
Life Among the Lowly*), James Joyce (1922, *Ulysses*), the English novelist Wyndham Lewis (1930, *The Apes of God*), and the English fantasy writer J. R. R. Tolkien (1937, *The Hobbit*). The saying has
been repeated in print frequently during the twentieth century.

Out of the frying pan into the fire. Among Aesop's *Fables* (sixth
century B.C.) is an amusing tale of some unfortunate slave girls
whose zealous mistress forced them to work long hours. Soon
after the rooster crowed each morning, the girls were put to
work, until finally, exhausted and blaming the rooster's predawn
crowing for their troubles, they wrung the offending bird's neck.
But their desperate act only made the situation worse. Not knowing when to start the day without the rooster, the mistress now
put her slave girls to work even earlier than before.

This notion of going from a bad situation to still worse mis-fortune provided the basis for the more recent saying, which first appeared in Sir Thomas More's *A Dyaloge Concerning Heresyes* (1528) as "They lepe lyke a flounder out of the fryenge panne into the fyre." Essentially this form of the saying was repeated soon after in John Heywood's *A Dialogue Conteinyng the Number in Effect of All the Prouerbes in the Englishe Tongue* (1546), George Pettie's *Civil Conversation of M. Stephen Guazzo* (1581), and Edmund Spenser's *View of the Present State of Ireland* (1596). Among those who subsequently adapted or repeated the saying were the English churchman Robert Burton (1621, *The Anatomy of Melancholy*), the writer John Bunyan (1684, *The Pilgrim's Progress*), George Washington (1793, in his writings), Thomas C. Haliburton (1843, *The Old Judge, or Life in a Colony*), George Bernard Shaw (1903, *The Revolutionist's Handbook*), O. Henry (1907, *Cupid a la Carte*), James Joyce (1922, *Ulysses*), and the American novelist James Gould Cozzens (1940, *Ask Me Tomorrow*).

Oysters are only in season in the R months.   Oysters, this curious old saying declares, should only be eaten in months that have an R in them—that is, from September to April. The caution was first recorded in *Description of England* (1577) by the English clergyman William Harrison as "Our oisters are generallie for-borne in the foure hot monethes of the yeare, that is, Maie, Iune, Julie, and August." At the close of the sixteenth century, Henry Buttes rendered a version closer to the modern in *Dyets Drie Dinner* (1599), "The Oyster . . . is vnseasonable and vnholesome in all the monethes, that have not the letter R in their name." John Ray's *A Collection of English Proverbs* (1678) quoted it as "Oysters are not good in a moneth that hath not an R in it." The exact wording of the current version appeared in a letter (1764) written by Lord Chesterfield: "no domestic news of changes and chances in the political world, which like oysters, are only in season in the R months, when the Parliament sits." That same century, the American statesman John Adams mentioned a Philadelphia law in his writings (1774) to the effect that "whereas oysters, between the Months of May and Sept[ember] were found to be unwholesome food, if any were brought to Markett they should be forfeited and given to the Poor." Apart from localized health problems resulting from pollution or spoilage, oysters could in fact be eaten all year round. The proverbial advice against eating them probably arose from the noticeable change in the flavor of oysters during their summer spawning season.

Peck of March dust is worth a king's ransom, A.   What could possibly make dust worth so much during March, much less any other month? This curious old saying is in fact a witty comment on March weather, which is usually windy and rainy. Day after day of March rain not only dampens the spirits but also turns the ground to mud, thereby making dust a fond memory of drier times. "A peck of March dust..." first appeared in John Heywood's *The Play of Wether* (1533) as "One bushell of march dust is worth a kynges raunsome," and was repeated in that form with the added note, "So infrequent is dry Weather during that Month," in Robert Boyle's *Experimental Discourse on the Insalubrity and Salubrity of Air* (1685). The saying has since been quoted in some collections of proverbs, including the recent *Oxford Dictionary of English Proverbs* (1970), but has otherwise appeared in print only infrequently.

Pen is mightier than the sword, The.   A perennial favorite of writers, this saying can be traced back to the sixteenth century when the line, "There is no sworde more to bee feared than the Learned pen," appeared in *Institution of a Christian Prince* (1571) by Tigurinus. Similarly, the English playwright George Whetstone wrote in *Heptameron* (1582) a few years later, "The dashe of a Pen, is more greeuous then the counter use of a Launce." The English poet William King echoed the sentiment over a century later in *The Eagle and the Robin* (c. 1712) with "A sword less hurt does, than a pen." In a letter dated 1796, Thomas Jefferson urged the pamphleteer Thomas Paine to "Go on doing with your pen what in other times was done with the sword," and soon after that the English writer Lord Bulwer-Lytton rendered the exact wording of the modern saying in the play *Richelieu* (1838). The saying has been quoted in print frequently during the twentieth century.

Penny saved is a penny earned, A.   [A penny saved is a penny got.] Though this proverb has the ring of something straight out of *Poor Richard's Almanack*, Benjamin Franklin never penned any-

147

thing more than a clumsy approximation (1737): "A penny saved is two pence clear. A pin a day is a groat a year. Save and have." And he was by no means the first to work this ground, either. The English poet George Herbert gave the earliest known version in *Jacula Prudentum* (1640), "A penny spared is twice got," and soon after, Thomas Fuller's *History of the Worthies of England* (1662) rendered it as "A penny saved is a penny gained." Toward the end of the seventeenth century, John Ray's *A Collection of English Proverbs* (1678) recorded what became a well-known variant: "A penny saved is a penny got." That version was repeated by, among others, the writer Richard Steele (1711, in his contribution to *The Spectator*), Henry Fielding (1733, *The Miser*), George Washington (1792, 1793, 1797, in his writings), Lord Byron, (1811, *Hints From Horace*), and Charles Dickens (1852, *Bleak House*). The exact wording of the modern version was first recorded in *A Pedestrious Tour of Four Thousand Miles* (1819) by Estwick Evans, and this version was later repeated or adapted by the American detective story writer Dashiell Hammett (1929, *Red Harvest*), the English writer P. G. Wodehouse (1933, *Heavy Weather*), and others.

Penny wise and pound foolish. The English philosopher Francis Bacon recorded the earliest mention of this familiar proverb in his *Essays* (1597) as "Be not Penny-wise." Soon afterward, the English historian William Camden rendered the exact wording of the current version in *Remaines Concerning Britaine* (1605), and two years later, Edward Topsell further explained in *The Historie of Foure-Footed Beastes* (1607), "If by covetousnesse or negligence, one withdraw from them their ordinary foode, he shall be penny wise, and pound foolish." About the same time, Bishop John Hall's *Contemplations* (1612) put the matter on a higher plane with "Worldly hearts are penny-wise and pound-foolish," observing that they "shamefully undervalue" spiritual matters while greatly overvaluing the "trash of this world." The proverb was put to still other uses by subsequent writers, and was included in such collections of proverbs as James Howell's *Proverbs in English, Italian, French and Spanish* (1659) and John Ray's *A Collection of English Proverbs* (1670). The 1678 edition of Ray's collection contained an amusing note after the proverb, "He spares at the spigot, and lets it out at the bung-hole." The saying was repeated or adapted by Joseph Addison (1712, in a contribution to *The Spectator*), Benjamin Franklin (1747, *Poor Richard's Almanack*), Thomas Paine (1796, *American Crisis*), and, more recently, the American novelist John Dos Passos (1930, *The 42nd Parallel*) and the English novelist Grahame Greene (1973, *Honorary Consul*). The saying has been quoted in print frequently during the twentieth century.

People who live in glass houses should not throw stones.
According to a traditional story, the crowning of the Scotsman James I as king of England resulted in hordes of Scots moving to London. This turn of events particularly upset the Duke of Buckingham, whose many-windowed mansion just happened to be called the Glass House. About 1604, the duke decided to drive the Scotsmen out, organizing groups of vandals to break windows in Scottish houses as part of his scheme. The plan backfired when angry Scotsmen gathered at the duke's Glass House, and broke all his windows. No doubt outraged by the Scotsmen's temerity, not to mention their embarrassingly successful counterattack, the duke complained to the king, but was rebuffed there, too. King James handily disposed of the matter with the words, "Steenie, Steenie, those who live in glass houses should be carefu' how they fling stanes." Though the saying was probably common then, this rendering was the earliest known.

Some years later, George Herbert's *Jacula Prudentum* (1640) rendered the saying as "Whose house is of glass, must not throw stones at another," and Benjamin Franklin's *Poor Richard's Almanack* (1736) noted, "Don't throw stones at your neighbors' if your own windows are of glass." Thomas Jefferson advised in a letter (1820), "Men in glass houses should not provoke a war of stones," and George Bernard Shaw wrote a version close to the modern with the line, "People who live in glass houses have no right to throw stones," from his play *Widowers' Houses* (1892). The exact wording of the current saying appeared in Herbert Best's *Twenty-fifth Hour* (1940), though it probably was in use much earlier. The saying has been quoted in print frequently during the twentieth century.

Please your eye and plague your heart.
Here is one of those difficult compromises life sometimes forces on us, with conflicting wants demanding a price no matter which choice we make. The sentiment was first rendered by the playwright Anthony Brewer in the appropriately titled play *The Love-Sick King* (1655): "She may please your eye a little ... but vex your heart." The novelist Tobias Smollett gave the saying as "She was resolved to please her eye, if she should plague her heart," in *The Adventures of Roderick Random* (1748). The exact wording of the modern ver-

sion appeared during the next century in William Cobbett's *Advice to Young Men* (1829). Cobbett included an observation that the saying "is an adage that want of beauty invented, I dare say, more than a thousand years ago." The proverb has not been quoted frequently during the twentieth century.

Politeness costs nothing.   A sentiment generally forgotten during the daily trials of urban rush hours, this saying first appeared long ago as "Civility gains more than strength of arms," in John Florio's *Vocabolario Italiano & Inglese* (1659). The English poet Lady Mary Wortley Montagu rendered the exact wording of the current version in a letter dated about 1762, adding the further note, " . . . and gains everything." The saying appeared in Vincent Lean's *Collectanea* (1904), and in such major collections of proverbs as Burton Stevenson's *Home Book of Proverbs, Maxims, and Famous Phrases* (1948) and *The Oxford Dictionary of English Proverbs* (1970). But it has been quoted in print infrequently during the twentieth century. The English writer Edgar Wallace repeated the saying in *Frightened Lady* (1932).

Politics makes strange bedfellows.   Politics is but one of the forces that brings together unlikely allies, as the earlier versions of this familiar proverb attest. William Shakespeare observed in *The Tempest* (1611), "Misery acquaints a man with strange bedfellows," and over two centuries later, Charles Dickens noted in *Pickwick Papers* (1837) that "adversity brings a man acquainted with strange bedfellows." John Lockhart wrote in his *Memoirs of the Life of Sir Walter Scott* (1838), "Literature, like misery, makes men acquainted with strange bed-fellows," and Henry James spoke of "poverty, and the strange bedfellows it makes" in *Princess Casamassima* (1886). The first mention of "Politics makes . . . " was recorded by the American businessman and diarist Philip Hone in an 1839 diary entry: "But party politics, like poverty, bring men acquainted with strange bedfellows." The exact wording of the current version appeared later that century in Charles D. Warner's *My Summer in a Garden* (1870). The saying was quoted in print frequently during the twentieth century.

Possession is nine points of the law.   How many arguments over some prized possession have been won by invoking this proverbial truth? Though it is not clear (and may never have been) what exactly the points of law were, an English attorney named George Selwyn conjured up a less than official list of them in about 1750: "1. A good cause; 2. A good purse; 3. An honest and skilful attorney; 4. Good evidence; 5. Able counsel; 6. An upright judge; 7. An intelligent jury; 8. Good luck." The upshot was that having possession of an item was probably preferable to having to prove ownership in court.

The earliest version of the current saying appeared in *Edward III*, published in 1596, and contained the phrase " 'Tis you are in possession of the Crowne, And thats the surest poynt of all the Law." Virtually the modern wording appeared soon after in Thomas Draxe's *Bibliotheca Scholastica Instructissima, or A Treasurie of Ancient Adages* (1616), "Possession is nine points in the Law." A few years later, a parallel variant noting eleven points of the law appeared in Thomas Adams's *Works* (1630) as "The deuill hath eleuen poynts of the law against you; that is, possession." This variant appeared in John Ray's *A Collection of English Proverbs* (1670) and was quoted by, among others, the English satirist Jonathan Swift (1738, *Polite Conversation*). The "nine points" version was repeated or adapted by Sir Walter Scott (1817, *Rob Roy*), James Fenimore Cooper (1846, *The Redskins*), the English novelist Richard D. Blackmore (1880, *Mary Anerley*), and Agatha Christie (1935, *Boomerang Clue*). The saying has been quoted in print frequently during the twentieth century.

Practice makes perfect.   The Greek ruler Periander wrote in *Apothegm* (c. 600 B.C.), "Practice is everything," and fellow Greeks in later centuries apparently also saw the value of practice in the learning of all manner of things. One of the earliest English versions appeared in Thomas Norton's *The Ordinall of Alchimy* (1477) as "Use [practice] maketh Masterie," a version repeated later in John Heywood's *A Dialogue Conteinyng the Number in Effect of All the Prouerbes in the Englishe Tongue* (1546). Thomas Wilson's *Arte of Rhetorique* (1560) noted, "Before arte was inuented, eloquence was used, and through practise made perfect." The exact wording of the modern version was recorded in the diary of John Adams in 1761 and was later repeated or adapted by, among others, Andrew Jackson (1831, in correspondence), James Fenimore Cooper (1848, in correspondence), Charles Dickens (1870, *The Mystery of Edwin Drood*), and James Joyce (1922, *Ulysses*). The saying has been quoted in print frequently during the twentieth century.

Practice what you preach.   Appropriately enough, it was the Chinese sage Confucius who recorded this saying in its earliest known form. Describing the superior man in *Analects* (c. 500 B.C.),

Confucius said, "He first practices what he preaches, and then preaches according to his practice." The Irish missionary Columban observed in his Latin text *Carmen Monostichon* (c. 600), "He is a great teacher who practices what he teaches," and the legendary William Langland is credited with the first version in English, "If ye lyuen as ye leren[teach] vs, we shal leue [believe] you the bettere," which appeared in *Piers Plowman* (c. 1377). William Shakespeare noted in *The Merchant of Venice* (1596), "It is a good divine that follows his own instructions," and in the next century, the English writer Sir Roger L'Estrange rendered virtually the current saying with "We must practise what we preach" in *Seneca's Morals by Way of Abstract* (1678). The exact wording was quoted in William Combe's poem *Tour of Dr. Syntax in Search of the Picturesque* (1812). Among the writers who made use of the saying in one form or another were John Dryden (c. 1700, *The Character of a Good Parson*), Benjamin Franklin (1733, *Poor Richard's Almanack*), Samuel Richardson (1748, *Clarissa*), Thomas Jefferson (1791, in his writings), Charles Dickens (1840, *The Old Curiosity Shop*), William Makepeace Thackeray (1853, *The Newcomes*), Louisa May Alcott (1868, *Little Women*), P. G. Wodehouse (1915, *Something Fresh*), James Joyce (1922, *Ulysses*), and the English novelist Wyndham Lewis (1930, *The Apes of God*). "Practice what you preach" has been quoted in print frequently during the twentieth century.

Pretty is as pretty does.   *See* **Handsome is as handsome does.**

Pride goes before a fall.   This familiar saying dates back to the Old Testament Proverbs (c. 350 B.C.), which rendered it as "Pride goeth before destruction, and an haughty spirit before a fall." A medieval manuscript (c. 1350) recorded the earliest English version of the saying as "Pryde goyth before [the fall] and shame comyth after." Similarly, the Scottish clergyman Alexander Barclay gave the saying as "Pryde goth before, but shame do it ensue," in *The Shyp of Folys* (1509), a sentiment repeated with but slight wording changes in John Heywood's *A Dialogue Conteinyng the Number in Effect of All the Prouerbes in the Englishe Tongue* (1546). Over two centuries later, Sir Walter Scott gave a shortened version in *The Antiquary* (1816), "Pride goeth before destruction," and soon after, Herman Melville rendered essentially the modern version in *The Piazza Tales* (1856): "And so pride went before the fall." The exact wording appeared the next decade in Louisa May Alcott's *Little Women* (1868). "Pride goes..." was quoted in print frequently during the twentieth century, and among those writers using the proverb were W. Somerset Maugham (1930, *Cakes and Ale*) and Ogden Nash, who adapted the saying with a witty and very contemporary turn for his poem titled *Pride Goeth Before a Raise* (1933).

Promises are like pie crust, made to be broken. Who has not experienced a broken promise, and does anyone really believe it will not happen again? We find out soon enough in life that some promises are broken because of changing circumstances, while others are made to be broken by liars, unscrupulous lovers, and con artists. William Shakespeare warned in *Henry V, Part II* (1599) that "oaths are straws, men's faiths are wafercakes," and almost a century later, the earliest reference to the current saying appeared in *Heraclitus Ridens* (1681) by E. Rawlings: "He makes no more of breaking Acts of Parliament, than if they were like Promises and Pye-crust, made to be broken." The English satirist Jonathan Swift wrote in *Polite Conversation* (1738), "Promises and pie-crust are made to be broken," and the writer George Watterson rendered essentially the modern version of the saying in *Wanderer in Washington* (1827) with the line, "His promises ... were like pie-crusts, made to be broken." Though probably in use much earlier, the exact wording of the current version was quoted by the English novelist Joseph S. Fletcher in *Safety Pin* (1924). *See also* **Honesty is the best policy.**

Proof of the pudding is in the eating, The. Like the metaphorical dessert in this old proverb, many ideas look good in the abstract, but the ultimate comes when they are put into practice—too often it turns out ideas are not particularly good, much less good for you. The earliest version of the current saying was recorded by the English historian William Camden in *Remaines Concerning Britaine* (1605) as "All the proof of a pudding is in the eating." The exact wording was rendered just a few years later by the English playwright Henry Glapthorne in *The Hollander* (1635). "The proof of the pudding ... " later appeared in collections of proverbs, such as Giovanni Torriano's *A Common Place of Italian Proverbs and Proverbial Phrases* (1666) and John Ray's *A Collection of English Proverbs* (1678). It was also quoted or adapted by, among others, the English poet Joseph Addison (1714, in a contribution to *The Spectator*), the satirist Jonathan Swift (1738, *Polite Conversation*), George Washington (1784, in his writings), George Bernard Shaw (1908, *Doctor's Dilemma*), James Joyce (1922, *Ulys-*

ses), John Galsworthy (1924, *White Monkey*), and W. Somerset Maugham (1940, *The Mixture as Before*). The saying has been quoted in print frequently during the twentieth century.

Put your best foot forward.   The English writer Henry Medwall rendered in *A Goodly Interlude of Nature* what was apparently the earliest version of this familiar saying: "Set out the better legge I warne the[e]." Similarly, Anthony Munday wrote in *The English Romayne Lyfe* (1582), "Wee sette the better legge before," and William Shakespeare apparently introduced the notion of the foot with the line, "Come on, my lords, the better foot before," in *Titus Andronicus* (1593). John Ray's *A Collection of English Proverbs* (1678) quoted the saying as "To set the best foot forward," and William Congreve rendered virtually the modern wording in *The Way of the World* (1700) with "put your best foot foremost." That version was repeated by, among others, Thomas Jefferson (1789, in his writings), Washington Irving (1809, *History of New York*), and James Fenimore Cooper (1843, in correspondence). Robert Louis Stevenson gave it as "I set my best foot forward," in *Kidnapped* (1866), and the exact wording of the current version was quoted in Joseph S. Fletcher's *Heaven-sent Witness and Other Stories* (1930), though it was probably in use before then.

Rabbit's foot brings luck.   Dating back to about the sixth century B.C. this superstition could have arisen from a number of rabbit characteristics; certainly, the rabbit's ability to produce large numbers of offspring is a prime candidate. In any event, over the centuries, the rabbit's foot has been believed to have various powers, including curing cramps and rheumatism, and warding off attacks by witches. Apparently, it was also once a custom to brush a newborn baby's face with a rabbit's foot. Even today, some people still carry a rabbit's foot as a lucky charm, and at the very least they *feel* a bit luckier for it. Perhaps they are, but as one English writer recently noted in *Sunday People*, "I always carried a rabbit's foot for luck until someone said: 'Well, the rabbit wasn't lucky, was he?' "

Rain before seven, fine before eleven.   Although this amusing rhyme might not always be true, it apparently was often enough to establish the proverb by the end of the nineteenth century. Or perhaps the rhyme itself made the saying easy to remember and therefore to repeat. Whatever the reason, the saying was first recorded in *Notes and Queries* (1853) in the current form and was repeated toward the end of the century in *Weather Lore* (1893) by R. Inwards. A few years later, the proverb was quoted in *Notes and Queries* (1899) with an added line, "If it rains at eleven, 'Twill last till seven."

Red sky at night, sailors' delight; red sky at morning, sailors take warning.   One of today's better known weather proverbs, this saying appeared in the New Testament Gospel According to Matthew (A.D. c. 65) as "When it is evening, ye say, It will be fair weather: for the sky is red. And in the morning, It will be foul weather today; for the sky is red and lowring." The earliest version mentioned outside the Bible gave only the proverb's second part, "The skie was very red this mornyng, Ergo we are like to haue rayne or nyght," and appeared in *Rule of Reason* (1551) by Thomas Wilson. Soon after, a version containing both parts was rendered as "The element redde in the euenyng, the next daye fayr, but in the morning redde, wynde and rayne," in *Prognostication to Judge of the Weather* (1555) by Leonard Digges. The English author Reginald Scot gave another version, combining both elements in *The Discouerie of Witchcraft* (1584): "The skie being red at evening Foreshews a faire and clear morning; But if the morning riseth red, Of wind or raine we shall be sped." A version closer to the modern appeared in R. Inwards's *Weather Lore* (1893) as "Sky red in the morning Is a sailor's sure warning; Sky red at night Is the sailor's delight." The current version with the word "shepherd" substituted for "sailor" was recorded in the magazine *Punch* (1920). Versions using "sailor" and "shepherd" (usually just the first or second part) were quoted in print frequently during the twentieth century.

Reformed rake makes the best husband, A.   Though a reformed rake probably would make a more passionate husband, a wife may have good reason to worry about just how "reformed" the rake really is. True or not, the saying apparently was recorded for the first time in *The Coquette* (1797) by Hannah W. Foster. Foster quoted the current wording, adding the warning that it was "a trite, but very erroneous maxim." The saying, which appeared in V. S. Lean's *Collectana* (1904), generally has not been included in collections of proverbs and has not been quoted in print frequently during the twentieth century. In one reference, Saki (H. H. Munro) made a witty and perhaps truer use of the proverb in *The Square Egg* (1924): "A relapsed husband makes the best rake."

Revenge is sweet.   Revenge is probably as old as mankind, and the notion of its being "sweet" dates back at least to ancient Greece. In the *Iliad* (c. 850 B.C.), the poet Homer wrote that revenge "is sweeter far than flowing honey," but not all the ancient writers voiced such unabashedly vengeful sentiments; for example, the Roman writer Juvenal declared, "Revenge is always the delight of a little, weak and petty mind," in his *Satires* (c. 120). Centuries later, the first English version was rendered in William Painter's *The Palace of Pleasure* (1566) as "Vengeance is sweete." The dramatist Ben Jonson wrote the line, "O revenge, how sweet thou art!" in his play *Silent Woman* (1609), and the poet John Milton wisely noted in *Paradise Lost* (1667), "Revenge, at first, though sweet, Bitter ere long, back on itself recoils." The exact wording of the modern version appeared in *The Whole Duty of Man* (1658, author unknown) and was later repeated by, among others, the English dramatist William Wycherly (1672, *Love in a Wood*, the Irish dramatist Richard Sheridan (1775, *St. Patrick's Day*), the poet Lord Byron (1818, *Don Juan*), and Sir Walter Scott (1819, *A Legend of Montrose*).

Road to hell is paved with good intentions, The.   The French cleric and mystic Saint Bernard of Clairvaux was credited with having first recorded this familiar saying in *Apothegm* (c. 1150): "Hell is full of good intentions or desires." One might have wondered what could be bad about having good intentions, but that was just the point of the proverb—hell was full of good wishes, while heaven was full of good deeds. Centuries later, a translation of *Guevara's Familiar Epistles* (1574) by Edward Hellowes quoted the earliest English version as "Hell is full of good desires." William Gurnall's *The Christian in Compleat Armour* (1655) further explained the proverb with "Hell is full of good wishes—of such, who now, when it is too late, wish they had acted their part otherwise." The first mention of the word "paved" appeared in the journal (1736) of John Wesley, the English clergyman and founder of Methodism: "Hell is paved with good intentions." This version was later repeated or adapted by a number of writers, including James Boswell (1775, *Life of Samuel Johnson*), Sir Walter Scott (1819, *Bride of Lammermoor*), Charles Dickens (1865, *Our Mutual Friend*), William James (1890, *The Principles of Psychology*), George Bernard Shaw (1903, *Maxims for Revolutionists*), and Aldous Huxley (1944, *Time Must Have a Stop*).

The idea of good intentions paving "the road to" hell apparently did not appear until the nineteenth century, when James A. Froude referred to it in *Shadows of the Clouds* (1847) with the line, "intentions—what they say the road to the wrong place is paved with." The exact wording of the modern version was quoted just a few years later in the *Hand-Book of Proverbs* (1855) by Henry G. Bohn. The proverb has appeared in print frequently during the twentieth century.

Rolling stone gathers no moss, A.

The Greek satirist Lucian (second century) first recorded this ancient proverb as "The stone which is rolling gathers no seaweed," an apparent allusion to stones rolled and polished by waves along the shoreline. The Dutch scholar Desiderius Erasmus recorded the modern form in *Adagia* (1523), giving the Latin as "*Saxum volutum, non obducitur musco.*" The underlying assumption here held that gathering moss was desirable, and constantly moving about was not. That began to change by the mid-1800s, though, possibly reflecting attitudes of a new, more mobile society. Charles Dickens wrote in *Barnaby Rudge* (1841), " 'Roving stones gather no moss, Joe.' 'Nor mile-stones much,' replied Joe." At about the same time, a Scotsman complained, "But can ye tell me what guid the fog [moss] does to the stane?" George Bernard Shaw took up the cause in *Misalliance* (1914): "We keep repeating the silly proverb ...as if moss were a desirable parasite."

But in 1931, Herbert Adams struck out for the middle road in *Paulton Plot*: "They say a rolling stone gathers no moss, but it isn't always true. It may roll until it strikes something good." Later, J. R. R. Tolkien wrote in *The Return of the King* (1956), "He is a moss-gatherer, and I have been a stone doomed to rolling." Nevertheless, "rolling stone" became the romantic role model for many people in the sixties and early seventies. Then in the 1980s, with yet another new age dawning, the old proverb reappeared in Charlotte MacLeod's *The Palace Guard* (1981) as "He's the original rolling stone, though I expect he's fairly mossy as far as money goes."

Rome was not built in a day. Invoked when a task is too big to be accomplished quickly, this familiar saying was originally a French proverb, "Rome was not made all in one day," which was recorded in *Li Proverbe au Vilain* (c. 1190). The English version did not appear until three centuries later, when it was included first in Richard Taverner's translation of *Erasmus' Adages* (1545) as "Rome was not buylt in one daye," and then a year later in John Heywood's *A Dialogue Conteinyng the Number in Effect of All the Prouerbes in the Englishe Tongue* (1546) as "Rome was not bylt on a daie (quoth he) & yet stood Tyll it was fynysht." "Rome was not built..." was subsequently quoted or adapted by, among others, the English novelist Tobias Smollett (1748, *The Adventures of Roderick Random*), Sir Walter Scott (1822, *The Fortunes of Nigel*), the American novelist James Fenimore Cooper (1823, *The Pioneers*), Charlotte Brontë (1849, *Shirley*), Arthur Conan Doyle (1893, *The Stock-Broker's Clerk*), Saki (H. H. Munro; 1913, *When William Came*), E. B. White (1914, in correspondence), T. H. White (1939, *The Sword in the Stone*), and Gore Vidal (1952, *The Judgment of Paris*). The proverb has been quoted in print frequently during the twentieth century.

S

Sadness and gladness succeed each other. Nothing in life is permanent, and this bromide reminds us that those sometimes difficult passages from happiness to sorrow and back again are just that—passages. In *Amphitruo* (c. 200 B.C.), the Roman comic playwright Plautus wrote the line, "It is heaven's will for sorrow to follow joy." Centuries later, Chaucer observed in *Canterbury Tales* (c. 1387), "Joy after wo, and wo after gladnesse." G. Delamothe in *The French Alphabet* (1592) rendered nearly the modern saying with "Gladnesse and sadnesse, doth rule one after another," and a short time later the exact wording of the current version appeared in John Clarke's *Paroemiologia Anglo-Latina* (1639). The saying has since been included in such books of proverbs as John Ray's *A Collection of English Proverbs* (1670) and

Thomas Fuller's *Gnomologia: Adagies and Proverbs* (1732), but has been quoted only infrequently outside them.

Sauce for the goose is sauce for the gander.   "Goose" and "gander" here stand for women and men generally, and accordingly the proverb declares that what is good for a woman is also good for a man. An earlier saying based on the same logic, "As well for the coowe as for the bull," appeared in John Heywood's *A Dialogue Conteinyng the Number in Effect of All the Prouerbes in the Englishe Tongue* (1546), and the first rendering of the current saying was recorded in John Ray's *A Collection of English Proverbs* (1670) as "That that's good sawce for a goose, is good for a gander." Ray added a further explanatory note, "This is a woman's Proverb." The English writer Roger L'Estrange gave virtually the modern version in his translation of *Aesop's Fables* (1692), quoting it as "Sauce for a Goose is Sauce for a Gander." The English satirist Jonathan Swift used essentially this version in *Polite Conversation* (1738), as did Benjamin Franklin in his papers (1764). Lord Byron quoted the exact wording of the modern version in *Don Juan* (1824), and the saying in this form was repeated or adapted by, among others, Richard Blackmore (1894, *Perlycross*), James Russell Lowell (1848, *The Bigelow Papers*), James Joyce (1922, *Ulysses*), Wyndam Lewis (1930, *The Apes of God*), John Updike (1941, *Between Two Worlds*), and Peter DeVries (1981, *Sauce for the Goose*). The saying has been quoted in print frequently during the twentieth century.

Seeing is believing.   According to this old maxim, you can in fact believe your eyes. The Greek playwright Aristophanes recorded what was probably the earliest such saying in *The Ecclesiazusae* (c. 393 B.C.) as "I saw it and believed." Centuries later, a manuscript (1609) by Simon Harward contained the first English version, "Seeing is leeving," and just a few years later, John Clarke's *Paroemiologia Anglo-Latina* (1639) quoted the exact wording of the current version: "Seeing is beleeving." The maxim was used widely thereafter, appearing in such collections of proverbs as Giovanni Torriano's *A Common Place of Italian Proverbs and Proverbial Phrases* (1666), John Ray's *A Collection of English Proverbs* (1670), and Thomas Fuller's *Gnomologia: Adagies and Proverbs* (1732). Fuller, by the way, included the note, "Seeing's Believing, but Feeling's the Truth." Among the writers who repeated or adapted the maxim were Washington Irving (1855, *Wolfert's Roost*), Mark Twain (1872, *Roughing It*), Agatha Christie (1924,

Man in the Brown Suit), and J. P. Marquand (1946, *B. F.'s Daughter*). *See also* **Believe only half of what you see and nothing that you hear.**

Silence is golden.   *See* **Speech is silver, silence is golden.**

Silence is wisdom, when speaking is folly.   The Greek biographer Plutarch wrote in *Moralia* (A.D. c. 95), "There is wisdom in timely silence that is better than all speech." Although this left open the question of determining just when it was timely not to speak, Plutarch's sentiment was echoed centuries later in English by Chaucer, who advised in *Troilus and Criseyde* (c. 1385) that "firste vertu is to kepe tonge." About a century later, a manuscript titled *Poems* (c. 1470) by George Ashby contained the line, "Grete wisdam is, litil to speke," and George Pettie's *Civil Conversation of M. Stephen Guazzo* (1581) rendered the idea as "That to use silence in time and place, passeth all well speaking." Some years later, the text of *Two Merry Milkmaids* (1620, author unknown) recommended, "Silence lady is the best part of wisdom."

The exact wording of the current version was recorded in Thomas Fuller's *Gnomologia: Adagies and Proverbs* (1732) and was repeated by the English clergyman Charles Spurgeon in *John Ploughman's Talks* (1869), a collection of sayings. The saying has been quoted in print only infrequently during the twentieth century, though other variations on this same theme have gained somewhat greater currency. *See also* **Speech is silver, silence is golden; A still tongue makes a wise head.**

Six hours of sleep for a man, seven for a woman, and eight for a fool.   How much sleep is enough? This particular proverb notwithstanding, there have been a number of rigid formulas prescribed in similar sayings from centuries past. Certainly among the earliest was "Six hours in sleep is enough for youth and age; Seven for the lazy, but eight are allowed to none," which was recorded in a medieval manuscript titled *Regimen Sanitatis* (c. 1100). Giovanni Torriano's *A Common Place of Italian Proverbs and Proverbial Phrases* (1666) recommended a different set of hours for sleep: "Five hours sleepeth a traveller, seven a scholar, eight a merchant, and eleven every knave." Meanwhile, Thomas Fuller's *Gnomologia: Adagies and Proverbs* (1732) warned, "Seven Hours' Sleep will make a Clown forget his Design."

In *The Gentle Life* (1864), James H. Friswell gave essentially the current proverb, which he reported was a favorite of English

King George III: "six hours [of sleep] for a man, seven for a woman, and eight for a fool." Not surprisingly, the saying has appeared in print only rarely during the twentieth century, though it has been included in such recent collections of proverbs as Burton Stevenson's *Home Book of Proverbs, Maxims and Familiar Phrases* (1948) and *The Oxford Dictionary of English Proverbs* (1970).

Slice from a cut cake is never missed, A. Though perhaps not the most laudable, this bit of proverbial wisdom offers sound advice: Before purloining an extra piece of any nearby (and always irresistible) cake, wait until a few slices have been removed, and your thievery will remain undiscovered. Probably reflecting tougher economic times, the early form of this proverb mentions bread instead of cake, but the intent is the same. William Shakespeare apparently revealed the secret of this skulduggery in *Titus Andronicus* (1592), writing, "Easy it is Of a cut loaf to steal a shive [slice]." Some years later, John Clarke's *Paroemiologia Anglo-Latina* (1639) advised matter-of-factly, " 'Tis safe taking a shive of a cut loafe," a version repeated in essentially that form in Thomas Fuller's *Gnomologia: Adagies and Proverbs* (1732). The cut loaf version in various forms continued in use up to modern times, while the cut cake variant apparently came into use only recently. Essentially the modern version was quoted in *The Wrong House* (1937) by Cecil F. Gregg as "like a slice from a cut cake ... it's never missed."

Slow and steady wins the race. This familiar proverb is the subject of perhaps the best-known of Aesop's fables, the race between the tortoise and the hare. The hare, certain he was the fastest, stopped to nap during the race. Meanwhile, the tortoise plodded along slowly but steadily, eventually passing the still sleeping hare and winning the race. Probably the earliest version of the current proverb was "Slow but sure," which first appeared in *Accedence of Armorie* (1562) by Gerard Legh: "Although the Asse be slowe, yet is he sure." William Shakespeare echoed that sentiment in *Romeo and Juliet* (1595) with the line, "Wisely and slow; they stumble that run fast." With minor variations, this form of the saying was used by the English dramatist Thomas Middleton (1608, *The Widow*), Oliver Goldsmith (1768, *The Vicar of Wakefield*), Charles Dickens (1865, *Our Mutual Friend*), Richard Blackmore (1882, *Christowell*), and Mark Twain (1884, *The Adventures of Huckleberry Finn*). The exact wording of the proverb in its current form was first recorded by the English poet Robert Lloyd in *The Hare and Tortoise* (1762).

Soft answer turns away wrath, A.   The Old Testament Proverbs (c. 350 B.C.) gave us this saying as "A soft answer turneth away wrath," though John Wycliffe's English translation of the Bible (c. 1388) rendered it as "A soft answere breakith ire." The exact wording of the modern version appeared over three centuries later in Gersolm Bulkeley's *Will and Doom* (1692), with the added observation, "but grievous words stir up anger." "A soft answer . . . " was adapted or quoted by, among others, the American clergyman Cotton Mather (1692, *The Wonders of the Invisible World*), John Quincy Adams (1814, in his memoirs), and James Joyce (1922, *Ulysses*).

Spare the rod and spoil the child.   Hardly one to be popular with children, this proverb nevertheless comes to us from the Old Testament Proverbs (c. 350 B.C.), which rendered it as "He that spareth his rod, hateth his son." *Homilies* by Aelfric recorded the saying in English for the first time as "Se [He] the sparath his gyrde, he hateth his cild," and *Piers Plowman* (1377) by William Langland warned, "Who-so spareth the sprynge [switch], spilleth his children." The exact wording of the modern version was quoted over two centuries later in John Clarke's *Paroemiologia Anglo-Latina* (1639) and subsequently was quoted in other collections of proverbs, including John Ray's *A Collection of English Proverbs* (1670) and Thomas Fuller's *Gnomologia: Adagies and Proverbs* (1732). Among the notable writers who repeated or adapted the saying were the English poet Samuel Butler (1664, *Hudibras*), the American writer Washington Irving (1820, *The Sketch Book of Geoffrey Crayon, Gent.*), the English writer Thomas C. Haliburton (1843, *The Old Judge, or Life in a Colony*), and the English novelist Samuel Butler (1901, *The Way of All Flesh*).

Speak softly and carry a big stick.   The implied threat of force is often as effective as outright war in dealing with other nations, and this observation has been the subject of various sayings over the centuries. In *Jacula Prudentum* (1640), the English writer George Herbert recorded one of the earlier proverbs in this vein, "One sword keeps another in the sheath." Similarly, a French variant said, "Who carries a sword, carries peace," and a medieval Latin saying noted, "Where there is good guarding, there is good peace." The current saying, believed to be a West African proverb, was apparently used for the first time in English by President Theodore Roosevelt during a speech at the Minnesota State Fair (1901). The saying became a well-known slogan for Roosevelt's conduct of American foreign policy during his administration.

Speech is silver, silence is golden.   The value placed upon saying less, rather than more, as reflected in this proverb can be traced as far back as the early Egyptians, who recorded one such saying: "Silence is more profitable than abundance of speech." The current proverb was rendered for the first time in the Judaic Biblical commentaries called the *Midrash* (c. 600), which gave the proverb as "If speech is silvern, then silence is golden." The poet Thomas Carlyle quoted this version in German in *Sartor Resartus* (1831), and soon after, the American poet James Russell Lowell quoted the exact wording of the modern version in *The Bigelow Papers* (1848). Perhaps more familiar in the shortened version "Silence is golden," the saying has been quoted in print frequently during the twentieth century. One witty adaptation in Brian Aldiss's *The Primal Urge* (1961) seems particularly appropriate to modern times: "Speech is silver; silence is golden; print is dynamite." *See also* **Silence is wisdom, when speaking is folly; A still tongue makes a wise head.**

Spilling salt brings bad luck.   Salt has been valued as a food preservative and flavor enhancer probably at least since 6500 B.C., and the practice of throwing a pinch of spilled salt over the left shoulder to prevent bad luck was known to the ancient Sumerians, Egyptians, and Greeks. Superstitions about spilling salt were common in Europe from the sixteenth century, and in subsequent times, people believed that it could portend a dispute with a friend or spouse, or even a broken bone. Others said each spilled grain stood for a tear the spiller would someday shed. The satirist Jonathan Swift included the superstition in *Polite Conversations* (1738) with the passage, "Mr. Neverout, you have overturn'd the salt, and that's a sure sign of anger: I'm afraid, miss and you will fall out." As to the reason for throwing the spilled salt, a twentieth-century writer explained it this way in *Walnut Tree* (1951): "One must never spill the salt without taking the precaution to blind the devil by throwing a pinch at him over the left shoulder."

Squeaking wheel gets the oil, The.   Here the squeaking wheel, or in earlier versions the creaking spoke of a wheel, is a metaphor for a troublesome person who gets attention because of noisy complaining, rather than because of need or merit. The earliest version was recorded in a medieval manuscript (c. 1400) as "Euer the worst spoke of the cart krakes." Almost two centuries later, George Pettie's *Civil Conversation of M. Stephen Guazzo* (1581) observed that "the brokenest wheele of the charriot maketh alwaies the greatest noyse," and some years after, Thomas Fuller declared in *An Appeal of Injured Innocence* (1659), "That spoke in the wheel which creaketh most doth not bear the greatest burden in the cart. The greatest complainers are not always the greatest sufferers." Benjamin Franklin's *Poor Richard's Almanack* (1737) put it more succinctly: "The worst wheel of the cart makes the most noise."

Versions closer to the modern apparently did not come into use until the 1900s, and an edition of Bartlett's *Familiar Quotations* published in the 1930s included the passage, "The wheel that squeaks the loudest Is the one that gets the grease." The saying, "But the wheel that does the squeaking is the one that gets the grease," appeared in Burton Stevenson's *Home Book of Proverbs, Maxims, and Familiar Phrases* (1948), and the exact wording of the current version was quoted in a 1959 edition of the *Bangor Daily News*. The saying has gained a wide currency in modern times.

Sticks and stones will break my bones, but names will never hurt me.

A familiar rhyme probably heard more often in the schoolyard than anywhere else, this saying is a last defense for those on the receiving end of a name-calling attack. But earlier sayings in this vein sometimes came to the opposite conclusion on the ill effects of foul words. The fifteenth-century *How the Good Wyf Taugte His Doughtir* (c. 1450) recorded the saying, "Ne fayre [fair] wordis brake neuer [never] bone," and the English playwright Robert Greene wrote in 1584, "Wordes breake no bones, so we cared the lesse for his scolding." But Thomas Fuller's *Gnomologia: Adagies and Proverbs* (1732) gave the rhyme, "Fair Words never broke a Bone, / Foul Words have broke many a one." The following century, the modern saying was quoted by G. F. Northall in *Folk Phrases of Four Counties* (1894), with the added note, "Said by one youngster to another calling names." The saying has been quoted in print frequently during the twentieth century.

Still tongue makes a wise head, A.

The English epigrammatist John Heywood recorded the earliest version of this proverb in *Epigrams* (1562) as "Hauyng a styll toung he has a besy head." A closer variant, "A quiet tongue makes a wise head," appeared over two centuries later in Thomas Cogan's *John Buncle, Jr.* (1785), and the exact wording of the modern version was quoted in W. C. Hazlitt's *English Proverbs* (1869). The nineteenth-century also saw the rendering of an opposite, and perhaps truer, saying—"A wise head makes a still tongue"—that was quoted in *Notes and Queries* (1865). *See also* **Silence is wisdom, when speaking is folly; Speech is silver, silence is golden.**

Still waters run deep. Now often used to describe those who conceal a passionate nature beneath a calm exterior, the saying was first recorded in a medieval text titled *Cursor Mundi* (c. 1400) as "Ther the flode is deppist the water standis stillist." The English poet John Lyly rendered the saying as "Water runneth smoothest, where it is deepest," in *Sapho and Phao* (1584), and William Shakespeare wrote in *Henry VI, Part II* (1590), "Smooth runs the water where the brook is deep." James Kelly's *A Complete Collection of Scotish Proverbs* (1721) gave essentially the modern version, "Smooth Waters run deep," with the added note, "Spoken to or of them who seem demure, yet are suspected to be roguish." Samuel Richardson repeated the sentiment with "The stillest waters is the deepest," in *Clarissa* (1748), and in the next century, *A Woman's Thoughts About Women* (1858) by Dinah Mulock mentioned "those 'still waters' which run deep." Though probably in use much earlier, the exact wording of the saying appeared in 1915, in Ronald Firbank's *Vainglory*. "Still waters..." has been quoted in print frequently during the twentieth century.

Stitch in time saves nine, A. Who has not heard this clever rhyme before, much less repeated it? Easily among the most widely known of all proverbs today, "A stitch in time..." cautions us to take care of little problems right away, before they become bigger and require even more work to fix. The saying itself was first recorded as "A Stitch in Time may save nine," in Thomas Fuller's *Gnomologia: Adagies and Proverbs* (1732), and the exact wording of the current version appeared some years later in Francis Baily's *Journal of a Tour in Unsettled Parts of North America in 1796 & 1797*. The proverb was used in one form or another by George Washington (1797, in his writings), the English writer Thomas C. Haliburton (1837, *The Clockmaker, or The Sayings and Doings of Samuel Slick of Slickville*), Herman Melville (1849, *Mardi and a Voyage Thither*), Ogden Nash (1938, *A Stitch Too Late Is My*

Fate), the American detective story writer Erle Stanley Gardner (1943, *The Case of the Drowsy Mosquito*), and the American novelist Peter DeVries (1956, *Comfort Me With Apples*).

Stolen fruit is sweet.   Human nature being what it is, many people enjoy stolen or illicit pleasures all the more because they are forbidden. The Old Testament Proverbs (c. 350 B.C.) rendered the saying, "Stolen waters are sweet, and bread eaten in secret is pleasant," which no doubt helped inspire the English clergyman John Lydgate to write the lines, " 'Much sweeter,' she saith, 'more acceptable / Is drinke, when it is stolen privily,' " in *The Remedy of Love* (c. 1430). The Biblical "Stolen waters are sweet" continued in use up to the present day, and other stolen pleasures, from "fruits" to "glances," also appeared. The French writer Rabelais mentioned in *Pantagruel* (1533) what he called a medieval proverb, "Sweeter is fruit after many dangers have been undergone for it," and some years later, the *Divil's Banket* (1614) by Thomas Adams noted, "Apples are sweet, when they are plucked in the Gardiners absence. Eve liked no Apple in the Garden so well as the forbidden." The English dramatist Philip Massinger wrote in *The City-Madame* (1632), "Stolen pleasures being sweetest." *The English Rogue* (1671) by Richard Head and Francis Kirkman advised, "Stolen meat is sweetest," and Lord Byron's *Don Juan* (1818) pointed to "Stolen glances, sweeter for the theft." Essentially the current saying was quoted in Henry G. Bohn's *Handbook of Proverbs* (1855) as "Forbidden fruit is sweet," and in one form or another ("Stolen fruit is always sweet"; "Stolen fruit is sweetest"), the saying has been quoted in print during the twentieth century.

Stretch your legs according to the length of your blanket.
An amusing and quite apt metaphor for keeping within limits of one sort or another (as in living within your means), this proverb was first recorded in Robert Grosseteste's *Boke of Husbandrie* (c. 1240) as "Whoso streket his fot forthere [farther] that the whitel [blanket] will reche, he schal streken in the straw." The idea of feet pushed beyond the blanket (or sheet) winding up in the bedding straw also appeared in William Langland's *Piers Plowman* (1377). The Spanish novelist Miguel de Cervantes gave the saying as "Stretch not your leg beyond the sheet," in *Don Quixote* (1615), and George Herbert rendered a version closer to the modern in *Jacula Prudentum* (1640) with "Every one stetcheth his legs according to his coverlet."

Essentially the modern version was quoted by John Ray as "Stretch your legs according to your coverlet," in *A Collection of English Proverbs* (1670), and Johann von Goethe observed in *Spruche in Reimen* (c. 1825), "He who does not stretch himself according to the coverlet finds his feet uncovered." Some years later, the English clergyman Charles Spurgeon gave the exact wording of the modern version in *John Ploughman's Pictures* (1880), with the added explanation, "Never spend all you have." Though quoted in such recent collections of proverbs as Burton Stevenson's *Home Book of Proverbs, Maxims, and Familiar Phrases* (1948) and *The Oxford Dictionary of English Proverbs* (1970), the saying has been repeated outside them only rarely during the twentieth century.

Strike while the iron is hot.   Take action while the circumstances remain favorable, or so this familiar proverb advises, by way of a metaphorical iron heated and ready for the blacksmith. Chaucer rendered an early version of the saying in *Troilus and Criseyde* (c. 1385) as "Whil that iren is hoot, men sholden smyte," and almost two centuries later, a similar variant, "And one good lesson... From the smithis forge, whan thyron is hote stryke," appeared in John Heywood's *A Dialogue Conteinyng the Number in Effect of All the Prouerbes in the Englishe Tongue* (1546). The exact wording of the current version was recorded just a few years later in George Pettie's *A Petite Pallace of Pettie His Pleasure* (1566) and was used widely thereafter.

Among the writers who repeated or adapted the saying were William Shakespeare (1591, *Henry VI, Part III*), the English writer John Bunyan (1682, *The Holy War*), John Dryden (1697, *Aeneis*), Benjamin Franklin (1763, in his papers), Tobias Smollett (1771, *The Expedition of Humphrey Clinker*), James Fenimore Cooper (1823, *The Pioneers*), Charles Dickens (1841, *Barnaby Rudge*), William Makepeace Thackeray (1848, *Vanity Fair*), Louisa May Alcott (1868, *Little Women*), William McFee (1932, *The Harbormaster*), and the English novelist Kingsley Amis (1954, *Lucky Jim*). *See also* **Make hay while the sun shines.**

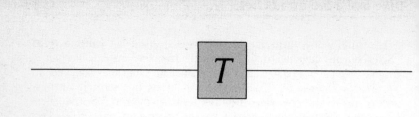

T

Take care of the minutes and the hours will take care of themselves. This proverb appears to be a variant of the somewhat earlier "Take care of the pence and the pounds will take care of themselves," which the English statesman Lord Chesterfield attributed (1747) to William Lowndes, secretary of the Treasury under King William, Queen Anne, and King George I. This version was later included in collections of proverbs and was repeated by George Bernard Shaw (1912, *Pygmalion*), among others. Lord Chesterfield also recorded the parallel "Take care of the minutes..." for the first time in a letter written in 1747. A century later, the English writer Thomas Haliburton repeated the saying in *Wise Saws* (1843), and the next year, Ralph Waldo Emerson wrote, " 'Tis an old and vulgar maxim, Take care of the minutes, and the hours will take care of themselves; but like many vulgar things 'tis better than gold of Ophir, wisely used." "Take care of the minutes..." has been quoted in print only infrequently during the twentieth century.

Take the good with the bad. The Greek lyric poet Alcaeus observed in *To Mytilene* (c. 600 B.C.), "There is something bad in everything that is good." Over fifteen hundred years later, the Icelandic manuscript on Scandinavian mythology, the *Poetic Edda* (c. 900), rendered a similar sentiment: "None so good that faults he has none; none so bad that he is nothing worth." In the sixteenth century, the French moralist Michel de Montaigne noted, "Of the pleasures and goods that we have, not one is free from some mixture of bad." The idea of "taking" the one with the other did not appear until the nineteenth century, however, when it was used in a loosely related saying, "You must take the fat with the lean," quoted in the 1813 edition of John Ray's *A Collection of English Proverbs*. Soon afterward, essentially the current saying was rendered in James Fenimore Cooper's *The Pathfinder* (1840) as "We must take the bad with the good." The exact modern wording was recorded in 1936, in a line from *The Big Money* by John Dos Passos. The saying has been quoted in print only infrequently during the twentieth century. *See also* **Every cloud has a silver lining.**

Talk is cheap.   A familiar maxim today, this straightforward version is a fairly recent invention, but an earlier form, "Talking pays no toll," can be traced back to the seventeenth century. George Herbert's *Jacula Prudentum* (1640) recorded this older version for the first time, and the saying was included in such later collections as John Ray's *A Collection of English Proverbs* (1670) and Thomas Fuller's *Gnomologia: Adagies and Proverbs* (1732). The current version did not appear until the mid-nineteenth century, when the English writer Thomas C. Haliburton used it in a line from *The Attache, or Sam Slick in England* (1844): "Talk is cheap, it don't cost nothing but breath." Haliburton adapted the saying in *Season-Ticket* (1860), and the writer Andy Adams repeated the current version in *The Outlet* (1905). Twentieth-century writers who have quoted the maxim include Norman Mailer (1948, *The Naked and the Dead. See also* **There is a difference between saying and doing; Easier said than done; Actions speak louder than words.**

Tell your lawyer and doctor the whole truth.   *The Garden of Pleasure* (1573) by James Sanford recorded the earliest version of this proverb as "Conceale not the truthe From the Phisition and Lawyer," and five years later, *First Fruites* by the English lexicographer John Florio rendered it as "From the Phisition & Attorney, keepe not the truth hidden." George Herbert's *Jacula Prudentum* (1640) advised, "Deceive not thy Physitian, Confessor, nor Lawyer," a sentiment echoed in John Ray's *A Collection of English Proverbs* (1670): "Hide nothing from thy minister, Physician and Lawyer." Ray further explained in a note, "He that doth so, doth it to his own harm or loss, wronging thereby either his soul, body, or estate." In the next century, Benjamin Franklin quoted the saying as "Don't misinform your doctor nor your lawyer," in *Poor Richard's Almanack* (1737). A version closer to the current one appeared in Maria Edgeworth's novel *Helen* (1834): "Always tell your confessor, your lawyer, your physician, your friend, your whole case." The exact wording of the current version was given in Erle Stanley Gardner's *Case of the Sulky Girl* (1933). The proverb has been quoted in print only infrequently during the twentieth century.

There are more ways than one to skin a cat.   This proverb is considerably less harmful than its barbaric imagery suggests; it simply means that something can be accomplished in more than one way. Earlier versions of the proverb were only a little less grim, and John Ray's *A Collection of English Proverbs* (1678) gave what was probably the first: "There are more ways to kill a dog than hanging." With slight differences in wording, this version appeared in James Kelly's *A Complete Collection of Scotish Proverbs* (1721) and in Jonathan Swift's writings (1725). A new torture was added by W. T. Thompson in *Chronicles of Pineville* (1845): "There's more ways to kill a dog besides choking him with butter." About this time, the first version involving a cat appeared in *John Smith's Letters* (1839) by S. Smith: "There's more ways to kill a cat than one." Charles Kingsley's *Westward Ho!* (1855) rendered the saying as "There are more ways of killing a cat than choking her with cream," and Mark Twain recorded the first version using skinning—"She knew more than one way to skin a cat"—in *A Connecticut Yankee in King Arthur's Court* (1889). Though probably in use earlier, the exact wording of the current version appeared, interestingly enough, in *Morals for Moderns* (1939) by Ralph A. Habas. The proverb has been quoted in print frequently during the twentieth century.

There are two sides to every question.   The Greek philosopher Protagoras recorded this saying for the first time in *Aphorism* (c. 435 B.C.), but it apparently was either little used or forgotten by English writers until the nineteenth century. A book titled *The Other Side of the Question*, by James Ralph, did appear in 1742, but it was John Adams who rendered essentially the modern English version in his writings (1802): "There were two Sides to a question." Some years later, Thomas Jefferson rendered the exact wording in a letter (1817), and the saying was subsequently repeated or adapted by the English novelist Charles Kingsley (1863, *Water Babies*), Oscar Wilde (1891, *The Critic as Artist*), O. Henry (1907, *The Trimmed Lamp*), and Ogden Nash (1938, *Don't Grin*). The saying has been quoted in print frequently during the twentieth century, though a humorous variant may be even closer to the truth: "There are three sides to every question—your side, my side, and the right side."

There is a difference between saying and doing.   The Greek philosopher Plato urged in *Laws* (c. 345 B.C.), "By all means let us do as we say." Centuries later, an early form of the current proverb, "Saiyng and dooyng are two thingis," appeared in John Heywood's *A Dialogue Conteinyng the Number in Effect of All the Prouerbes in the Englishe Tongue* (1546). The French moralist Michel de Montaigne wrote in *Essay* (1580), "Saying is a different thing from doing," and the English writer John Bunyan came to a like conclusion in *Pilgrim's Progress* (1678): "I see that saying and doing are two things." Essentially the current version was recorded a few years earlier in Giovanni Torriano's *A Common Place of Italian Proverbs and Proverbial Phrases* (1666): "There's a great deal of difference twixt doing and saying." The saying has been quoted only infrequently during the twentieth century. *See also* **Easier said than done.**

There is a sucker born every minute.   A proverbial truth as far as hucksters and con artists are concerned, this saying is often attributed to the American showman Phineas T. Barnum. Barnum supposedly made the remark, "A sucker is born every minute," based on his years as a circus showman. Short story writer O. Henry repeated that sentiment in *Babes in the Jungle* (1910): "In the West a sucker is born every minute." The exact wording of the current version was recorded in the *New Yorker* magazine (1956), though it was probably in use well before then. An allusive form of the saying, "There is one born every minute," is also sometimes used.

There is a time and a place for everything.   This proverb is often repeated as a mild reprimand when someone's actions are in fact ill-timed or out of place. The English poet Alexander Barclay recorded the earliest version of the saying in *The Shyp of Folys* (1508), noting that "there is tyme and place for euery thynge." The Quaker William Penn, founder of the Pennsylvania colony, rendered essentially the modern version in *Some Fruits of Solitude* (1693) with the line, "There should be a Time and a Place for everything." Almost two centuries later in *Never the Time and the Place* (1883), Robert Browning lamented, "Never the time and the place / And the loved one all together!" Though probably in use earlier, the exact wording of the current version appeared in *Death at the Manor* (1938) by Molly E. Corne. The saying was later adapted by, among others, the American writer J. P. Marquand in *Melville Goodwin, USA* (1951).

There is many a good tune played on an old fiddle.   Of fairly recent vintage, this saying is tailor-made for those refusing to surrender to the stereotypes of old age. Apparently originated by the English novelist Samuel Butler in *The Way of All Flesh* (1903), it was subsequently included in J. C. Bridge's *Cheshire Proverbs* (1917) and such other collections of proverbs as Burton Stevenson's *Home Book of Proverbs, Maxims, and Familiar Phrases* (1948) and *The Oxford Dictionary of English Proverbs* (1970). Among the writers who quoted or adapted the saying were the Irish novelist Liam O'Flaherty (1926, *Mr. Gilhooley*) and Anthony Burgess (1964, *The Eve of Saint Venus*).

There is more to marriage than four bare legs in bed.   This clever saying first appeared as "Whan folks wyll needis wed / Mo thyngs belong, than foure bare legs in a bed," in John Heywood's *A Dialogue Conteinyng the Nomber in Effect of All the Prouerbes in the Englishe Tongue* (1546). Almost a century later, William Camden rendered another version with "[Be]longs more to marriage then foure bare legges in a bed," in *Remaines Concerning Britaine* (1623). The dramatist Ben Jonson referred to a shortened version, "Four bare legs in a bed," in the play *New Inne* (1631), and John Ray's *A Collection of English Proverbs* (1670) offered "More longs to marriage, then four bare legs in bed." In the nineteenth century, Sir Walter Scott wrote in *The Fortunes of Nigel* (1822), "A sort of penny wedding it will prove, where all men contribute to the young folks' maintenance, that they may not have just four bare legs in a bed together." The exact wording of the current version was recorded in Dorothy L. Sayers's *Busman's Honeymoon* (1937). Not surprisingly, the proverb has been quoted in print only infrequently during the twentieth century.

There is no accounting for taste.   Noting the often sharp differences in taste between various people, the English writer John Bunyan wrote in *The Pilgrim's Progress* (1678), "Some love meat, [and] some love to pick the bone." The English prelate Jeremy Taylor recorded an early version of the current proverb, the Latin saying, "There is no disputing about tastes," which he included in *Reflections Upon Ridicule* (c. 1667). Later in the next century, the novelist Ann Radcliffe gave the exact wording of the modern version in *The Mysteries of Udolpho* (1794). Among other writers who later repeated or adapted the saying were James Fenimore Cooper (1845, *Satanstoe*), Charles Dickens (1865, *Our Mutual Friend*), Anthony Trollope (1867, *The Last Chronicle of Barset*), George Bernard Shaw (1903, *Man and Superman*), James Joyce (1922, *Ulysses*), and P. G. Wodehouse (1937, *Laugh-*

ing Gas). The proverb has been quoted in print frequently during the twentieth century.

There is no harm in trying.   A fairly recent saying, this one was apparently first recorded in Herman Melville's *The Confidence Man: His Masquerade* (1857): "No harm in trying." Vincent Lean's *Collectanea* (1902) rendered it with "asking" instead of "trying," as did the detective story writer Erle Stanley Gardner in *The Case of the Dangerous Dowager* (1937). F. Scott Fitzgerald's *The Great Gatsby* (1925) repeated the earlier "No harm in trying." The exact wording of the current version appeared in A. A. Fair's *Bedrooms Have Windows* (1949), though the saying probably was in use earlier. The saying has been quoted in print frequently during the twentieth century. *See also* **If at first you don't succeed, try, try again.**

There is no honor among thieves.   That no special morality exists among thieves seems a recent discovery; for centuries, writers stubbornly clung to the romantic notion that, in fact, "There *is* honor among thieves." Perhaps a strong sense of honor once existed within the society of rogues, and none other than the Roman statesman Cicero noted in *De Officiis* (c. 45 B.C.), "They say that thieves even have a code of laws to observe and obey." Centuries later, Shakespeare adapted this notion in *Henry IV, Part I* (1597) with the line, "A plague upon it when thieves cannot be true to one another!" Daniel Defoe helped perpetuate the idea with "Thieves make a point of honour ... of being honest with one another," which appeared in *The History of Colonel Jack* (1721). Sir Walter Scott in *Redgauntlet* (1824) and Herman Melville in *The White Jacket, or The World in a Man-of-War* (1850) likewise affirmed notions of "honor among thieves," but at the close of the nineteenth century, some doubt began to surface. While writing about the notorious buccaneer Henry Morgan— who in fact even robbed his own crewmen—Andrew Lang declared in *Essays in Little* (1891), "There is not even honour among thieves." In *Terrible People* (1926), the English writer Edgar Wallace took the middle road on the question with "There is no honour among thieves, only amongst good thieves," but in a later book, *Fourth Plague* (1930), he noted "the falsity of the English adage that there is honour amongst thieves." "There is no honor ..." has since been quoted in print frequently.

There is no place like home.   Long ago, the Roman statesman Cicero expressed a sentiment similar to this familiar homily: "No place is more delightful than one's own fireside," a line that appeared in *Ad Familiares* (46 B.C.) In about 800, a Norse proverb echoed that idea in "Home is best, though it be small," and the sixteenth-century English writer Thomas Tusser rendered the saying, "Though home be but homely, yet huswife is taught, That home hath no fellow to such as haue aught," which appeared in *A Hundreth Good Pointes of Husbandrie* (1571 edition). The exact wording of the modern version first appeared as the line, "Be it ever so humble, there's no place like home," for the song "Home Sweet Home" (1822) by J. H. Payne. "There is no place like home" has been in common usage ever since.

There is no wisdom below the girdle.   Girdle once meant a belt or sash about the waist and was sometimes taken to be the dividing line between a person's better qualities (those of head and heart) and the coarser sexual impulses emanating from below the girdle. William Shakespeare made an early reference to such notions in *King Lear* (1605) with the lines, "Down from the waist they are Centaurs, Though women all above. But to the girdle do the gods inherit, Beneath is all the fiend's." Some years later, *Apothegm* (c. 1670) by Sir Matthew Hale rendered a close variant of the modern saying with "No wisdom below the girdle." Later, a work titled *England's Vanity* (1683) noted that an early Christian heretical sect called the Paterniani believed "that the upper Parts of a mans Body were made indeed by God, but the lower Parts from the Girdle, they held was made by the Devil." *Virtues* (1691) by John Hartcliffe reported, "It was a favourable and merry Conceit of the Cardinal of Rome, that there was no Law beneath the Girdle." Lord North later quoted the exact wording of the modern version, apparently taken from *The New English Dictionary* (c. 1734). North wrote of a well-to-do man who "married his own servant maid and then for excuse, said there was no wisdom below the girdle." The saying has appeared in print only rarely during the twentieth century.

There is safety in numbers.   The Old Testament Proverbs (c. 350 B.C.) gave this saying as "In the multitude of counsellors there is safety," and some centuries later, the Roman writer Juvenal rendered the shorter version, "Number is their defence," in his *Satires* (c. 120). The clergyman John Bunyan repeated the biblical proverb in English in *The Life and Death of Mr. Badman*

(1680), and Charles C. Colton declared in *Lacon* (1822) that the idea of safety in numbers was "the maxim of the foolish." In her novel *Emma* (1816), Jane Austen included the passage, "She determined to call upon them and seek safety in numbers," and Theodore Dreiser used virtually the exact wording of the current version in *The Titan* (1914): "There was safety in numbers." The saying has been quoted in print frequently during the twentieth century.

There's many a slip between the cup and lip.   This proverb is generally said to have originated with the ancient Greek story of Ancaeus, son of Neptune. As the story went, Ancaeus was planting a vineyard when a seer predicted he would not live long enough to drink the wine. Much later, as he was about to taste the first wine from his now prosperous vineyard, Ancaeus mocked the prophecy and raised the cup of wine to his lips. But before he could drink, word came that a wild boar was loose in the vineyard. Ancaeus immediately set out to kill the animal, but in the fray was himself set upon and killed by the boar, thus fulfilling the prophecy. Alluding to just such a circumstance, the Roman statesman Marcus Cato wrote (c. 175 B.C.), "Many things may come between the mouth and the morsel." Centuries later, the Dutch scholar Desiderius Erasmus gave the Latin saying in *Adagia* (1523): "Manye thynges fall betwene the cuppe and the mouth." This wording was later repeated by, among others, the English writer John Lyly (1580, *Euphues and His England*) and the dramatist Ben Jonson (1633, *Tale of a Tub*).

Virtually the modern version, "There's many a slip 'Twixt the cup and the lip," was quoted for the first time in *The Ingoldsby Legends* (1840) by Richard H. Barham, and the saying was later adapted by, among others, James Joyce (1922, *Ulysses*). The proverb has been quoted in print frequently during the twentieth century. *See also* **Don't count your chickens before they hatch.**

They who live longest will see most.   Here is a proverb that seems perfect for the modern world, where youth and longer lives are prized so highly, and where there is great promise of so much more to see. First recorded in English by Thomas Shelton in his translation of *Don Quixote* (1620), the early version said simply, "It was needful to live long to see much." Later that century, John Ray's *Proverbs: Scottish* (1678) rendered the saying as "The langer we live we see the mae ferlies [wonders]." The exact wording of the current saying was quoted in *John Plough-*

man's Talk (1869) by the English clergyman Charles H. Spurgeon. Interestingly, the proverb has been quoted only infrequently in the twentieth century, perhaps because of a cynical truism about long life that Randle Cotgrave recorded in *A Dictionary of French and English Tongues* (1611): "The longer the life, the greater griefe."

Things are not what they seem.   The freed Roman slave Phaedrus recorded what was essentially the Latin version of the current saying in *Fabulae Aesopiae* (c. 25 B.C.) as "Things are not always what they seem." The earliest English versions were only distant approximations, as in Richard Edwards's *The Paradyse of Daynty Devises* (1576), which rendered the saying as "Things proue not as they seeme." About this time William Shakespeare also used the theme of misleading appearances in *The Rape of Lucrece* (1594): "Thou art not what thou seem'st; and if the same, Thou seem'st not what thou art, a god, a king." The saying in its current form appeared over two centuries later in Henry Wadsworth Longfellow's *A Psalm of Life* (1838), and was later adapted by, among others, Charles Dickens (1865, *Our Mutual Friend*) and the playwright William S. Gilbert (1878, *H. M. S. Pinafore*). The poet William Wordsworth rendered yet another version in *Ecclesiastical Sonnets* (1822), one well worth remembering when times turn for the worse: "All things are less dreadful than they seem."

Think before you speak.   Here is a maxim for preventing those red-faced moments when you ask yourself, "Why didn't I just keep my mouth shut?" The saying itself apparently originated in the sixteenth century, appearing in Roger Edgeworth's *Sermons Very Fruitfull, Godly, and Learned* (1557) as "Thinke well and thou shalt speake well." In the next century, Thomas Draxe's *Bibliotheca Scholastica Instructissima, or A Treasurie of Ancient Adages* (1616) rendered the saying as "A man must first think, and then speak," and John Clarke's *Paroemiologia Anglo-Latina* (1639) gave "First think, and then speak." The unrealistic advice, "Think today and speak tomorrow," was included in H. G. Bohn's *Handbook of Proverbs* (1855), and a French proverb from about this time recommended glossal acrobatics with "Turn the tongue seven times in the mouth before speaking." Such exotic exercises aside, the modern version finally appeared in Richard Neely's *The Walter Syndrome* (1970), though it was probably in use before then. The saying has been quoted in print only infrequently during the twentieth century.

Three may keep a secret if two of them are dead.   The Roman dramatist Seneca probably gave the best advice of all in *Hippolytus* (A.D. c. 60): "If you would have another keep a secret, keep it first yourself." But if you must talk, remember the warning given in the *Poetic Edda* (c. 900), a collection of Scandinavian tales: "Tell thy secret to one, but beware of two; what is known to three is known to everyone." Similar advice has been given in English sayings dating from medieval times. Chaucer wrote in *Romaunt of the Rose* (c. 1370), "Tweyn [two] in nombre is bet than three / In every counsel and secree," while almost two centuries later the deliberately humorous "Three maie kepe a counsayle if two be away," appeared in John Heywood's *A Dialogue Conteinyng the Nomber in Effect of All the Prouerbes in the Englishe Tongue* (1546). Similarly, George Herbert's *Jacula Prudentum* (1640) declared, "Three can hold their peace if two be away," a version essentially repeated in John Ray's *A Collection of English Proverbs* (1670). The current version of "Three may keep a secret..." appeared some years later in Benjamin Franklin's *Poor Richard's Almanack* (1735) and has not been improved on since. The proverb has been quoted in print only infrequently during the twentieth century.

Three things are not to be trusted...   There are many things not to be trusted today, but the modern reader will no doubt find these thoughts from other times both amusing and sometimes oddly insightful. Perhaps the earliest of them was a thirteenth-century French saying, "A dog's tooth, a horse's hoof, and a baby's bottom are not to be trusted." A fourteenth-century manuscript recorded the earliest English version, which singled out a horse's foot (by which a man might be kicked), a hound's tooth (by which he might be bitten), and a woman's faith (no comment!). The sixteenth century English lexicographer John Florio warned in *First Fruites* (1578), "Trust not to much four things, that is, A strange dogge, an vnknowen horse, a talkative woman, & the deepest place of a riuer." William Shakespeare set his thoughts to an amusing rhyme in *Timon of Athens* (1608): "Grant I may never prove so fond, / To trust man on his oath or bond; / Or a harlot, for her weeping, / Or a dog, that seems a-sleeping; / Or a keeper with my freedom; / Or my friends, if I should need 'em." Nearly two centuries later, the English poet Robert Southey returned to the "Three things..." theme in *Madoc in Aztlan* (1805): "Three

things a wise man will not trust, / The wind, the sunshine of an
April day, / And woman's plighted faith." Lastly, in our own
century, T. H. White gave us still other things to watch out for
in *Elephant and Kangaroo* (1948): "Four things not to trust...a
dog's tooth, a horse's hoof, a cow's horn, and an Englishman's
laugh."

Time and tide wait for no man.   A familiar saying from the
days of sailing ships (when tides determined departure times),
this maxim was recorded in its earliest form as "For wete you
well the tyde abydeth no man," which appeared in *Everyman*
(c. 1500). By the end of the century, a more complete version,
"Tyde nor time tarrieth no man," was quoted in Robert Greene's
A Disputation Between a Hee Conny-Catcher and a Shee Conny-Catcher
(1592). Both this and another version, "Time and tide stayeth
for no man" (1630, *The English Gentleman* by Richard Brathwait),
were in use during the next centuries. James Howell's *Proverbs
in English, Italian, French and Spanish* (1659) and James Kelly's *A
Complete Collection of Scotish Proverbs* (1721) both quoted the
maxim with "stays," for example, and John Ray's *A Collection of
English Proverbs* (1670) and Thomas Fuller's *Gnomologia: Adagies
and Proverbs* (1732) used "tarry." Virtually the modern saying
appeared at the end of the eighteenth century in Andrew Barton's *The Disappointment or The Force of Credulity* (1796). Barton
rendered the saying as "Time and tide waits for no one," and
the exact modern wording was recorded a few years later by Sir
Walter Scott in *Fortunes of Nigel* (1822). Among the writers who
quoted or adapted the saying were Robert Burns (1791, *Tam
O'Shanter*), James Fenimore Cooper (1823, *The Pioneers*), and
Charles Dickens (1844, *Martin Chuzzlewit*). The maxim has appeared in print frequently during the twentieth century.

Time heals all wounds.   The Greek dramatist Menander wrote
in about 300 B.C., "Time is a healer of all ills." Chaucer rendered
that sentiment in English for the first time in *Troilus and Criseyde*
(c. 1385): "As tyme hem hurt, a tyme doth hem cure." Richard
Taverner quoted a shortened version, "Tyme taketh away greu-
ance," in *Proverbes or Adagies* (1539), and Thomas Draxe gave it
as "Time cures every disease," in *Bibliotheca Scholastica Instructissima or A Treasurie of Ancient Adages* (1616). Over a century later,
Benjamin Franklin's *Poor Richard's Almanack* (1738) compared
time to "an herb that cures all diseases," and the statesman Benjamin Disraeli later repeated the saying in *Henrietta Temple* (1837)

as "Time is the great physician." Though probably in use well beforehand, the exact wording of the current version was recorded by Dave Smalley in *Stumbling* (1929). The saying was adapted by, among others, D. H. Lawrence (1930, in correspondence) and Agatha Christie (1942, *The Body in the Library*), and has been quoted in print frequently during the twentieth century.

Time is money.   While this familiar maxim may seem an invention of our hectic and impersonal modern society, it actually comes to us from the ancient Greeks. Antiphon, an orator who wrote speeches for defendants in court cases, recorded the earliest known version of the saying in *Maxim* (c. 430 B.C.) as "The most costly outlay is time." Centuries later, the notion of time's value appeared in English as "Tyme is precious," which was included in Sir Thomas Wilson's *A Discourse Upon Vsurye* (1572) and John Fletcher's *The Chances* (1647). A century after Fletcher, Benjamin Franklin rendered the exact wording of the current version in *Advice to a Young Tradesman* (1748), and the saying afterward came into wide use. Among those who quoted or adapted the maxim were George Washington (1797, in his writings), James Fenimore Cooper (1823, *The Pioneers*), Charles Dickens (1839, *Nicholas Nickelby*; 1841, *Barnaby Rudge*), Lord Bulwer-Lytton (1840, *Money*; 1863, *Caxtoniana*), Mark Twain (1873, *The Gilded Age*), Oscar Wilde (1894, *Phrases for the Young*), James Joyce (1922, *Ulysses*), and the detective story writer Erle Stanley Gardner (1952, *Top of the Heap*). "Time is money" has been quoted in print frequently during the twentieth century.

Times change and we with them.   The Roman emperor and philosopher Marcus Aurelius wrote in *Meditations* (c. 174), "Everything changes. Thou thyself art undergoing a continuous change." Similarly, the medieval German King Lothair I (a grandson of Charlemagne) is believed to have said, "All things change and we change with them" (c. 840), and a later medieval text titled *Gesta Romanorum* (c. 1440) made the more cynical observation, "Times change and men deteriorate." The English dramatist John Lyly rendered the saying in *Euphues, The Anatomy of Wit* (1579) as "The tymes are chaunged ... and wee are chaunged in the times." The exact wording of the current version finally appeared in Giovanni Torriano's *A Common Place of Italian Proverbs and Proverbial Phrases* (1666). The proverb has been quoted in print infrequently during the twentieth century.

To bite off more than you can chew.   Used metaphorically to describe times when we take more than we can possibly handle (chew in one mouthful), the expression is at least related to an early English saying that appeared in *Brut* (c. 1200) by the Middle English poet Layamon: "The man is a fool who takes to himself more than he can manage" ("The mon is muchel sot The nimeth to him-seoluen Mare thonne he mayen wolden"). Later, Chaucer noted in *Melibeus* (c. 1386), "He that to muche embraceth, distreyneth litel," and Sir Thomas Urquhart in his translation of *Rabelais* (1653) rendered the saying, "He that gripes [grips] too much, holds fast but little." The current expression probably did not come about until the nineteenth century, however, and the earliest known version of it appeared in a book called *Chinese Vocabulary* (1872), which contained the English translation, "If you bite off too much you can't chew it thoroughly." The expression next appeared in John H. Beadle's *Western Wilds* (1877) as "Men, you've bit off more'n you can chaw." In *Pygmalion* (1912), George Bernard Shaw noted "the mistake we describe metaphorically as 'biting off more than they can chew.'" Shaw adapted the expression again in *Heartbreak House* (1913), and James Joyce repeated it in *Ulysses* (1922).

To bite the hand that feeds you.   No doubt an expression particularly familiar to those given to ingratitude, this one was apparently first recorded in 1711 by the English writer Joseph Addison as "He will bite the Hand that feeds him" in one of his contributions to the *Spectator*. Later that century, the statesman and author Edmund Burke noted in *Thoughts on the Cause of the Present Discontents* (1770): "We set ourselves to bite the hand that feeds us." Adapting the expression in a second work, *Thoughts and Details on Scarcity* (1795), Burke wrote, "And having looked to Government for bread, on the very first scarcity they will turn and bite the hand that fed them." The American statesman Alexander Hamilton wrote in his correspondence of 1792, "It is thought ungrateful for a man to bite the hand that puts bread in his mouth." The expression has been repeated or adapted regularly in the twentieth century, notably by Irish writer Liam O'Flaherty in *Martyr* (1933, "A cur bites the hand that feeds him") and with a clever turn by Elizabeth Dean in *Murder Is a Collector's Item* (1939, "Feeling as though he had been bitten by the hand that was feeding him"). But the award for the most "biting" wit here belongs to Mark Twain, who wrote in *Pudd'nhead Wilson's Calendar* (1893), "If you pick up a starving dog and make him prosperous, he will not bite you. This is the principal difference between a dog and a man."

To burn your bridges.   A now familiar caution against leaving yourself without any alternative (or avenue of retreat) in the event of failure, this expression apparently originated in the twentieth century. The earliest known citation appeared in Aleister Crowley's *Confessions of Aleister Crowley* (1923) as "She wouldn't burn her bridges." The English-born American writer Talbot Mundy included the line, "If I burn all my bridges," in his adventure story *Om* (1923), and among other subsequent references was "He had burned every bridge to his past" in Edwin P. Hoyt's *Horatio's Boys* (1974).

To cut off your nose to spite your face.   *See* **Don't cut off your nose to spite your face.**

To each his own.   Each person has a right to individual likes and dislikes according to this maxim, an early version of which first appeared in John Lyly's *Euphues and His England* (1580) as "Euery one as he lyketh." William Shakespeare included the Latin "*Suum cuique* [To every man his own]" in *Titus Andronicus* (1593), and Randle Cotgrave's *A Dictionary of the French and English Tongues* (1611) rendered the version, "Every one as hee likes." Two centuries after that, Lord Bulwer-Lytton declared in *The Caxtons* (1849), "Every man to his taste in the Bush." Though it was probably in use much earlier, the modern wording of "To each his own" was recorded in Benjamin Benson's *Silver Cobweb* (1955). The maxim was adapted by Irving Wallace (1960, *The Chapman Report*), among others.

To kill the goose that laid the golden egg.   Used metaphorically for people who want to get rich too quickly, this expression came to us from one of Aesop's *Fables*, written in the sixth century B.C. Aesop's story told of a poor man whose goose one day began laying golden eggs. Impatient for still greater riches, and supposing the goose had a horde of golden eggs in its belly, the man slit the bird open to find nothing more than the innards of a normal—and now very dead—goose. The first English rendering of the fable appeared in the fifteenth-century *Aesope* (1484), a translation published by William Caxton, the first English printer. Almost a century later, the lexicographer John Florio wrote in his grammar *Florio His First Fruites* (1578), "There be many that wyl have both the egge and the hen," and the dramatist John Lyly recounted the tale in his tract *Pappe With a Hatchet* (1589): "A man . . . kild his goose, thinking to haue a mine of golde in her bellie, and finding nothing but dung . . . wisht his goose aliue."

The saying, "Gone is the goose that the great egg laid," was included in James Kelly's *A Complete Collection of Scotish Proverbs* (1721), and a letter written by Benjamin Franklin (1768) gave us essentially the current wording: "To kill the goose which lays the golden eggs." The expression has been in regular use up to the present day, and among the noted writers who have adapted it are Thomas Jefferson (1781, in correspondence), novelist Sir Walter Scott (1824, *St. Ronan's Well*), and American philosopher Henry David Thoreau (1860, in his journal).

To lengthen thy life, lessen thy meals.   Here is a proverb that anticipated by centuries part of the message that modern-day medical experts have been touting for the past few decades—you will live longer if you eat less (today we also have to exercise and watch what we eat). The Roman poet Ovid rendered one of the earliest such advisories on eating in *Artis Amatoriae* (c. 1 B.C.), "Stop short of your appetite; eat less than you are able." Given what one reads about gluttony in Roman times, this must have been a radical point of view for some, but the *Babylonian Talmud* (c. 450) recommended an even more severe regimen, "Eat a third [oe what your stomach will hold], drink a third, leave a third empty." The Muslim *Sunnah* (c. 630) warned, "Kill not your hearts with excess of eating and drinking."

The earliest such advice in English appeared as a rhyme in John Heywood's *A Dialogue Conteinyng the Nomber in Effect of All the Prouerbes in the Englishe Tongue* (1546): "Temprance teacheth this, where he kepeth scoole, / He that knoweth whan he enough is no foole. / Feed by measure, and defie the physician, / And in the contrary marke this condition, / A swyne ouer fatte is cause of his owne bane, / Who seeth nought herein, his wit is in the wane." *Civile Conversation* (1574) by Stephen Guazzo stated the case more simply with "The lesse one eates, the more he eates. I meane he liveth longer to eat more." Simpler still was "Feed sparingly and defy the physician," which appeared in John Ray's *A Collection of English Proverbs* (1670). The exact wording of the current version was rendered in Benjamin Franklin's *Poor Richard's Almanack* (1733), and though restraint at mealtime was probably good advice, it was never easy or popular. Not surprisingly, the saying has been quoted in print only infrequently.

To put the cart before the horse. The Greek satirist Lucian noted in his *Dialogues of the Dead* (c. 180), "The cart often draws the ox," which is to say that things sometimes do get out of the natural order. The medieval Englishman Dan Michel in his *Ayenbite of Inwyt* (c. 1340)—a translation of a French work—included the passage, "Moche uolk of religion zetteth the zuols be-uore the oksen," while Richard Whitinton in *Vulgaria* (c. 1520) criticized a similar tendency among teachers: "That techer setteth the carte before the horse that preferreth imitacyon before preceptes." About the same time, the philosopher Sir Thomas More wrote, "Muche like as if we woulde go make the carte to drawe the horse" (1529); the French satirist Rabelais rendered the expression in *Gargantua* (1534) as "He would put the plow before the oxen"; and the Dutch scholar Desiderius Erasmus included it in *Apophthegms* (1542) as "The tale...also setteth the carte before the horses." In 1589, the English courtier George Puttenham wrote in *Arte of English Poesie*, "We call it in English prouerbe, the cart before the horse." Not long after, William Shakespeare asked in *King Lear* (1605), "May not an ass know when the cart draws the horse?" Thus established, the expression subsequently appeared in collections of proverbs and has been quoted regularly up to the present day.

In the United States, Ben Franklin gave us the witty adaptation, "Some People always ride before the Horse's Head" (1773). A year later, the young James Madison used the expression to describe an embarrassing but not uncommon difficulty: "He put the Cart before the horse: he was a father before he was a husband." Among the other notable writers who used the expression were Thomas Paine in *Remarks* (1804), Washington Irving in *History of New York* (1809), Robert Louis Stevenson in *Catronia* (1893), and, more recently the American detective story writer Erle Stanley Gardner in *Dubious* (1954). Lastly, and perhaps reflecting the uncertainties of the 1960s, English writer Leonard Woolf observed in his autobiography *Downhill All the Way* (1967), "The real question...is: which was the cart and which the horse?"

To wash dirty linen in public. Napoleon Bonaparte is believed to have originated this expression during a speech before France's Legislative Assembly, following his return in 1815 from exile on the island of Elba. "It is at home, not in public, one

washes one's dirty linen," Napoleon reminded his listeners. Some
years later, the English statesman and author Thomas Macaulay
wrote in his *Essays* (1842), " 'See,' exclaimed Voltaire, 'what a
quantity of his dirty linen the king sends me to wash,' " and
Anthony Trollope in *the Last Chronicle of Barset* (1867) wrote that
"there is nothing, I think, so bad as washing one's dirty linen in
public." Oscar Wilde, in *The Importance of Being Earnest* (1895),
gave the expression a witty turn with "The amount of women in
London who flirt with their husbands is perfectly scandalous. It
looks so bad. It is simply washing one's clean linen in public."

**Toad beneath the harrow knows where each tooth point
goes, A.**   This grimly humorous saying tells us that the person
getting run over in a raw deal (the toad) is in the best position
to know exactly where he or she is being hurt. Originally a medieval Latin saying with a broader meaning, it was first recorded
in *Political Songs John to Edward II* (c. 1290) as "Said the toad
under the hurdle, 'Curses upon all masters.' " Almost a century
later, the English religious reformer John Wycliffe rendered a
similar sentiment in *English Works* (c. 1380) with the saying, "The
frog seide to the harwe, cursed be so many lordis." Thomas
Fuller's *Gnomologia: Adagies and Proverbs* (1732) gave the saying
as "Many Masters, quoth the Toad to the Harrow, when every
Tine turned her over," a version repeated in essentially that form
by Sir Walter Scott (1818, *Rob Roy*). Another variant, "To live
like a toad under a harrow," was included in *Teesdale Glossary*
(1849) with the note, "an expression denoting extreme personal
wretchedness." The modern version was rendered by Rudyard
Kipling in *Pagett, M. P.* (1886): "The toad beneath the harrow
knows / Exactly where each tooth-point goes; / The butterfly upon
the road / Preaches contentment to that toad." Quoted in print
frequently during the twentieth century, the saying was repeated
or adapted by, among others, the detective writer Dorothy Sayers
(1936, *Gaudy Night*) and P. G. Wodehouse (1958, *Cocktail Time*).

Tomorrow is another day.   A familiar bromide usually heard
at the end of a trying or very busy day, it says, in effect, that
there will be time tomorrow for a fresh start, or for completing
whatever work remains to be done. The earliest version appeared
as a line in the sixteenth-century play *Calisto and Meliboea* (c. 1520)
by an unknown author: "Well, mother, to-morrow is a new day."
This version apparently came into wide use, being repeated by,
among others, the English poet and playwright John Lyly (1594,

Mother Bombie), John Florio (1603, *Montaigne*), the satirist Jonathan Swift (1738, *Polite Conversation*), and Sir Walter Scott (1824, *St. Roman's Well*).

Virtually the modern wording of the saying, "Tomorrow will be another day," was recorded in Charles Cahier's *Six Mille Proverbes* (1856), and the exact wording apparently was first recorded a half century later in Earl D. Biggers *Seven Keys to Baldpate* (1913). The saying has been quoted in print frequently during the twentieth century.

Tongue returns to the sore tooth, The.   Anyone with a toothache knows the literal truth of this old saying, but the proverb actually refers to the habit people have of talking about whatever is bothering them at the time. A translation of Stefano Guazzo's *Civile Conversation* (1574) recorded the first English version of the saying as "The tongue rolles there where the teeth aketh." Almost a century later, James Howell's *Proverbs in English, Italian, French and Spanish* (1659) gave the saying, "Where the tooth pain, the toung is commonly upon it," and a version closer to the modern, "The Tongue is ever turning to the aching Tooth," appeared in Thomas Fuller's *Gnomologia: Adagies and Proverbs* (1732). Benjamin Franklin repeated the latter version in *Poor Richard's Almanack* (1746). A similar version, "The tongue touches where the tooth aches," was rendered by the American James Paulding in a letter of 1816, who noted the saying meant "that people are apt to talk of what annoys them most at the moment." Though it was probably in use earlier, the exact wording of the current version appeared in William Krasner's *Walk the Dark Streets* (1949). The proverb has appeared in print only infrequently during the twentieth century.

Too many cooks spoil the broth.   "Broth" here is a metaphor for any sort of undertaking, while the cooks are those who will have a say in how it is to be done (and who will presumably ruin things because of their conflicting opinions). Apparently already a common proverb in the sixteenth century, the saying was first recorded in John Hooker's *Life of Sir Peter Carew* (c. 1580) as "The more cookes the worse pottage."

The closest wording to our current version appeared the next century in Sir Balthazar Gerbier's *Principles of Building* (1662), which rendered it, "Too many cooks spoils the broth." The proverb was later repeated or adapted by, among others, Jane Austen (1804, *The Watsons*), Mark Twain (1869, *The Innocents Abroad*),

P. G. Wodehouse (1914, *Little Nugget*), and James Joyce (1922, *Ulysses*). "Too many cooks..." has been quoted in print frequently during the twentieth century.

Trouble shared is a trouble halved, A.   About the only thing worse than trouble itself is trying to endure it all alone. That is not to say one should pass off the responsibility on others when things go wrong, but there is no better way to ease the burden and sort through solutions than by talking out a problem with a friend. Perhaps the earliest saying in this regard was recorded by the Spanish Jesuit Baltasar Gracian in *Oraculo Manual* (1647): "Search out some one to share your troubles."

Interestingly, neither this saying nor, apparently, any variants of it appeared in collections of proverbs published subsequently in the eighteenth and nineteenth centuries. In fact, the current saying "A trouble shared..." seems to have sprung up whole in a line from the 1931 detective novel *Suspicious Characters* by Dorothy Sayers. The saying was later quoted in Burton Stevenson's *Home Book of Proverbs, Maxims, and Familiar Phrases* (1948) and was repeated outside collections of proverbs as well. By the 1950s, one mention of the saying even referred to it as an "old adage."

Truth is not to be spoken at all times, The.   The Greek poet Pindar wisely observed in *Nemean Odes* (c. 485 B.C.), "Not every truth is better for having its face unveiled." Centuries later came an early English version by the religious reformer John Wycliffe, who wrote in *English Works* (c. 1380), "Sumtyme it harmeth men to seie the sothe [truth demonstrated] out of couenable tyme." This sentiment was echoed in *Parlament of Byrdes* (c. 1550) with the rhyme, "All soothes be not for to saye, / It is better some be lefte by reason / Than truth to be spoken out of season." The French moralist Michel de Montaigne noted in *Essays* (1580), "A man must not always tell the whole truth," and in the next century George Herbert's *Jacula Prudentum* (1640) included the saying, "All truths are not to be told." The exact wording of the current version appeared in a pamphlet printed in the American colonies (1764), and was repeated with a slight difference in wording by John Quincy Adams (1798, in his writings). Sir Walter Scott also quoted the proverb in his journal (1827) and Thomas C. Haliburton adapted it in *The Old Judge, or Life in a Colony* (1843).

Truth will out.   Perhaps this is true because at least a few people always seem to be looking for the truth. As to the maxim itself, Richard Taverner's *Proverbes or Adagies* (1539) rendered the earliest words in this vein with "The thyng that good is (as trouth and justice) thoughe it be suppressed and kepte and vnder for a tyme . . . at length wyll breake out agayne." Another sixteenth-century work, *Wealth & Health* (1558) stated the case more succinctly with "Truth wyll appeare," and by the end of the century, William Shakespeare rendered the exact wording of the maxim in a passage from *The Merchant of Venice* (1596): "Murder cannot be hid long—a man's son may, but in the end truth will out." The English dramatist Ben Jonson (1633, *Tale of a Tub*) and the American essayist Henry David Thoreau (1851, in his journal) both rendered their own versions of this saying, and Herman Melville (1857, *The Confidence Man: His Masquerade*) and others quoted the current version. The parallel saying "Murder will out," which today amounts to a credo of detective fiction, appeared even earlier than "Truth will out." Chaucer apparently recorded this saying in the *Nun's Priest's Tale* (c. 1390) as "Mordre wol out."

Turnabout is fair play. This saying is usually invoked by those who have been waiting for a chance to pay back someone else's lack of consideration (or, alternatively, who have been waiting for a chance to have the advantage at some enterprise). The modern form of the saying was first recorded in *The Life of Captain Dudley Bradstreet* (1755), and was later repeated by, among others, John Quincy Adams (1823, *Memoirs*), and Robert Louis Stevenson (1892, *The Wrecker*). The saying remains current in the twentieth century.

Two can live as cheaply as one. A now familiar, fanciful deflection of financial worries, this saying was once (and perhaps still is) conjured up by lovers as they approached the altar. The idea, if ever true of itself, ignored age-old marital mathematics, namely that one plus one equals not two, but three or more. The saying itself apparently originated in this century, appearing first in Ring Lardner's *Big Town* (1921), though it may have been in use already. Interestingly, references challenging the truth of this saying began to appear in the late 1930s, and today the saying probably should be rewritten. After all, it now takes two incomes to live as cheaply as one person once did.

Two heads are better than one. The Greek philosopher Aristotle (whose own head was probably better than a dozen) wrote in *Politics* (c. 330 B.C.), "Two good men are better than one."

Centuries later, the English poet John Gower recorded the earliest English version in *Confessio Amantis* (c. 390) with the line, "Two have more wit than one." About a century and a half later, the exact wording of the modern version appeared in John Heywood's *A Dialogue Conteinyng the Number in Effect of All the Prouerbes in the Englishe Tongue* (1546). The proverb has been quoted in print frequently during the twentieth century, and among those who have repeated or adapted it were Edgar Rice Burroughs (1930, *Fighting Man of Mars*), the detective story writer Erle Stanley Gardner (1949, *Case of the Dubious Bridegroom*), Agatha Christie (1951, *They Came to Baghdad*), and P. G. Wodehouse (1960, *Jeeves*).

Two is company and three is a crowd. Here is a saying for lovers and others who want to get rid of a third person so that they can talk privately between themselves. Originally, the proverb was rendered as "Company consisting of three is worth nothing," in J. Stevens's *A New Spanish and English Dictionary* (1706). The English writer Thomas C. Haliburton mentioned, "Three is a very inconvenient limitation, constituting... no company," in *The Season Ticket* (1860), and W. Carew Hazlitt's *English Proverbs* (1869) renders the saying as "Two is company, but three is none." Although the latter form has remained in use, the more common "Two is company and three is a crowd" was apparently first quoted in Joseph C. Lincoln's *Cap'n Eri* (1904). Adapted by James Joyce (1922, *Ulysses*), among others, the saying has been quoted in print frequently during the twentieth century.

Two wrongs do not make a right. This familiar proverb means that when people wrong you, you are not necessarily justified in repaying the disservice by doing some wrong to them. What so often complicates matters, though, is that "getting even" *feels* so right, even though we may know we are being childish or small about it (compare **Revenge is sweet**). The earliest known version of "Two wrongs..." appeared in a letter written (1783) by the American statesman and physician Benjamin Rush, who noted, "Three wrongs will not make one right." A few years later, a letter written to Aaron Burr (1802) included the line, "If two wrongs could make one right, this account might be squared," and virtually the exact wording of the current version appeared in Jacob Kerr's *The Several Trials of the Reverend David Barclay*

(1814, "Two wrongs don't make one right"). The saying was later quoted or adapted by, among others, the English novelist Thomas C. Haliburton (1840, *The Clockmaker, or Sayings and Doings of Sam Slick*) and James Joyce (1922, *Ulysses*). *See also* **An eye for an eye.**

United we stand, divided we fall.   A maxim that arose during the years before the American Revolution, this saying originally appeared as a line in John Dickinson's *Liberty Song*, first published in the *Boston Gazette* (1768): "Then join hand in hand, brave Americans all. / By uniting we stand, by dividing we fall!" In other writings that same year, Dickinson penned a somewhat different version of the maxim, "United we conquer, divided we die," and it fell to the American statesman Elbridge Gerry to record the exact wording of the version we know today in his correspondence (1772). As might be expected, "United we stand..." was quoted frequently during the Revolution and in the years afterward. Most Americans today recognize the maxim as part of their national heritage.

Variety is the spice of life.   The Greek playwright Euripides observed in *Orestes* (c. 410 B.C.), "Variety is sweet in all things," and centuries later, Richard Taverner's *Proverbes or Adagies* (1539) rendered the first English version in the blandly worded "Man is much delyted wyth varietie." A restrained version, "Variety is pleasant," appeared in *Holland's Leaguer* (1632), but it was the English poet William Cowper whose seasoned hand finally provided the missing spice; "Variety's the very spice of life, / That gives it all its flavour." The lines appeared in *The Task* (1784). The saying remains current in the twentieth century and has on occasion been adapted with a witty turn. In *Much Ado About Nothing* (1940), for example, Phyllis McGinley cleverly suggested, "Variety is the vice of wives."

Virtue is its own reward.   This lofty ideal first appeared in the Latin text of Ovid's *Tristia* (A.D. c. 11), though it was not until the sixteenth century that English sayings on the subject were recorded. Alexander Barclay's *Shyp of Folys* (1509) included the line, "Virtue hath no rewarde," and Edmund Spenser's *The Faerie Queene* (1596) wrote, "Your vertue selfe her owne reward shall breed." The dramatist and poet Ben Jonson rendered the saying as "Vertue...she being his owne reward," and Sir Thomas Browne observed in *Religio Medici* (1642), "Vertue is her own reward, is but a cold principle." The exact wording of the modern version first appeared as a line in John Dryden's *The Assignation* (1673), and the saying was later repeated or adapted by, among others, Tobias Smollett (1771, *The Expedition of Humphrey Clinker*), John Adams (1786, in correspondence), Sir Walter Scott (1827, in his journal), Thomas Carlyle (1828, *Miscellanies*), Ralph Waldo Emerson (1841, *Essays*), Charles Dickens (1850, *Martin Chuzzlewit*), and Louisa May Alcott (1868, *Little Women*). The saying has been quoted in print frequently during the twentieth century.

Voice of the people is the voice of God, The.   Originally a Latin proverb, this saying was recorded in Latin by the English scholar Alcuin in *Admonitio ad Carolum Magnum* (c. 800). But Alcuin doubted the proverb, declaring that "the voice of the people is near akin to madness." Though the Latin *Vox populi, vox dei* continued in use up to the twentieth century, the first English version was recorded in Thomas Hoccleve's *Regiment of Princes* (c. 1412) as "Peples vois is goddes voys." The exact wording of the modern version appeared soon after in Thomas Wright's *Political Poems* (1450). Although the saying was used with some frequency thereafter (in one form or another), writers continued to voice some skepticism. Francis Bacon allowed in *De Augmentis Scientiarum* (1605), "The voice of the people hath some divineness in it," but the American statesman Alexander Hamilton complained in a speech before the Federal Convention

(1787) that the proverb "is not true in fact. The people . . . seldom judge or determine right." William Tecumseh Sherman was even less forgiving in a letter to his wife (1863): "The voice of the people is the voice of humbug." Despite such misgivings, the proverb has nevertheless been quoted in print frequently during the twentieth century, including one instance by George Bernard Shaw (1914, *Misalliance*).

Walls have ears.   A Judaic scriptural commentary called the *Babylonian Talmud* (c. 450) apparently recorded this proverb for the first time in the passage, "They hold counsel only in the open fields for, says the Rashi, 'walls have ears.' " The poet George Gascoigne rendered an early, approximate English version in *Supposes* (1573) with "The tables . . . beds, portals, yea and the cupboards themselves have eares," and later that century in *A Midsummer Night's Dream* (c. 1594), William Shakespeare penned, "No remedy, my lord, when walls are so willful to hear without warning." In 1592, G. Delamothe's *The French Alphabet* gave the saying as "The walles may have some eares," and the English satirist John Harington (banished from Queen Elizabeth's court because of his ribald tales) wrote in *No-body and Somebody* (c. 1600), "There is a way: but walls have earrs and eyes." Thomas Shelton's translation of *Don Quixote* (1620) rendered the saying in the modern form ("They say walls have ears"), as did playwright James Shirley in *The Bird in a Cage* (1633).

   Since then the saying has been in regular use. Among the writers who quoted it were Jonathan Swift in *Polite Conversations* (1738), the dramatist William Wycherly in *Love in a Wood* (1672), Sir Walter Scott *Fortunes of Nigel* (1822), James Joyce in *Ulysses* (1922), and the American novelists J. P. Marquand in *The Late George Apley* (1937) and John O'Hara in *Ourselves* (1960).

Waste not, want not.   Thomas Fuller's *Gnomologia: Adagies and Proverbs* (1732) rendered this familiar maxim as "Waste makes want," and later that century, a letter (1772) written by John

Wesley, the founder of Methodism, recorded a similar sentiment with "He will waste nothing; but he must want nothing." The exact wording of the current version appeared some years afterward in Maria Edgeworth's *The Poet's Assistant* (1800). The maxim was subsequently repeated by, among others, the English novelist Charles Kingsley (1855, *Westward Ho!*), Thomas Hardy (1872, *Under the Greenwood Tree*), the American writer Thorne Smith (1932, *Topper Takes a Trip*), and the English writer Anthony Burgess (1962, *The Wanting Seed*).

Watched pot never boils, A.   Worry not, the laws of physics remain intact: A pot will in fact boil even if you watch, but it will *seem* to take forever, and that is really the point of this amusing proverb. So if you must wait for something to happen, take your mind off the waiting by doing something else. It's amazing how much faster "the pot" seems to reach a boil. As for the saying itself, the English novelist Elizabeth Gaskell first rendered it in *Mary Barton* (1848), giving the exact wording of the current version. The saying was later repeated in Alan B. Cheales's *Proverbial Folk-Lore* (1875) and has been quoted or adapted frequently during the twentieth century.

Way to a man's heart is through his stomach, The.   The evolution of this saying appears to be almost as indirect as the route to a man's heart. The American statesman John Adams wrote in a letter (1814), "The shortest road to men's hearts is down their throats," and some years later Richard Ford's *A Handbook for Travellers in Spain* (1845) advised, "The way to many an honest heart lies through the belly." A few years later, Miss Mulock observed in *John Halifax, Gentleman* (1857) that the stomach was the way to an Englishman's heart. Fifteen years after that, the writer Fanny Fern broadened the idea to include all men in *Willis Parton* (c. 1872), rendering the saying in its current form. Among those who later repeated the saying were Ring Lardner (1921, *Big Town*). Finally, in a last twist, the detective writer Erle Stanley Gardner turned the saying upside down in *The Case of the Drowsy Mosquito* (1943), creating a clever new truism: "The way to a man's stomach is through his heart." After all, many's the man who endured burned toast—and worse—for the sake of love.

What a neighbor gets is not lost.   Earlier versions of this saying mentioned friends instead of neighbors, as in *Mary Magdalene* (1566) by Lewis Wager: "There is nothyng lost that is done for such a friende." James Kelly's *A Complete Collection of Scotish Proverbs* (1721) echoed that sentiment a century and a half later with "It is no tint [not lost], a friend gets." The exact wording of the current version was recorded in *Beast and Man* (1891) by John L. Kipling, father of the writer Rudyard Kipling. The proverb has been quoted in print only infrequently during the twentieth century.

What can you expect from a hog but a grunt?   An expression used to register disapproval of an ill-mannered or otherwise loutish person, this saying was first recorded in *Poor Robin Almanack* (1731) as "If we petition a Hog, what can we expect but a grunt." Sir Walter Scott rendered another version a century later in his journal (1827), while complaining about a financial matter: "What can be expected of a sow but a grumph?" H. G. Bohn's *Handbook of Proverbs* (1855) replaced the "grunt" with "bristles," in "What can you expect of a hog but his bristles?" The exact wording of the modern version appeared about a half century later in F. E. Hulme's *Proverb Lore* (1902). The saying has been quoted in print infrequently during the twentieth century.

What can't be cured must be endured.   In *Sententiae* (c. 43 B.C.), the Roman writer Pubilius Syrus rendered an early version of this saying as "What you cannot change, you should bear as it comes." Centuries later, *Piers the Plowman* (1377) by William Langland conjured up a grimmer scene with "When *Must* comes forward, there is nothing for it but to *Suffer*." Edmund Spenser's *The Shepheardes Calender* (1579) advised, "Such il as is forced mought nedes be endured," and William Shakespeare adapted the saying in *The Merry Wives of Windsor* (1601) with the line, "What cannot be eschew'd must be embraced." Robert Codrington's *A Collection of Many Select and Excellent Proverbs* (1664) gave a version closer to the modern, "That which cannot be cured, must with patience be endured." The exact wording appeared later in the seventeenth century in John Ray's *A Collection of English Proverbs* (1670). Among the writers who later quoted or adapted the saying were Tobias Smollett (1771, *The Expedition of Humphrey Clinker*), Charles Dickens (1837, *The Pickwick Papers*), Andrew Jackson (1833, in correspondence), Thomas C. Haliburton (1853, *Wise Saws and Modern Instances*), George Bernard Shaw (1904, *John Bull's Other Island*), and Agatha Christie (1953, *Pocket Full of Rye*).

What goes up must come down.   The coincidence in this case is almost too perfect: "What goes up . . . , a surprisingly recent invention, was apparently first recorded in 1929, the same year the stock market everyone thought would keep going up and up, finally came tumbling down in the Great Crash of 1929. Though the saying may well have been in use beforehand, Frederick A. Pottle's *Stretchers* (1929) apparently recorded it for the first time, and in the current form. Norman Mailer (1949, *The Naked and the Dead*) was among the writers who later quoted the saying. And Fred J. Singer complained in *Epigrams at Large* (1967) that the saying was "really a time-worn statement which wore out after the Venus and Mars probes." With our exploration of outer space, what goes up now does not necessarily come down, however, "What goes up . . . " has continued in wide use.

What is yours is mine and what is mine is my own.   The original version of this saying was far more generous than its modern counterpart. The Roman playwright Plautus recorded the first, praiseworthy sentiment in *Trinummus* (c. 196 B.C.) with the line, "What's yours is mine, and of course all mine is yours." Later, perhaps anticipating the direction the modern saying was to take, the *Babylonian Talmud* (c. 450) declared, "He who says, What is yours is mine and what is mine is mine is a wicked man." The English writer George Pettie advised selflessness in *A Petite Pallace of Pettie His Pleasure* (1576) with "That which is mine should bee yours and yours your own," and in *Measure for Measure* (1604), William Shakespeare urged the more equitable, "What's mine is yours and what is yours is mine." Things took a turn toward the selfish with "What's mine is my own; what's my Brother's is his and mine," which appeared in Thomas Fuller's *Gnomologia: Adagies and Proverbs* (1732). Soon after, the exact wording of the unabashedly grasping, modern version was recorded in Jonathan Swift's *Polite Conversation* (1738). That was not the last or worst of it, however, because in the next century, Collis Huntington's *Epigram* (c. 1890) gave us this witty, albeit outlandishly selfish bit: "Whatever is not nailed down is mine. Whatever I can pry loose is not nailed down." "What is yours is mine . . . " has been quoted in print only infrequently during the twentieth century.

What must be must be.   This and the related "What will be will be" both probably stem from an earlier version, "That whiche muste be wyll be," which was recorded in W. Horman's *Vulgaria*

(1519). A few years later, the similar "That shalbe, shalbe" appeared in John Heywood's *A Dialogue Conteinyng the Number in Effect of All the Prouerbes in the Englishe Tongue* (1546). William Shakespeare wrote in *Romeo and Juliet* (c. 1595), "What must be shall be," and just over two decades later, the exact wording of the current version was recorded in Beaumont and Fletcher's *Scornful Lady* (1616). The saying was repeated by, among others, the founder of Methodism, John Wesley (1768, in correspondence) and more recently by Saki (H. H. Munro; 1914, *When William Came*). *See also* **What will be will be.**

What the eye does not see, the heart does not grieve.   The early form of this proverb, "That the eie seeth not, the hert rewth [rues] not," was first recorded in John Heywood's *A Dialogue Conteinyng the Number in Effect of All the Prouerbes in the Englishe Tongue* (1546). With some variation in wording (sometimes beginning with "what" instead of "that," for example), this version was repeated in such collections of proverbs as Thomas Draxe's *Bibliotheca Scholastica Instructissima, or A Treasurie of Ancient Adages* (1616), James Howell's *Proverbs in English, Italian, French and Spanish* (1659), and John Ray's *A Collection of English Proverbs* (1670). Meanwhile, the Spanish writer Miguel de Cervantes echoed the sentiment in *Don Quixote* (1615) with "If eyes don't see, [the] heart won't break," and William Penn, the founder of Pennsylvania, wrote in *No Cross, No Crown* (1669), "What the eye views not, the heart craves not, as well as rues not."

The exact wording of the current version appeared almost a century and a half later in J. L. Burckhardt's *Arabic Proverbs* (1817). Quoted in print frequently during the twentieth century, "What the eye does not see..." was repeated by, among others, James Joyce (1922, *Ulysses*), D. H. Lawrence (1928, *Lady Chatterley's Lover*), and William McFee (1928, *Pilgrims of Adversity*). *See also* **Out of sight, out of mind; What you don't know won't hurt you.**

What will be will be.   The saying, "That the whiche muste be wyll be," recorded for the first time in W. Horman's *Vulgaria* (1519), apparently gave rise to both the current maxim and the related "What must be must be." John Heywood's *A Dialogue Conteinyng the Number in Effect of All the Prouerbes in the Englishe Tongue* (1546) echoed that sentiment a few years later with "That shalbe, shalbe." Toward the end of the century, Christopher Marlowe's *The Tragedy of Dr. Faustus* (first performed 1588) gave a closer version in the line, "What doctrine call you this, Che sera, sera, What will be, shall be." The exact wording of the current saying appeared later in James Howell's *Proverbs in English, Italian, French and Spanish* (1659). "What will be..." was subsequently repeated by, among others, Charles Dickens in *David Copperfield* (1850). *See also* **What must be must be.**

What you don't know won't hurt you.   You certainly can't be upset by what you don't know, although in the long run not knowing about—and therefore not doing anything about—a problem may eventually lead to grief anyway. George Pettie's *A Petite Pallace of Pettie His Pleasure* (1576) recorded the earliest version of the proverb as "So long as I know it not, it hurteth mee not." Apparently, the saying was little used thereafter, however, until the early 1900s when it finally become widely used. A version close to the modern appeared in J. C. Lincoln's *Cy Whittaker* (1908) as "What they don't know won't hurt 'em," and the exact wording was rendered soon after in Earl D. Biggers's *Seven Keys to Baldpate* (1913). The proverb has been quoted in print frequently during the twentieth century. *See also* **Where ignorance is bliss, 'tis folly to be wise.**

What you never had, you don't miss.   [You cannot lose what you never had.] The current proverb may have derived from an earlier, parallel saying, "You cannot lose what you never had." The earlier proverb first appeared as "No man can lose what he never had" in *The Compleat Angler* (1653). This was an altogether appropriate beginning, considering all those fishermen's stories about the "big one" that got away. Over a century later, the English church reformer and founder of Methodism, John Wesley, repeated this version in a sermon (1788), but the saying did not gain wide currency thereafter.

In the twentieth century, *The Oxford Dictionary of English Proverbs* (1970) rendered the saying in revised form as "You cannot lose what you never had." But even this was a shade different from the modern version, which spoke of not missing what you never had and which apparently did not appear until the twentieth century. Though it may well have been in use earlier, the modern proverb was first recorded in Dorothy L. Sayers's *Documents in the Case* (1931), and in the current form. It has since been repeated in print, with some variation in wording.

When in doubt, don't.   According to Hoyle's *A Short Treatise on Whist* (1742), "When in doubt win the trick." Although winning is almost always agreeable, life often presents situations far more complex than those at cards, sometimes making it difficult to know what to do. Enter the current proverb, which probably will not help you get ahead of the game, but at times such caution may keep you from getting into more trouble than you already have. A recent invention, the saying was first recorded in J. C. Bridge's *Cheshire Proverbs* (1917) as "When in doubt, do nowt [nothing]." Bridge commented that the saying revealed "the cautious Cheshireman at his best." A few years later, Joseph S. Fletcher's *Annexation Society* (1925) advised, "When in doubt, count twenty before you act or speak," but it was Peter Cheyney's *This Man Is Dangerous* (1936) that recorded the exact wording of the current proverb. *See also* **Think before you speak.**

When in Rome, do as the Romans do.   Saint Ambrose apparently originated this proverb while advising Saint Augustine on what to do about observing different church practices when in Rome and Milan. In *Advice to St. Augustine* (387), Saint Ambrose wrote, "When I am at Rome, I fast on a Saturday. Follow the custom of the church where you are." Centuries later, the *Common-place Book* (c. 1530) by Richard Hills urged, "When thou art at Rome, do after the dome; / And when thou art els wher, do as they do ther." A few years later, Richard Taverner's *Erasmus' Adagies* (1552 edition) rendered the proverb as "When you art at Rome, do as they do at Rome," a sentiment echoed in one form or another by the Spanish writer Miguel de Cervantes (1615, *Don Quixote*), William Penn (1669, *No Cross, No Crown*), and Lord Byron (1817, *Beppo*). Virtually the exact wording of the current version was recorded by Herman Melville in *Typee: A Peep at Polynesian Life* (1846): "When at Rome do as the Romans do." The saying was later used in one form or another by Charlotte Brontë (1849, *Shirley*), Mark Twain (1880, *A Tramp Abroad*), and George Bernard Shaw (1905, *Major Barbara;* 1908, *Getting Married*), but it was Shaw who finally used the exact wording of the modern version in a radio address in 1932. "When in Rome..." has appeared in print frequently during the twentieth century.

When it rains in sunlight, the devil is beating his wife.   An amusing weather superstition that one writer attributed to the Normans, this proverb was recorded for the first time as "When it rains and the sun shines at the same time the devil is beating his wife," a version that appeared in Giovanni Torriano's *A Common Place of Italian Proverbs and Proverbial Phrases* (1666). Almost a century later, the English satirist Jonathan Swift gave an even more fantastic explanation, saying that rain and sunshine together meant "the devil was beating his wife behind the door with a shoulder of mutton." Lord Bulwer-Lytton repeated Swift's shoulder-of-mutton imagery in *Pelham* (1828), and Richard Inwards introduced yet another explanation for sunshowers: "If it rains while the sun is shining the devil is beating his grandmother. He is laughing and she is crying." The exact wording of the current version appeared in John Updike's *Couples* (1968). The proverb has been quoted in print only rarely during the twentieth century.

When poverty comes in at the door, love flies out the window.   Sad, but sometimes true, this proverb was first recorded by William Caxton in *The Game and Playe of the Chesse* (1474) as "Loue lasteth as longe as the money endureth." Richard Braithwait's *The English Gentlewoman* (1631) observed that "as poverty goes in at one doore, love goes out the other," and John Clarke's *Paroemiologia Anglo-Latina* (1639) gave the saying a still more fanciful turn with "When povertie comes in at doores, love leaps out at windows." The exact wording of the current version was recorded a few years later in Robert Codrington's *A Collection of Many Select and Excellent Proverbs* (1664). The proverb was repeated with slight variations during the eighteenth and nineteenth centuries, but was quoted in print only rarely during the twentieth century.

When the cat's away, the mice will play.   Perhaps the best proof of this familiar saying is an elementary school classroom on a day when the teacher is sick. Many are the substitute teachers who have dealt with a roomful of rambunctious children—the mice—while covering for an absent teacher—the cat. The Roman playwright Plautus gave an early rendering of the saying in *Persa* (c. 200 B.C.): "Sport as you may while the master's away." The first recorded English version, complete with the cat as a metaphor for authority, appeared in a manuscript from about 1470: "The mows [mouse] lordchypythe [plays the lord] ther a cat ys nawt." A century later, John Florio's *First Fruites* (1578) repeated the saying as "When the Cat is abroade, the Mise play," and soon after that, the English dramatist Thomas Dekker used essentially the modern version in *Batchelors Banquet* (1603): "When the cat's away the mouse will play." Similarly, close variants were rendered by John Ray's *A Collection of English Proverbs* (1670, "...the mice play") and in *Bleak House* by Charles Dickens (1852, "The cat's away and the mice they play"). Though probably in use beforehand, the exact wording was recorded in Isabella Banks's *Manchester Man* (1872). Repeated by James Joyce (1922, *Ulysses*), among others, the saying has been quoted in print frequently during the twentieth century.

When the cows lie down, it's a sign of rain. Not an uncommon belief in rural areas where there are cows, this notion does seem to have some truth to it—but only some. Cows (and cattle) can be seen lying down in the pasture before a rainstorm, but as often as not it is only some of them. Does that mean there is just a good chance of rain? Also, some cows stubbornly remain standing even while it is raining, which may or may not mean anything at all. Although the belief appears fairly common in the oral tradition, the saying has rarely been quoted in print. Among the collections of proverbs, only Bartlett Whiting's *Modern Proverbs and Proverbial Sayings* (1989) includes it. Whiting gives just a single citation (1957), which refers to the saying as an "old American proverb."

When the wine is in, the wit is out. Chaucer's contemporary, John Gower, wrote in *Confessio Amantis* (c. 1390), "For wher that wyn [wine] doth wit awei [away], / Wisdom hath loste the rihte weie [way]." A version closer to the modern, "When ale is in, wyt is out," was included in John Heywood's *A Dialogue Conteinyng the Nomber in Effect of All the Prouerbes in the Englishe Tongue* (1546). The exact wording of the current version was recorded just a few years later in Thomas Becon's *Catechesme* (1560), and in one form or another, the proverb appeared in many collections of proverbs, including Thomas Draxe's *Bibliotheca Scholastica Instructissima, or A Treasurie of Ancient Adages* (1616) and John Ray's *A Collection of English Proverbs* (1670). Among those who later repeated or adapted the saying were William Shakespeare (1598, *Much Ado About Nothing*), Henry Wadsworth Longfellow (1835, in his correspondence), and Charles Dickens (1839, *Nicholas Nickleby*) *See also* **In wine there is truth.**

When thieves fall out, honest men come to their own. The idea here is that an argument among thieves will expose their crimes and lead to the return of goods stolen from honest men.

The earliest version of the proverb, "When theeues fall out, true men come to their goode," was included in John Heywood's *A Dialogue Conteinyng the Nomber in Effect of All the Prouerbes in the Englishe Tongue* (1546). A version closer to the modern saying appeared in John Day's *The Blind-Beggar of Bednal-Green* (1600) as "When false thieves fall out true men come to their own." Later, the somewhat more explicit "When thieves fall out, then true men come to their goods again" was given in Giovanni Torriano's *A Common Place of Italian Proverbs and Proverbial Phrases* (1666).

Benjamin Franklin rendered the saying in *Poor Richard's Almanack* (1742) as "When Knaves fall out, honest Men get their goods: When Priests dispute, we come at the Truth," and Charles Dickens wrote in *Martin Chuzzlewit* (1844), "When rogues fall out, honest people get what they want." Though it was probably in use well beforehand, the exact wording of the current version was recorded about 1923 by Aleister Crowley. The proverb has been quoted in print frequently during the twentieth century, including one instance by Lincoln Steffens (1931, *Autobiography*).

When your neighbor's house is on fire, beware of your own.   This old proverb is fraught with dilemma. On the one hand, a fire next door could always spread to your own house, making it in your interest to go help the neighbor. But while you are away helping that unfortunate neighbor, your house may also catch fire and burn. Should you stay at home to protect your house, while your neighbor's is consumed by the fire? At the very least—and that is really the point here—you cannot stand idly by while your neighbor suffers, because the very same may happen to you. The Roman poet Horace posed the question in *Epistles* (20 B.C.) with the line, "Your own property is at stake when your neighbor's house is on fire," and the first mention of it in English appeared in William Horman's *Vulgaria* (1519) as "Whan my neybours house is a fyre, I can nat be out of thought for myne owne." John Clarke warned, "Look to thyself when thy neighbor's house is on fire," in *Paroemiologia Anglo-Latina* (1639), and a few years later, virtually the exact wording of the modern saying appeared as "When thy neighbor's house is on fire, beware of thine own," which was included in John Ray's *A Collection of English Proverbs* (1670). Among those who subsequently used the saying were the American colonial William Lee, who noted that "the prudent man" should not stand by "coldly" waiting until his own house caught fire (1768, in correspondence); and Thomas

Jefferson (1791, in his papers). The saying has been quoted in print only infrequently during the twentieth century.

Where ignorance is bliss, 'tis folly to be wise. [Ignorance is bliss.] The Greek dramatist Sophocles wrote in *Ajax* (c. 409 B.C.), "In knowing nothing is the sweetest life," a sentiment echoed centuries later by the Dutch scholar Erasmus in *Moriae Encomium* (1524) with "To know nothing is the happiest life." The current version of the saying first appeared as the last lines to *Ode on a Distant Prospect of Eton College* (1742), by the English poet Thomas Gray. A century later, the English poet Thomas Hood expanded on the thought in *Sentimental Journey From Islington to Waterloo Bridge* (1845): "Hys was the Blisse of Ignorance, but We, being born to bee learned, and unhappye withal, have noght but the Ignorance of Blisse." The saying was adapted by the detective story writer Erle Stanley Gardner in *The Case of the Drowsy Mosquito* (1943) and was repeated by Robert Penn Warren in *All the King's Men* (1946). The saying, shortened in recent years to "Ignorance is bliss," has been quoted in print only infrequently during the twentieth century.

Where there is a will, there is a way. A testimony to the fact that those with determination generally get what they are after, this saying dates back to the seventeenth century when George Herbert's *Jacula Prudentum* (1640) rendered it as "To him that will, ways are not wanting." The exact wording of the current version appeared over a century and a half later in the *New Monthly Magazine* (1822), and was repeated or adapted by, among others, Lord Bulwer-Lytton (1836, *The Caxtons*), James Fenimore Cooper (1845, *Satanstoe*), George Bernard Shaw (1903, *Man and Superman*; 1911, *Fanny's First Play*), the detective story writer Erle Stanley Gardner (1933, *The Case of the Sulky Girl*), and Wyndham Lewis (1940, in correspondence). "Where there is a will..." has been quoted in print frequently during the twentieth century. *See also* **If at first you don't succeed, try, try again.**

Where there is smoke, there is fire. Unfounded rumors are no harder to start today than they ever were, though they do seem to travel farther and faster. What this familiar proverb tells us, however, is that where there is suspicion, there must be some wrongdoing. In fact, the suspicion that there is truth in others' suspicions has been around for a long time. The Roman writer Pubilius Syrus, for example, wrote in *Sententiae* (c. 43 B.C.),

"Never, where there has been fire for any length of time, is smoke lacking." Centuries later, that sentiment was echoed in the saying, "There is no fyre without some smoke," which appeared in John Heywood's *A Dialogue Conteinyng the Number in Effect of All the Prouerbes in the Englishe Tongue* (1546). A few years later, John Florio transposed the elements in *Florio His Firste Fruites* (1578) to render the saying as "There is no smoke without some fire." In the seventeenth century, John Ray gave it as "No smoke without some fire" in *A Collection of English Proverbs* (1670) and included the note, "There is no strong rumour without some ground for it." Virtually the exact wording of the modern version was recorded (1773) in papers belonging to James Madison and read, "Where there is smoke there must be some fire." With slight variations, both this and the earlier "No smoke without some fire" have been in use up to the present day. Among the writers who repeated or adapted a form of the saying were Anthony Trollope (1869, *He Knew He Was Right*), William McFee (1932, *The Harbourmaster*), Agatha Christie (1942, *The Moving Finger*), and Erle Stanley Gardner (1942, *The Case of The Drowning Duck*). The proverb has been quoted in print frequently during the twentieth century.

While the grass grows, the horse starves. By using the metaphor of a starving horse waiting for its fodder to grow, this proverb warns us that our plans or hopes for the future may sometimes take too long to bring to fruit. First recorded in Latin, the saying was included in *Epigram* (c. 1238) by Simeon of Chieti as "While the grass grows, the horse dies." A century later, essentially the modern version appeared in a medieval English manuscript (c. 1350) as "While the grasse growes, the goode hors sterues [starves]." With minor variations in wording—one version substituted "steed" for "horse," for example—the saying was subsequently repeated in major collections of proverbs, including John Heywood's *A Dialogue Conteinyng the Nomber in Effect of All the Prouerbes in the Englishe Tongue* (1546), John Ray's *A Collection of English Proverbs* (1670), and Thomas Fuller's *Gnomologia: Adagies and Proverbs* (1732).

In addition, the saying was repeated or adapted by, among others, William Shakespeare (1600, *Hamlet*), the English writer Robert Burton (1621, *The Anatomy of Melancholy*), the satirist Jonathan Swift (1738, *Polite Conversation*), Andrew Jackson (1845, in correspondence), and George Bernard Shaw (1906, *The Doctor's*

Dilemma). The proverb has been quoted in print infrequently during the twentieth century.

While there is life, there is hope.   This proverb reminds us that no matter how bad the circumstances, as long as you are alive, you will always have hope and the chance somehow to make things better. A common saying in ancient times (when there was plenty to despair), the proverb was rendered in *Ad Atticum* (49 B.C.) by Cicero, who gave the Latin equivalent of the modern form. The first English version, "The sycke person whyle he hath lyfe, hath hope," appeared in *Proverbes or Adagies* (1539) by Richard Taverner, and the French writer Michel de Montaigne gave the saying in *Essays* (1580) as "All things . . . may be hoped for by a man as long as he is alive."

The exact wording of the current version was recorded in the next century by John Ray's *A Collection of English Proverbs* (1670). Among those who later repeated or adapted the saying were the poet and playwright John Gay (1728, *Fables*), James Fenimore Cooper (1821, *The Spy*), Thomas Carlyle (1841, *On Heroes and Hero Worship*), Robert Louis Stevenson (1888, *The Black Arrow*), and T. H. White (1939, *The Sword in the Stone*). The saying has been quoted in print frequently during the twentieth century.

Who marries for love without money has good nights and sorry days.   A raffish bit of rustic wisdom, this proverb reminds headstrong young lovers that there are practical as well as romantic considerations to marriage. The saying arose early in the seventeenth century as "Fy on Loue without Mony!" which appeared in John Wodroephe's *The Spared Houres of a Souldier* (1623). The exact wording of the current version was recorded a few years later in *Select Italian Proverbs* (1642) by Giovanni Torriano and was repeated in such collections of proverbs as John Ray's *A Collection of English Proverbs* (1670) and Thomas Fuller's *Gnomologia: Adagies and Proverbs* (1732). Repeated infrequently since then, the saying has been quoted in print only rarely during the twentieth century. *See also* **You can't live on love.**

Whom the gods love dies young.   *See* **Good die young, The.**

Wise man changes his mind, a fool never will, A.
Perseverance and determination are important in life, but as this proverb tells us, a wise man recognizes when he is wrong and changes accordingly. The English writer William Baldwin ap-

parently recorded the saying for the first time in *Beware the Cat* (1570) as "A wise man may in some things chaunge his opinion," and over a half century later, James Mabbe's *Celestina* (1631) provided the further explanation, "A wise man altereth his purpose, but a foole persevereth in his folly." Included in James Howell's *Proverbs in English, Italian, French and Spanish* (1659) as "The wise man changeth counsel, the fool perseveres," the saying was quoted in its current form by the playwright Richard Steele in one of his contributions to *The Spectator* (1711). Apparently not widely used since then, the saying has been quoted in print only infrequently during the twentieth century.

Woman can throw out more with a spoon than a man can bring in with a shovel, A.   The proverb talks about how easily a woman can spend money, compared to what a man can bring home in wages. The saying is similar to the earlier "A nice wife and a back door oft do make a rich man poor," the back door being the entrance (and exit) used by the tradespeople and servants who were once major household expenses. First recorded in the fifteenth century, it was included in James Clarke's *Paroemiologia Anglo-Latina* (1639) and James Kelly's *A Complete Collection of Scotish Proverbs* (1721), the latter giving the additional note, "The Wife will spend, and the Servants purloyn."

The current saying was apparently first recorded in Ralph Waldo Emerson's *Journal* (1831) as "A woman could throw out with a spoon faster than a man could throw in with a shovel." The woman's point of view was better represented in C. S. Burne's *Shropshire Folk-Lore* (1883): "Don't throw your property out through the door with a spade, while your husband is bringing it in through the window with a spoon." The exact wording of the current version of "A woman can throw out more . . ." was recorded in the *Bangor Daily News* (1957), though it was probably in use before then. The saying has not been quoted in print frequently during the twentieth century.

Woman's place is in the home, A.   Nowadays, this saying is virtually guaranteed to raise the hackles of liberation-minded American women, especially those who view marriage and home as a gilded cage. It was surely used by men as a means of keeping women "in their place" at home, but sayings of this type were almost always double-edged. Until recent times, the saying was also repeated by women to justify their then prevalent way of life and right to be supported by men, instead of going off to work. Whatever its uses, the notion of women staying at home was apparently quite old, though it was not quoted in written form with any frequency.

The earliest version appeared in *Seven Against Thebes* (467 B.C.) by the Greek dramatist Aeschylus, who wrote, "Let women stay at home and hold their peace." Perhaps the earliest English version was rendered in George Pettie's *Civile Conversation* (1574) as "A dishonest woman can not be kept in, and an honest ought not." In *Don Quixote* (1615), the Spanish writer Miguel de Cervantes penned the downright ghoulish "The respectable woman should have a broken leg and keep at home," and an English version rendered in the next century was no better. Thomas Fuller's *Gnomologia: Adagies and Proverbs* (1732) gave this variant as "A Woman is to be from her House three times: when she is Christened, Married and Buried." By comparison, the nineteenth-century "A woman's place is her own house, taking care of the children" (1844, *High Life* by J. Slick) seemed comparatively mild. Though it was probably in use earlier, the exact wording of the modern version appeared in R. A. J. Walling's *The Corpse With the Dirty Face* (1936). A few years later, Agatha Christie railed against the saying in *The Moving Finger* (1942), calling it a "silly old-fashioned prejudice" and thereby heralding changed attitudes that came in the next decades.

Woman's work is never done, A.   The English agricultural writer Thomas Tusser recorded the earliest version of this familiar adage as "Some respit to husbands the weather may send, / But huswives affaires have never an end," which appeared in *Five Hundreth Pointes of Good Husbandrie* (1573). The modern wording was quoted some years later in a passage from *The Roxburghe Ballads* (c. 1655): "Man's work lasts till set of sun, / Woman's work is never done." John Ray's *A Collection of English Proverbs* (1670) rendered the saying as "Woman's work is never at an end," while James Kelly's *A Complete Collection of Scotish Proverbs* (1721) quoted it as "Women's work is never done." The current version was repeated by Benjamin Franklin (1722) in his correspondence. Quoted in print frequently during the twentieth century, the maxim was used by the English novelist C. S. Lewis (1948, in correspondence), among others.

Word to the wise is sufficient, A.   The Roman playwright Plautus wrote in *Persa* (c. 200 B.C.), "A word to the wise is enough," a sentiment echoed centuries later by Thomas à Kempis with

"To the intelligent man a word is enough," which appeared in *De Imiatione Christi* (c. 1420). A closer version, "Fewe woord is to the wise suffice to be spoken," was rendered in John Heywood's *A Dialogue Conteinyng the Nomber in Effect of All the Prouerbes in the Englishe Tongue* (1546). Early in the next century, William Camden's *Remaines Concerning Britaine* (1614) gave the saying as "Few words to the wise suffice," while Roger Williams, a clergyman and founder of Rhode Island, apparently recorded the exact wording of the modern version for the first time in 1676. The saying was later repeated or adapted by, among others, Joseph Addison (1711, contribution to *The Spectator*), Benjamin Franklin (1729, in his writings; 1757, *Poor Richard's Almanack*), James Madison (1780, in his writings), Thomas Jefferson (1786, in his writings), George Washington (1789, in his writings), Laurence Sterne (1794, *A Sentimental Journey*), John Adams (1819, Latin form, in his writings), Sir Walter Scott (1819, *Bride of Lammermoor*), Andrew Jackson (1828, in correspondence), Charles Dickens (1841, *The Old Curiosity Shop*), John O'Hara (1934, *Appointment in Samarra*), and Isaac Asimov (1950, *Pebble in the Sky*). The proverb has been quoted in print frequently during the twentieth century.

Workman is as good as his tools, A.   According to this proverb, the workman whose tools are worn, dull, or inadequate for the job can be expected to do shoddy work. The point is that if he cannot take care of his tools, which are so important to his livelihood, he is not likely to be much concerned about doing a good job, either. What was probably the earliest version of this proverb was recorded in *The Art of Angling* (1577) as "Like workman, like tool," while about this time John Heywood's *A Dialogue Conteinyng the Nomber in Effect of All the Prouerbes in the Englishe Tongue* (1546) asked, "What is a workman without his tooles?" A version close to the modern appeared the next century in John Clarke's *Paroemiologia Anglo-Latina* (1639), which gave it as "A workman is known by his tooles." But that version was not repeated in subsequent collections of proverbs during the eighteenth and nineteenth centuries. Instead, "An ill workman never had good tools" (from Jonathan Swift's *Polite Conversation*, 1738) and other variants were rendered. Though possibly in use beforehand, the modern version was first recorded in Robertson Davies's *Diary of Samuel Marchbanks* (1947). The proverb has apparently been quoted in print only rarely during the twentieth century.

You are only young once. Implied but unspoken here is the advice that you should enjoy your youth while you have it, because it comes but once. The Greek poet Theocritus wrote in *Idyls* (c. 270 B.C.), "Youth cannot be recaptured once it is fled," a thought echoed centuries later by Johann Friedrich von Schiller with "The May of life blooms once and never again" (c. 1800, *Resignation*). Not long after Schiller, Henry Wadsworth Longfellow rendered the saying in *Hyperion* (1839) as "Youth comes but once in a lifetime." Though probably in use beforehand, the exact wording of the current version was recorded in James T. Farrell's *Judgement Day* (1935).

You can lead a horse to water, but you can't make him drink. Although you may be able to show a person what is best, according to this proverb, you cannot force him to it—even though it is in his interest. An early version of the saying, "A man maie well bring a horse to the water, But he cannot make him drinke without he will," was rendered in John Heywood's *A Dialogue Conteinyng the Number in Effect of All the Prouerbes in the Englishe Tongue* (1546). George Herbert's *Jacula Prudentum* (1640) gave another version, "You may bring a horse to the river, but he will drink when and what he pleaseth." Benjamin Franklin later wrote in his papers, "Though one man may lead a horse to water, ten can't make him drink." James Boswell related a real-life incident involving the proverb in *Life of Samuel Johnson* (1791). Upon hearing Boswell was worried his father might make him become a lawyer, Johnson told him not to be afraid, adding "One man may lead a horse to water, but twenty cannot make him drink."

The closest wording to the modern version appeared some years later in Frederick Marryat's *The King's Own* (1830) as "You may take a horse to the water, but you can't make him drink." One version or another of the proverb was repeated by, among others, Sir Walter Scott (1818, *Heart of the Midlothian*), Anthony Trollope (1857, *Barchester Towers*), Saki (H. H. Munro, 1924, *The Square Egg*), and W. Somerset Maugham (1930, *Cakes and Ale*).

The proverb has been quoted in print frequently during the twentieth century.

You can't get blood out of a stone.   The stone here is a metaphor for a person who simply does not have (or would never give up) what is being sought—usually money. Over the centuries, various objects, such as a stone, a turnip, and even a wall, have been used in versions of the saying. The earliest known rendering, which appeared in John Lydgate's *Minor Poems* (c. 1435), mentioned marble—"Harde to likke hony [honey] out of a marbil stoon." The English poet Sir Thomas Wyatt wrote in *Defence* (c. 1542), "Thou shalt as soon find out oil out of a flint stone as find any such thing in me," and Giovanni Torriano in *A Common Place of Italian Proverbs and Proverbial Phrases* (1666) wrote "There's no getting bloud out of that wall." Charles Dickens first rendered the saying as "Blood cannot be obtained from a stone," in *David Copperfield* (1850) and then recorded the exact wording of the modern version in *Our Mutual Friend* (1865). The saying in one form or another has been quoted in print frequently during the twentieth century.

You can't have it both ways.   Life sometimes presents you with two opposing alternatives, and according to this maxim, you must choose between them. The saying itself appears to be of recent origin, the earliest recorded version probably being "You can't have anything both ways at once," which appeared in George Bernard Shaw's *Fanny's First Play* (1911). The exact wording of the current version was recorded some years later in Rex Stout's *Broken Vase* (1941), though it was likely in use beforehand. *See also* **You can't have your cake and eat it too.**

You can't have your cake and eat it too.   Once you've eaten your cake, this familiar proverb reminds us, you cannot cry as a child would about not having your cake anymore. The saying in its earliest form read, "Wolde you bothe eate your cake, and haue your cake?" which appeared in John Heywood's *A Dialogue Conteinyng the Number in Effect of All the Prouerbes in the Englishe Tongue* (1546). In the next century, Robert Heath's *Occasional Poems* (1650) rendered it as "I can't . . . Both eat my cake and have it too," while another version close to the modern was recorded as "You can't eat your cake and have your cake," in John Ray's *A Collection of English Proverbs* (1670). The English satirist Jonathan Swift wrote in *Polite Conversation* (1738), "She cannot eat her cake

and have her cake," and virtually the exact wording of the current
version appeared as "We cannot have our cake and eat it too,"
which was recorded in a document (1812) relating to the War of
1812. Later that century, the English novelist Anthony Trollope
used the exact wording, though he wrote, "You can't eat . . ." first
instead of "You can't have . . ." The saying was repeated in one
form or another by, among others, the American novelist Henry
James (1875, *The Passionate Pilgrim and Other Stories*), James Joyce
(1922, *Ulysses*), and Margaret Drabble (1980, *The Middle Ground*).
See also **You can't have it both ways.**

You can't keep a good man down.   Amen to that, but as Henry
B. Fuller asked in *Striking an Average* (1901), "Who wants to keep
a good man down?" Apart from that, the saying is apparently of
recent vintage and probably comes to us from the title of a song
popular in 1900, "You Can't Keep a Good Man Down," by M. F.
Carey. The saying continues to be familiar to most people up to
the present day.

You can't live on love.   This is another proverb aimed at tem-
pering the heat of love's passion with practical considerations.
An earlier saying, "Lovers live by love, as larks live by leeks,"
appeared in John Ray's *A Collection of English Proverbs* (1670),
with the added note, "This I conceive in derision of such expressions as living by love." Similarly, James Kelly's *A Complete Collection of Scotish Proverbs* (1721) rendered this saying as "You live
on Love as Laverocks [larks] do on Leeks. A Jest upon them that
eat little." George Washington gave another version in his writings (1794): "Love is too dainty a food to live upon alone," but
the current saying apparently was a product of the twentieth
century. Though it probably was in use beforehand, the saying
in its current form was first recorded in Peter Curtis's *No Question
of Murder* (1959). It has been quoted in print only infrequently
since then. *See also* **Who marries for love without money has
good nights and sorry days.**

You can't lose what you never had.   *See* **What you never had,
you don't miss.**

You can't make an omelet without breaking eggs.   Some
things just cannot be accomplished without creating hardships,
according to this proverb. The saying apparently was first ren-

dered in *Epigram* (c. 1790) by the French revolutionary Maximilien Robespierre, who himself created terrible hardships during the Reign of Terror in France. The first English version of the saying appeared long after Robespierre's own egg was broken, and was included in General T. P. Thompson's *Audi Alteram Partem* (1859). General Thompson wrote "The omelet will not be made without the breaking of some [eggs]," and not long afterward, Robert Louis Stevenson recorded the exact wording of the current version in *St. Ives* (1897). Among the writers who repeated the saying were Saki (H. H. Munro, 1924, *The Square Egg*) and Agatha Christie (1958, *Ordeal by Innocence*). "You can't make an omelet..." has been quoted in print frequently during the twentieth century.

You can't take it with you.   Money and other wealth have always been the subject of this old and familiar saying. For example, the Greek dramatist Aeschylus declared, "To the dead riches profiteth no jot," in *The Persians* (472 B.C.). Chaucer said essentially the same thing over eighteen hundred years later in *The Canterbury Tales* (c. 1387): "Whan he is deed, he shal nothing bere [bear] with him out of this world." William Shakespeare wrote in *Measure for Measure* (1604), "Like an ass whose back with ingots bows, / Thou bear'st thy heavy riches but a journey, / And death unloads thee." The exact wording of the current version appeared in the nineteenth century, however, as a line in Frederick Marryat's *Masterman Ready* (1841). Among the writers who later repeated or adapted the saying were Erle Stanley Gardner (1939, *The Case of the Rolling Bones*), the English novelist Edgar Wallace (1929, *Murder Book of J. G. Reeder*), Agatha Christie (1952, *Mrs. McGinty's Dead*), and P. G. Wodehouse (1961, *Ice in the Bedroom*). The saying has been quoted in print frequently during the twentieth century.

You can't teach an old dog new tricks.   A familiar proverb today, this saying apparently originated in the sixteenth century, when it was recorded in J. Fitzherbert's *The Boke of Husbandry* (1523) as "The dogge must lerne it when he is a whelpe... for it is harde to make an olde dogge to stoupe." John Heywood's *A Dialogue Conteinyng the Number in Effect of All the Prouerbes in the Englishe Tongue* (1546) repeated the "... make an old dog stoupe" version, and John Ray's *A Collection of English Proverbs* (1670) gave a more explicit version: "An old dog will learn no tricks. It's all one to physick the dead, as to instruct old men." The saying was adapted by Laurence Sterne (1767, *Tristram Shandy*), and finally appeared in the exact modern form in a letter written by the American statesman John Randolph (1806). Among those who subsequently repeated or adapted the saying were Sir Walter Scott (1819, *The Bride of Lamermoor*; 1823, *Peveril of the Peak*), Anthony Trollope (1857, *Barchester Towers*), Mark Twain (1876, *The Adventures of Tom Sawyer*), William McFee (1932, *The Harbourmaster*), and P. D. James (1963, *A Mind to Murder*). The saying has been quoted in print frequently during the twentieth century.

You catch more flies with honey than vinegar.   Being nice to others always gets better results than taking a harsh approach, though this truism sometimes seems all but lost nowadays. Apparently a favorite saying of French King Henry IV, it was rendered in English for the first time by Thomas Fuller in *Gnomologia: Adagies and Proverbs* (1732): "More Flies are taken with a Drop of Honey than a Tun of Vinegar." Benjamin Franklin repeated the saying in *Poor Richard's Almanack* (1744) as "Tart Words make no Friends; a spoonful of honey will catch more flies than a Gallon of Vinegar." In the next century, the not yet famous Abraham Lincoln gave the saying as "A drop of honey catches more flies than a gallon of gall" during a speech before the Washingtonian Temperance Society (1842). Essentially the current version was recorded in Carroll J. Daly's *Third Murder* (1931) as "You catch more flies with molasses than with vinegar," and the exact wording of it appeared in Hildegarde Dolson's *Beauty Sleep* (1978), though it was probably in use before then. The proverb in one form or another has been quoted in print frequently during the twentieth century.

You have to learn to walk before you can run.   This proverb reminds us that some basic skills have to be mastered before we can move on to the next level of responsibility or expertise. For example, the Greek playwright Aristophanes wrote in *The Knights* (424 B.C.), "One should learn how to row before trying to take the rudder." Centuries later, the first English version appeared in a medieval manuscript (c. 1350) as "Fyrst the chylde crepyth and after gooth [goes]." Almost two centuries later, the saying was rendered as "Children learne to creepe er they can learne to go" in John Heywood's *A Dialogue Conteinyng the Number in Effect of All the Prouerbes in the Englishe Tongue* (1546). In his writings (1794), George Washington adapted the saying while discussing the future of the new American nation: "We must walk as other countries have done before we can run." More recently, Victor S. Reid observed in *New Day* (1950), "You are no' forgetting you must creep 'fore you walk?"—which was along the lines of earlier versions of this saying. A few years later, however, Rae Foley adapted the modern form in *Last Gamble* (1956) to read, "The novice soprano had learned to run before she had learned to walk." Virtually the exact wording of the current version, probably in use well beforehand, was recorded in Dell Shannon's *Murder With Love* (1972) as "You got to learn to walk before you can run."

You never miss the water till the well runs dry.   This proverbial advice against taking things you have for granted can be traced back to ancient Greek times. According to an account in Plutarch's *Lives,* the Greek ruler Pericles became upset when his trusted counsel, the philosopher Anaxagoras, decided to commit suicide. Anaxagoras is said to have replied, "It's when they miss the lamp [that] men pour in oil." The first English version of the saying was rendered as "We'll never know the worth of water till the well go dry," in James Kelly's *A Complete Collection of Scotish Proverbs* (1721). Benjamin Franklin's *Poor Richard's Almanack* (1746) gave the saying as "When the well's dry, we know the worth of water." The exact wording of the modern version was recorded the next century as the title of what became a popular minstrel song (1876). The writer O. Henry was among those who later adapted the saying (1907, *The Pendulum*). The proverb has been quoted in print only infrequently during the twentieth century.

You only die once.   Implied in this maxim is a bit of battlefield bravado, namely that you (or preferably someone else) need not be afraid in a dangerous situation because you can only suffer death once. The Byzantine writer Agathias rendered an early version of the saying in *Epigram* (c. 575) as "Death cometh but once to mortals," and over a thousand years later, William Shakespeare wrote in *Henry IV, Part II* (1598), "A man can die but once." Charles Lamb shortened that to "Men die but once" in *John Woodvil* (1802), and Thomas Carlyle invoked a cosmic cataclysm to get his point across in a letter (c. 1866): "The crash of the whole solar and stellar systems could only kill you once." Meanwhile, essentially the modern version was recorded in Francis Hall's *Travels in Canada and the United States* (1818) as "You can die but once." The exact wording was recorded by Alfred

Kreymborg in *New American Caravan* (1929), and the saying was later adapted by, among others, Liam O'Flaherty (1933, *Martyr*) and Norman Mailer (1948, *The Naked And The Dead*).

You only live once.   Make the most of life, this maxim advises, because you have only one chance at it. There were earlier sayings along this line, as in "While we live, let us live," which appeared in Jan Gruter's *Inscriptiones Antiquae* (c. 1602), but the current saying appears to be a product of recent times. Henry James advised in *The Ambassadors* (1903), "Live all you can; it's a mistake not to," and Ring Lardner rendered essentially the modern saying in *Zone of Quiet* (1926) with "We only live once." The exact wording appeared in print just two years later in William McFee's *Pilgrims of Adversity* (1928).

Youth and white paper take any impression.   Young minds, any parent can tell you, are pliant and readily take to new ideas— as readily as the white paper of this proverb soaks up fresh ink. The English writer John Lyly rendered an early form of the saying in *Euphues, The Anatomy of Wit* (1579) with the line, "A childe is... apte to receiue any forme," while Shakespeare observed in *The Two Gentlemen of Verona* (1594), "Tender youth is soon suggested." The exact wording of the modern version was recorded just over a half century later in James Howell's *Proverbs in English, Italian, French and Spanish* (1659), and was repeated in John Ray's *A Collection of English Proverbs* (1670), Thomas Fuller's *Gnomologia: Adagies and Proverbs* (1732), and subsequent collections of proverbs up to modern times. The saying has not been quoted in print frequently during the twentieth century.

Youth will be served.   Like the previous proverb, the English writer John Lyly apparently recorded the earliest version of this saying in *Euphues, The Anatomy of Wit* (1579). Lyly rendered this saying as "Youth will haue his course," a sentiment echoed by Shakespeare in *Love's Labour's Lost* (1595) with the line, "Young blood doth not obey an old decree." In the next century, John Clarke's *Paroemiologia Anglo-Latina* (1639) gave the saying as "Youth will have his swing." The exact wording of the current version appeared in George Borrow's *Lavengro* (1851). Among the writers who later repeated or adapted it were Arthur Conan Doyle (1896, *Rodney Stone*; 1900, *The Green Flag*), and Steven Vincent Benet (1930, *Young Blood*).

Z

Zeal, when it is a virtue, is a dangerous one. Up to a point, enthusiasm for some cause or interest is quite natural and even praiseworthy, but there is danger in making passionate interest (the zeal) a virtue all by itself, detached from its object. This notion was recorded as the current proverb in Thomas Fuller's *Gnomologia: Adagies and Proverbs* (1732), though there were earlier parallel sayings. For example, John Davies noted in *Scourge of Folly* (1611), " 'Zeale without knowledge is sister of Folly': But though it be witlesse, men hold it most holly [holy]." Later, Thomas Fuller's *Gnomologia: Adagies and Proverbs* (1732) declared, "Zeal without Knowledge is Fire without Light." Indeed, there is an all-consuming, destructive potential in uncontrolled passion, just as with fire. Encouraging zeal for its own sake is akin to moving a burning log from the fireplace out onto the living room floor. Suddenly, the fire can spread in any direction, and most certainly will burn up the house if not extinguished in short order. Interestingly, the saying has been quoted in print only infrequently during the twentieth century.

Selected Bibliography

Apperson, G. L. *English Proverbs and Proverbial Phrases*. London: J. M. Dent & Sons, 1929.

Barbour, Frances M. *A Concordance to the Sayings in Franklin's Poor Richard*. Detroit: Gale Research, 1974.

Bartlett, John. *A New and Complete Concordance or Verbal Index to Words, Phrases and Passages in the Dramatic Works of Shakespeare*. London: Macmillan, 1894.

Beford, Emmett. *A Concordance to the Poems of Alexander Pope*. Detroit: Gale Research, 1974.

Benham, Gurney. *A Book of Quotations, Proverbs and Household Words*. Philadelphia: Lippincott, 1907.

Benham, Gurney, *Putnam's Complete Dictionary of Thought*. New York: G. P. Putnam's, 1929.

Bohn, Henry George. *A Hand-Book of Proverbs*. London: George Bell and Sons, 1905.

Cooper, Lane. *Concordance to Poems of W. Wordsworth*. London: Smith, Elder & Company, 1911.

Cotgrave, Randle. *A Dictionary of the French and English Tongues*. Menston: Scholar Press, 1968 (reprint of 1611 edition).

Davies, David William. *A Concordance to the Essays of Francis Bacon*. Detroit: Gale Research, 1973.

Draxe, Thomas. *Bibliotheca Scholastica Instructissima*. New Jersey: W. J. Johnson, 1976 (reprint of 1616 edition).

Florio, John. *First Fruites.* New York: Da Capo Press, 1969 (reprint of 1578 edition).

Fuller, Thomas. *Gnomologia: Adagies and Proverbs.* London: T. & J. Allman, 1814.

Harbottle, Thomas. *Dictionary of Quotations.* London: S. Sonnenschein & Company, 1897.

Hardwick, Michael. *The Charles Dickens Encyclopedia.* New York: Scribner, 1973.

Hazlitt, W. C. *English Proverbs and Proverbial Phrases.* London: Reeves & Turner, 1906.

Henderson, Alfred. *Latin Proverbs and Quotations.* London: S. Low Sons & Marton, 1869.

Heywood, John. *A Dialogue Conteinyng the Nomber in Effect of All the Prouerbes in the English Tongue.* Berkeley: University of California Press, 1963 (reprint of 1546 edition).

Howell, James. *Lexicon Tetraglotten, An English-French-Italian-Spanish Dictionary.* Microfilm of 1659 edition, Alderman Library collection, University of Virginia.

Hoyt, Jehiel. *The Cyclopedia of Practical Quotations, English and Latin.* New York: Funk & Wagnalls, 1890.

Ingram, William. *A Concordance to Milton's English Poetry.* Oxford, England: Clarendon Press, 1972.

Irey, Eugene F. *A Concordance to the Poems of Ralph Waldo Emerson.* New York: Garland, 1981.

Jacobe, Betty. *Wesley Quotations.* New Jersey: Scarecrow, 1990.

Johnson, Samuel. *Wit and Wisdom of Samuel Johnson.* Pennsylvania: Folcroft Library Editions, 1978.

Kelling, Harold D. *A KWIC Concordance to Jonathan Swift's A Tale of a Tub...* New York: Garland, 1984.

Kelly, James. *A Complete Collection of Scotish Proverbs*. Pennsylvania: Folcroft Library Editions, 1976 (facsimile, 1721 edition).

Lathem, Edward Connery. *A Concordance to the Poetry of Robert Frost*. New York: Holt, 1969.

Montgomery, Guy. *Concordance to the Poetical Works of John Dryden*. New York: Russell & Russell, 1967.

National Center for Constitutional Studies. *The Real Thomas Jefferson*. 1983.

Pettie, George. *A Petite Pallace of Pettie His Pleasure*. Oxford, England: Oxford University Press, 1970 (reprint of 1576 edition).

Pickles, J. D., and Dawson, J. L., *A Concordance to John Gower's Confessio Amantis*. Suffolk: John Gower Society, 1987.

Ray, John. *A Collection of English Proverbs*. Microfilm of 1678 edition, Alderman Library collection, University of Virginia.

Shinagel, Michael. *Concordance to the Poems of Jonathan Swift*. Ithaca: Cornell University Press, 1972.

Simpson, John A. *The Concise Oxford Dictionary of Proverbs*. Oxford, England: Oxford University Press, 1988.

Stevenson, Burton. *The Home Book of Bible Quotations*. New York: Harper, 1949.

Stevenson, Burton. *The Home Book of Shakespeare Quotations*. New York: Scribner, 1937.

Stevenson, Burton. *The Macmillan Book of Proverbs, Maxims, and Famous Phrases*. New York: Macmillan, 1976.

Swift, Jonathan. *Polite Conversation*. Oxford: Oxford University Press, 1963 (reprint of 1738 edition).

Taverner, Richard. *Proverbes or Adagies*. New York: Da Capo Press, 1969 (reprint of 1539 edition).

Taylor, Archer, and Whiting, Bartlett Jere. *A Dictionary of American Proverbs and Proverbial Phrases*. Cambridge, Massachusetts: Harvard University Press, 1958.

Tilley, M. P. *Dictionary of the Proverbs in England in the Sixteenth and Seventeenth Centuries.* Ann Arbor: University of Michigan Press, 1950.

Tilley, M. P. *Elizabethan Proverb Lore in Lyly's Euphues and Pettie's Petite Palace.* New York: Macmillan, 1926.

Tusser, Thomas. *A Hundreth Good Pointes of Husbandrie.* London: Lackington, Allen and Company, 1812.

Washington, George. *Maxims of Washington.* New York: D. Appleton, 1894.

Wegener, Larry Edward. *Concordance to Herman Melville's the Confidence Man.* New York: Garland, 1987.

Whiting, Bartlett Jere. *Chaucer's Use of Proverbs.* Cambridge, Massachusetts: Harvard University Press, 1934.

Whiting, Bartlett Jere. *Early American Proverbs and Proverbial Phrases.* Cambridge, Massachusetts: Harvard University Press, 1977.

Whiting, Bartlett Jere. *Modern Proverbs and Proverbial Sayings.* Cambridge, Massachusetts: Harvard University Press, 1989.

Wilson, F. P., (Editor). *The Oxford Dictionary of English Proverbs.* Oxford, England: Oxford University Press, 1970.